Michele Landsberg (signature)

PENGUIN BOOKS

Women & Ch

Michele Landsberg is one of the *Toronto Star's* best-loved and most widely read columnists and the first winner of the National Newspaper Award for column-writing. Before joining the *Star* in 1978, she worked as a staff writer and then as Articles Editor at *Chatelaine* magazine for seven years, winning an award for journalism in her first year there. This book is the climax of a twenty-year career as a writer, editor, and speaker, on topics ranging from the state of feminism in Argentina to children's television and literature.

Michele Landsberg lives in Toronto with her husband, Stephen Lewis, and their three children, Ilana, Avi, and Jenny.

Women & Children FIRST

Michele Landsberg

A provocative look
at modern Canadian women
at work and at home

PENGUIN BOOKS

Penguin Books Ltd., Harmondsworth, Middlesex, England
Penguin Books, 40 West 23rd Street, New York, New York 10010,
U.S.A.
Penguin Books Australia Ltd., Ringwood, Victoria, Australia
Penguin Books Canada Ltd., 2801 John Street, Markham, Ontario,
Canada L3R 1B4
Penguin Books (N.Z.) Ltd., 182-190 Wairau Road, Auckland 10,
New Zealand

Published by Macmillan of Canada,
A Division of Gage Publishing Limited, 1982

Published in Penguin Books, 1983

Copyright © Michele Landsberg, 1982

Manufactured in Canada

Canadian Cataloguing in Publication Data

Landsberg, Michele, 1939-
    Women and children first

Bibliography: p.
ISBN 0-14-006845-7

1. Women - Canada - Social conditions.   2. Children
- Social conditions.   I. Title.

HQ1453.L35 1983   305.4'2'0971   C83-098205-1

ACKNOWLEDGEMENTS

I would like to acknowledge the generosity of the *Toronto Star* in giving me time to finish this book, and in allowing me to reprint columns which first appeared in its pages.

Grateful thanks are also due to Esperanza Hellyn for her loyal help; Donna Lam, who assisted so sturdily with research; Kathy Miniaci, who types like the wind and thinks at the same time; my children — Ilana, Avi, and Jenny — for their loving encouragement; Nina Libeskind for early and astute advice; and, above all and always, my husband, Stephen Lewis, on whose wisdom, support, and judgement I leaned shamelessly.

DEDICATION

To the memory of my mother, Naomi Leah Landsberg, who unwittingly set me on the path to feminism by showing such grace and courage in her own life that, very early in my childhood, I was moved to love the unsung strength of women.

CONTENTS

Introduction   1

Drink Up Your Shrinking-Potion, Alice   7

Superwoman Can't Fly   24

Men Are Two-Fifths More Equal Than Women   41

Crusts in the Lunch Bucket   55

Paying the Price of Mythology   70

The Heavy Fist   82

Not Taking No for an Answer   101

Our Bodies, Men's Rules   124

But If It's My Body,
Why Am I Doing These Awful Things To It?   137

Birth and New Life   165

After the Pampers   181

Adolescents — the Rights of Passage   200

Suffer the Little Children   219

Heart of the Family   238

Bibliography   271

NOTE

Columns which previously appeared in the *Toronto Star* are designated by a vertical rule in the left margin.

INTRODUCTION

YEARS AGO, I HEARD A RADIO BROADCAST IN WHICH THE narrator, going on about geographic phenomena, used the word "riverine". What a lovely, liquid, evocative word, I thought, to describe that fertile blur of territory where earth meets water: the buzz and click, croak and ooze and rustle, of insects in rushes, frogs in mud. This year I met another phrase that links up with riverine. The edge effect, I read, describes the scientific principle that more life will be found where two ecosystems meet than at the heart of either of the two systems.

In gloomier moments, when I am aware of shortfalls in logic and inconsistencies in my feminism—when I reach down a tentative toe and can't touch bottom—I wonder how it happened that I'm floundering around out here in mid-stream. Neither a radical nor a traditionalist, I end up as a contradiction: a committed feminist who is also a monogamous wife and devoted mother. It's nice to think, at such moments, that there is more life here at the edge where several ecosystems meet than there is on either bank of this particular river.

Over there, on the left bank, I can see the sharp and fiery arguments of the radical feminists. I agree with them that marriage and the nuclear family are the props of capitalism and the underpinning of our consumer economy. Yes, there is an element of slavery in marriage. Who but a husband, after all, is legally entitled to rape? Yes, women who marry trade their freedom, their domestic and sexual services, and many of their human rights, just to receive a frail safety for themselves and their children. They're kept in a position of economic and emotional dependency by a complex social structure that has effectively kept them out of the best-paying jobs. Society runs on the unpaid work of wives and mothers. At the very least, every married woman must face a flicker of that humiliating truth

1

when the first sock argument happens—the first time her husband rages and scolds, as thought she were the lowliest servant, for not washing/darning/folding his socks fast or well enough. His superbly arrogant expectation of service is what burns so deeply into the wife's consciousness.

Yes, all that is true. And yet, I drifted away, emotionally, from that analysis—just about the time when I first became pregnant. Women like me, who accept much of the truth of that radical critique of marriage, and yet end up happily married, then find themselves in the riverine quicksands. We are pragmatically sound, but on perilous philosophic footing. Bit by bit, as our children are born, we have to give up the radical position, since marriage is still the best available framework in which to nurture new life. I have never read a radical attack on the family that takes the task of parenthood as seriously as it takes the self-fulfilment of the adults. Vague mutterings about communes won't do; for the foreseeable future, family communes will not be appealing or accessible to ordinary Canadian parents. Such hasty and ill-thought-out solutions are almost flippant, considering how important a question this must be for most women.

Neither is single parenthood a real answer. There may be, somewhere, a woman who is strong, skilled, brave, and resourceful enough to raise children from infancy, work for a living, put up the storm windows, file her own income tax, change diapers, pay the day care, and still have enough money, leisure, and buoyancy to enjoy her own life and enrich those of her children. If so, I've never met her. People are often forced into such lonely situations, but few of them would claim that it is an ideal set-up for child-rearing. From the viewpoint of the average mother, nothing could be more desirable than a loving and steady marriage, in which the new mother is freed to give intense and undistracted attention to her infant, with enough comfort, emotional support, and companionship from her husband to allow her to go on giving, albeit with diminishing intensity, over the next several years. (There's nothing in this approach to say that it can't work the other way around too, of course, with wife supporting the husband.)

Having cut loose from the left bank this way, I find myself looking the other way and wondering why all those women over there on the right are keeping their feet dry. Well back from the water's edge are women who may now and then concede the rightness of a feminist insight, but who nevertheless refuse the baptism. They do not call themselves feminists; they do not view events through the critical eyes of the women's movement. Is it cultural conditioning, I wonder? Is it the way we've all been taught to think of any group of strongly identified women — Amazons, bluestockings, teetotallers — as faintly ridiculous? After all, it still comes as a shock to youngsters today when they are prodded into realizing that the suffragettes were honourable democrats, not a bunch of demented extremists running around in funny bloomers to get — ha ha — the vote.

Feminism, I think, has been tinged with the same militant-governess overtone. Because feminism questions male and female sex-roles, the subliminal image of the feminist has come to be a mixture of the Dutch Cleanser woman and a prohibitionist — an angry battleaxe, bursting into an uproarious gin-mill with her scolding tongue and upraised rolling-pin, a spoilsport determined to put the damper on sex, booze, and fun.

But what of those women who see through these mocking stereotypes, who share feminism's commitment to justice and equality, but still decline to join forces with their sisters? I see them over there on the right bank, grazing peacefully in those green pastures, quite removed — they think — from the currents that buffet other women. Until the boss harasses them or the husband leaves them on the begging end of child-support payments, they simply cannot make the larger feminist analysis fit their own personal situation. Women have not been trained to think politically, to see themselves as pieces in a pattern. Besides, such an insight is poison to people who have been brought up in the North American daydream of limitlessly free individualism. Those women who have not joined forces with feminism are not necessarily antagonistic; they simply have not experienced that famous "click" of connection that entered our vocabulary from the pages of *MS.* magazine, that moment of astonished clarity when a woman sees that her life is shaped, not by random free choices, but by imposed and limiting gender roles.

So how did I become one of the protean inhabitants of the edge zone — now a mother, now a rebel — trying to reconcile opposing patterns, at home on neither bank? I am one of those feminists who was born, not made; a "cradle feminist", a girl who grew up with brothers.

Maybe you have to grow up with brothers to experience that primal moment when every fibre of your being shrieks out "UNFAIR!" as special privileges are poured like anointing oil on the head of the boy, while your young female life is fretted with restrictions and limitations. Virginia Woolf salved her chafed soul by writing long, brilliant essays about the education of England's young men—all those Geralds and Georges who were sent off to Eton and Oxford to be treated like young lords and heirs of the realm, while, at home, thousands of their sisters lived in genteel and uneducated penury, shouldering more than their weary share of household management. It was the sister who paid for it all, said Virginia Woolf, who was never allowed to go to school.

I've noticed among my friends that when the oldest child was a girl, she very often grew up oblivious to the unfair advantages heaped on boys. Since modern Canadians bask in universal education, the disparities are not so glaring at an early age, especially when the girl has the balancing advantage of seniority in the family. In my own family constellation, no different from most others in the suffocating conformity of the forties and fifties, it was easier to see the patterns emerge. I was no less loved than my older brothers, and they were no more materially favoured than I. But all the favours were pre-ordained by gender. I was given hair ribbons, smocked dresses, and ballet lessons, but what I missed (without quite being able to articulate it at the time) were my brothers' special burdens of responsibility and free- dom—the solemn importance of the Bar Mitzvah, the freedom to run outside to play after supper, their mysterious exemption from boring household duties, and a sort of tacit assumption that boys were wild, anarchic, hungry, bold, and always in danger of going over the line of restraint. Girls, in my family, were meant to be morally responsible, adult, calm, well behaved, and pretty. When my brothers climbed someone's tree or garage roof, I was scolded too, though I was younger and a non-participant, because "girls should know better". But I didn't want to be a moral force for good. I wanted to go to the special public high school for bright students, where my one brother went, but it was for boys only...though I was the more ardent student. And I wanted to be free from the cage of myself, my prettiness or non-prettiness, my lack of female skills. They went to camp and learned to canoe; I stayed home and listlessly tried to knit a doll's scarf. The "unfair" was burned into me, and it was only natural that by the age of twelve I was noticing how even the English language I loved so fiercely was skewed toward male dominance, with its supposedly neutral "he" that seemed to rule my particular gender right out of existence.

At twelve and thirteen, I began to write rambling "essays" defending free love, railing against marriage and babies, and dissecting male bias...all of it in the inflated rhetoric of an angry child, but all of it, I see now in looking back with surprise, the very substance of radical feminism. When, finally, at fourteen, I pried *The Second Sex* by Simone de Beauvoir from a reluctant librarian, who had it behind the desk at the Central Reference Library and didn't want to give it to me because I still didn't have an adult library card, I read de Beauvoir's sweeping and often poetic analysis with an almost delirious rush of exhilarated vindication. It was the first time in my life I had heard or read of another human being who even acknowledged that there existed such a thing as inequality between the sexes.

Sisterhood came along a little late for me. By the time the first peeps of rebellion sounded from those who were reading *The Feminine Mystique* (I thought it was old hat), I was already ensconced in my marriage home with babies, and coming to a lonely new realization. The radical feminists and I had parted company forever, and yet, babies or no babies, I could never see the world from the right bank.

Still, I would rather be here in the middle than in either of the two rigidly opposing camps: Housewives who stubbornly refuse to consider any of the radical questions about marriage strike me as dully defensive; radicals who are unrelenting about the human seductiveness of marriage and babies have often seemed to me to have a bitter fixity of viewpoint.

If I've had the hubris to bring together some of the columns in which I charted the messy ins and outs, ups and downs, of feminist life and perceptions, it's because I think there's a particular light shining here at the intersection of two ecosystems. And it shines most modestly and kindly, I think, through the filter of ordinary daily experience.

Of all the hundreds of columns I've written and issues I've tackled for the *Toronto Star*, I've chosen the ones that bear most directly on the lives and interests of Canadian women and children. It cost me some pangs to leave out material on women in other countries—genital mutilation in Africa, oppression in South Africa, Chile, and Argentina, and the Nestlé boycott. An even more ruthless decision, also dictated by space limitations, was to delay discussing children's literature, music, and television until another day and another book. I have kept to subject matter that touches all of us: the kindling of a feminist consciousness, mingled with delight in and concern for all our children.

Most Canadian women will, like me, go through marriage, motherhood, and paid employment. I hope that some of them, through seeing their own joys and trials mirrored here, will come to share my conviction that until we all enjoy a perfect social, cultural, legal, and financial equality with men, none of us—however privileged we may be individually or temporarily—is really anything more than a second-class citizen.

DRINK UP YOUR
SHRINKING-POTION, ALICE

ALICE IN WONDERLAND IS THE ONLY BOOK I HAVE EVER defaced. It frightened me so much when I was seven or eight years old that I scribbled over the Tenniel drawings and stuffed the book behind the others in the shelf. Still, at night, the images swam out of the dark at me. In a last effort at exorcism, I stole down to the cellar and hid my *Alice* among the blindly sprouting potatoes in the bottom of the wire vegetable bin.

Lewis Carroll and Tenniel's drawings still have the power to make me queasy. I think it's the way Alice, as curiously passive as a baby or as someone pinned in a nightmare, docilely gulps the potions that appear beside her. She metamorphoses as numbly as Kafka's man-bug. "Drink me!" commands a label, and Alice drinks. And Alice shrinks. She shrinks down to the size of a drowning mouse; she shoots up to a long-necked monstrosity bursting the walls of the rabbit's claustrophobic house; she shrinks agains so rapidly that she nearly disappears into the vanishing-point of nothingness. It is the hallucination of fever or anaesthetic.

It is also a distressingly apt metaphor. Our modern Alices — and there is a numb, acquiescent Alice in every one of us — still lap up the shrinking-potion of male culture. Even now, when legal equality is more tangible than ever before, when many barriers to freedom have been breached, women are still agreeing to be shrunk to a conveniently diminished stature. Because they hate to seem shrill, or humourless, or bad sports, women will uneasily co-operate with any number of demeaning feminine role requirements, ranging from polite laughter at anti-female jokes to getting the coffee for a roomful of male colleagues at work.

The English writer Brigid Brophy pointed out the paradox: "Modern society, like the modern zoo, has contrived to get rid of the bars without altering the fact of [women's] imprisonment. All the zoo architect needs to do is to run a zone of hot or cold air, whichever the animal concerned cannot tolerate, round the cage where the bars used to be. Human animals are not less sensitive to social climate." Human females are remarkably sensitive to the frosty blast of disapproval that greets us when we stray across our sex-role boundaries. Our culture makes it easy, even seductively appealing, to stay inside the limits of behaviour that are acceptable and comfortable to men. We are constantly reminded that we are supposed to please men physically and even to enjoy a little maltreatment: "Killing me softly with his song" moans the female singer ecstatically, and the commercials nag us endlessly about our wrinkles, our baggy stockings, our rough skin, our odours, our flyaway hair, and our telltale bulges. Our reward for conforming, for staying within the boundaries, is the warm zephyr of male admiration. But even the admiration can be demeaning. A Toronto restaurateur dangles reproductions of breasts in every corner of his restaurant, and is praised as a lusty lover of women. Imagine the chilly reception we would give a woman restaurateur who dared to hang inflatable testicles from the rafters and tried to pass herself off with a shy smile as "a lover of men". So thoroughly ingrained is our understanding of our sex roles and their limits that we immediately laugh off this idea as purely ludicrous.

How are we persuaded to drink up our shrinking-potion so tamely? How do we know our proper sex role limits with such intuitive certainty? Conditioning. Conditioning in all things, large and small. Male and female, we breathe in the culture as we breathe in the air, and we don't have inborn filters to screen out the distortions. Nobody, for example, cautioned me that the literature I studied at high school and then university presented an almost exclusively male view of the world. Naturally not. All our teachers were male, too. We questioned the bias no more than we questioned the arrangement of tables and chairs. Literature was simply literature, beyond partisan quibbles. Oh, I might have angrily rejected the masturbation fantasies of Henry Miller, and understood that there was something profoundly perverse about D.H. Lawrence's besotted religion of the phallus. But I went on thinking of literature as a sacred grove until I encountered a little paperback by Priscilla Galloway:

Until a few days ago, if you'd told me that high school English courses should be examined for sexism, I would have bristled with porcupine outrage.

"What a narrow-minded way to approach literature," I would have said, pronouncing the word "literature" with the special reverence I learned in university. "Art is far above such shallow ideological thinking."

So I would have said before I read Priscilla Galloway's gimlet-eyed and devastating study *What's Wrong With High School English?* O Galloway. I blush, I recant. And let every English teacher in this province similarly eat crow.

Galloway, an English consultant for the North York Board of Education, studied the 1,700 literary works offered on 42 courses at eight representative Ontario high schools, and her findings blast to smithereens my smug assumption that "great literature" necessarily reflects all of humanity. The literature taught in our high schools is written by men, selected by men (83 per cent of the English departments heads are male), features men in its leading roles, glorifies male accomplishments and attitudes, and, when it does get around to mentioning women, is most often disparaging, distorted or outright degrading. Of the "Top 26" literary works—that is, the 26 novels, plays, and anthologies most used in high schools—88 percent are written by men. Since male authors overwhelmingly choose to feature men as the chief protagonist, 79 per cent of the leading characters in the Top 26 are male. In such Top 26 books as *Lord of the Flies* by William Golding, Ray Bradbury's *Martian Chronicles*, and the openly sexist anthology *Man and His World*, women are entirely or almost entirely absent. In all Top 26, the most frequent social position of women was housewife; second most frequent was servant.

While female authors often write about strong, rebellious, or creative women, male authors tend to depict women as dulled and pliant domestic victims, thrilled masochists, or evil temptresses. The dominant woman in Ontario's high schools is Lady Macbeth, since Shakespeare's *Macbeth* is the single most-taught work. The next most popular book is John Steinbeck's *Of Mice and Men*, in which the sole woman does not even have a name. She is called "Curley's wife", or "the tart", or "the bitch". She is the destroyer in the book, because her tempting sexuality "lures" a helpless male to kill her and thus ruin all his dreams. *Her* dreams, of course, are terminated without a mention.

Why does it matter? Well, as both the Ministry of Education and Galloway stress, literature is a powerful influence in our lives. Particularly in adolescence, it helps to shape our sense of reality. But for girls in our high schools, literature is a distorting mirror. They will not see themselves reflected there. At best, the images men have created of them are a half truth, a male truth. At worst (and did you know they teach James Bond in some high schools?), those images are a slow poison, convincing girls that we are much different and much worse than we are.

Indoctrination is an amazing process. We take the male literature course absolutely for granted. It's "normal". But Galloway asks us to picture a high school course in which every novel, play, and poem just happened to be written by a woman and featured a woman. Wouldn't that seem "biased"? Can't you just hear the indignant howls for more "balance"? Why hasn't anyone pointed out, angrily, that Jane Austen, Virginia Woolf, Charlotte Brontë, Simone de Beauvoir, George Eliot, Doris Lessing, Alice Munro, Margaret Atwood—to name only a random handful—are routinely left out of high school courses?

Is this massive a bias acceptable to you?

No, that massive a bias was not acceptable to many readers, some of whom sent letters of outrage to their local schools. But deep down at the alluvial level of consciousness, where speech patterns have sunk into the sediment and hardened into bedrock, women as well as men are captives of a language that obliterates the female and exalts the male to the universal norm.

Shifts in language are not merely an ego sop to frivolous feminists. The power of language to alter perceptions is well known; it has been documented again and again. Students, it has been shown, when reading about "the history of man" or the "achievements of man", begin to form a mental image of a male person. The female half of the human equation fades out of history. Take the Case of the Five Edmonton Women Who Disappeared:

Five of the 12 aldermen elected in Edmonton in the fall of 1980 were women.

"I dislike the word 'alderperson' and anyone who addresses me as such loses points," said one of them, Olivia Butti.

"The term alderman has nothing to do with sex," said Louise Campbell. "It's just a word which designates a position."

"I never assumed to think that I am anything but a woman," said Betty Hewes, somewhat ambiguously. "I don't need a label to describe me."

"The right to be called alderman is something I have just finished fighting very hard for," said June Cavanagh.

Why is it, I thought, reading this litany, that nothing provokes more wrath, more fiery resistance, more clambering about on barricades and waving of swords, than simple evolutionary changes in the language? I'll tell you why. Because words are more powerful that anything armies can blast at each other. Long after the battlefields are buried in dust, a word or a phrase will drift down the centuries that may alter the meaning our outcome of that battle for all time to come.

Small wonder that when we're dizzy from the velocity of social change, we cling to language as to a rock in a flood. However we clutch, though, language won't stand still. And people who want to hasten social reform are right to insist on new vocabularies. The Edmonton politicos may say that names "don't matter", but they fight the change precisely because they know words matter more than almost anything else: Words can shape, as well as reflect, our perceptions of the world.

The change doesn't have to be painful. Do you remember how we all switched, in the course of a few years, from saying "negro" to saying "black"? That didn't undermine the use of correct English, or lead us all into grammatical crimes. It was simply the pruning from the language of a word that had racist and bigoted overtones to its hearers.

Verbal gardening goes on all the time. Grubbing back in the *Star* files, I unearthed an article from 1969 when June Rowlands, now a Toronto politician, was elected president of the Association of Women Electors. It referred to her twice as "a dishy blond", repeatedly called the association a group of "lady vigilantes", and ended by comparing it to "the dead chicken hung around the neck of a naughty dog". That brand of slighting innuendo would not be tolerated today, because its demeaning intent is all too clear.

Mind you, people who are afraid or ashamed to oppose women's fight for equality often fall back on a last-ditch struggle against the accompanying linguistic progress. They dimly sense, I suppose, that male-dominated English has been instrumental in holding women in second place for almost all of our recorded history. Think of it: mankind, brotherhood, the pronoun "he" to stand for all of the human race, man-made, alderman, chairman, one giant step for mankind, all men are created equal, a man's reach should exceed his grasp, a man's a man for a' that, God created man in his own likeness...

If you think this is not invisibly crushing to the aspirations and self-image of little girls, try to imagine a small boy growing up in a fictional Amazonia, where phrases like womankind, she, chairwoman, God created woman in her own image, all women are created equal, womanhood, and all of woman's history, are the dominant norm, and everything male is a kind of subvariant, afterthought or abnormality. Would you expect little George to grow up and apply for jobs as chairwoman of the board, or even waitress, actress, or alderwoman? In the interests of appropriateness and equality, may I suggest a return to the original "elder" or, more sensibly, a leap forward to the sexually neutral "councillor"?

The resistance to language change is understandable. Everyone who earns a living by language has a vested interest in the rules of grammar, spelling, and speech that have been learned with difficulty and upheld with fidelity. I empathize with that emotional commitment to fastidious usage. In a sea of North American illiteracy, we English-lovers cling stubbornly to our objective pronouns and conditional verbs. We scorn the orphaned "hopefully", set adrift on a tide of muddled meanings. Our goal is linguistic conformity to the rules; our banner is clarity. But outdated styles cease to be clear. Male-dominated language, traditional though it may be, is misleading and imprecise. "Man" may once have been an Anglo-Saxon synonym for "human being", as Miller and Swift trenchantly argue in *The Handbook of Nonsexist Writing,* but it has long since lost that universality in actual usage. If, they say, "man" simply means "person", then why do newspapers not record that "marathon swimmer Diana Nyad became the first man to swim the 60 miles from the Bahamas to Florida"? Because, as we all know, man mean adult male, woman means adult female, and person means adult of either sex.

That usage, struggle as the chauvinists may, is already enshrined in our common speech. If "charwoman" was acceptable for many years, why is "chairwoman" considered ridiculous? If precision is the goal, why does *Today* magazine blazon "Anchormen" across the article about male and female news announcers?

Language inaccuracy, as author Elaine Morgan points out in *The Descent of Women,* has led generations of scientists down the most embarrassingly false trails. Blinded by that universal application of the word "man", zoologists and anthropologists have twisted themselves into knots to explain "man's aggression", "man's love of war", "man's territoriality", and all of it based on a chest-thumping theory of "man the hunter". Of course, while man hunted, women gathered and dug and farmed and harvested, and this was the steadier and deeper underpinning of human evolution, the missing link that eluded anthropological theorists like Robert Ardrey, with his notion that we are governed by an atavistic urge to defend our territory, and Lionel Tiger, with his view of all social history shaped by male bonding. If these men could be so dazzled by the blinding glare of the universal "he", how much more so the lesser scribblers and toilers?

Something odd struck me about the *Time-Life* ad that slipped through my mailbox the other day. Something odd, that is, other than its hysterically excited prose. The ad consisted of four closely typed pages of burble about a new book called *The Canadians*, part of a series on the old west. Reading it through once more to pinpoint the source of my unease, I noted these phrases, among others, describing the original settlers of the Canadian west: "Lords of the lakes, Sinbads of the wilderness, lusty Canadian fur men, tireless French voyageurs, tough railroaders, crack shot Gabriel Dumont, rocksteady nerves of bold adventurers, strong-willed breed of men, Indian warriors, heroes, legendary leaders, hardriding hombres…"

In all that spate of cliché, where were the women? In the bordellos, that's where. Women were singled out in only one phrase: "Dancehall girls and lady bandits".

That was our role in settling the west? Horsefeathers. There must have been thousands of unsung women heroes of the west, women who rode and shot and nursed and farmed and swatted horseflies and trapped and prospected and endured it all, side by side with men, and then were promptly dropped from the records as we have always been dropped from the pages of male-written history.

I thought about this when I wrote about the five women in Edmonton who proudly cling to the title of "alderman" and won't think of changing it to something sexually neutral. After all, who can blame them, when maleness, in our culture, is the stamp of excellence? Researchers keep proving it. In one classic study, university students consistently gave higher marks to an essay signed with a male name, and lower marks to the *same* essay signed by a woman. At the University of Manitoba, researchers showed that even mildly sexist language (the use of the pronoun "he" in a career description of a psychologist) triggered, in students, a bias against women in that profession.

If you want to be shocked down to your toes, read *The First Sex* by Elizabeth Gould Davis, which documents not only the way women have been brutalized through the ages but the way we've been deliberately wiped off the historical slate. Did you know that there was, for example, a female Apostle, called Thecia, a companion of Saint Paul, and vouched for as authentic by Saint Jerome even after she was removed from the official New Testament? Did you know about Pope Joan, elected in 853, and expunged from the records as "mythical" 800 years later? Have you ever heard of Queen Philippa of England, who founded that country's wool and coal trade, on which its wealth was based for centuries after? No, you haven't. Because later historians altered the records to give the credit to her husband, Edward III.

You can see the female-obliterating process at work right now. According to author Davis, a recent textbook claims that radium was discovered by Pierre Curie—assisted, incidentally, by his wife-to-be. And all the while, we women eagerly co-operate in the process that makes us disappear. (Aldermen, indeed!) Next time you read a history book—any history book—remember that only half the story is there. The other half is lost.

There is more than linguistic passion and historical oversight behind the resistance to language change; there's bias. It may be unconscious, but the struggle to exclude women from sharing the language is a struggle to keep women from sharing the power. The bias occasionally rises to the surface, as it did, amusingly, in a *Globe and Mail* editorial reacting to changes in Roget's *Thesaurus*. The female editor of the thesaurus had announced that some sexist language was being cleaned up; "mankind", for example, was being changed to "humankind". The *Globe* was outraged. "Neutered!" exclaimed the headline of its editorial—a Freudian slip if there ever was one, since the *Globe* has always argued that "man" words like "mankind" *were* neuter, not masculine, to begin with.

The *Globe* still huffily disdains to call a woman Ms., insisting on the right to label all women by their marital status (Miss or Mrs.), though men, of course, are labelled only by their names and career titles. The *Globe* editorial writers also delight in referring to "women's lib" rather than to the feminist movement. Of course, it's easier to sneer at something called "lib" than to come right out in a manly sort of way and state that you are opposed to equality rights for women.

Of all forms of opposition to women's equality, sexual ridicule is the favourite weapon and, to most women, the most stinging form of rebuke. Nothing drives us back behind our invisible bars more effectively than the whip of sexual scorn. It is all the more effective because its opposite is so seductive: Which of us has not been young and, however fleetingly, beautiful? Which of us has not imagined basking in the easy warmth of male approval of our beauty? It is so much simpler than writing a Ph.D. thesis or becoming president of the company. And several thousand years of conditioning have taught us that sexual admiration is as heady a reward as we women are likely to grasp in this life.

How effective a slight, then (or so men think), to withdraw that approval, and to imply that a feminist is merely out of temper because she is ugly and not desirable to men. Their argument is fatuous (only ugly women want equality?), but even experienced writers and debaters use it. A Toronto freelancer, for example, who apparently prides himself on a dangerously masculine image, wrote a deliberately provocative article against what he predictably called "the libbers". He ended his argument with what he no doubt fancied was a killer of a thrust: he was going to knock off the debate, he said, and just go out "with a shapely blonde". This bit of pathetic swashbuckle was meant to reduce any unshapely brunette readers to a most painful state of envy.

Sometimes men don't even realize they are using sexual insult to keep women in their place. A *Toronto Star* entertainment reporter didn't like a clever satire (about music — not sex) with an all-woman cast. He ended his review this way: "It all brings to mind a term we used back in the '60s to describe girls who kept promising but never delivered: CTs. In a theatrical sense, nothing could be more appropriate for the Clichettes." CTs, in case you've forgotten the sixties, when girls were supposed to "deliver" themselves to men, means "cock-teasers". The assumption behind the phrase was that a sexually alluring girl had an obligation to relieve men of their genital tensions. In terms of theatrical criticism, this gem is equivalent, for example, to a female reviewer dismissing a male cast as "a bunch of premature ejaculators". It's preposterous. Yet, the next day, when the *Star* apologized for using the expression "CTs", it apologized for the rudeness of the language...not the deeper offensiveness of a reviewer relying on sexual taunts.

That such slighting innuendo is often unconscious is shown in another 1982 *Toronto Star* story about a crusading lawyer who pioneered a storefront law office in Toronto, to the chagrin of more conventional lawyers. The *Star* reporter referred to lawyer Jane Harvey's "thick, husky, bring-your-troubles-to-me voice, sounding like a concerned Mae West...". He calls her "bright and beautiful", says she is "passionate" about law reform, and, throughout, uses the language of sexual admiration to describe her style as lawyer. She "beams her luminous blue eyes", "breathes" rather than "says" the most matter-of-fact information, and "crosses and uncrosses an elegant set of model's legs" while talking about law school. However smitten the reporter may have been, and he clearly was, the steamed-up imagery obscures Harvey's role as a lawyer and leaves a predominant impression of a sexual adventurer on the fringes of respectability. No female reporter, in my experience, has ever referred to a male lawyer as having a truck-driver's torso, a wrestler's bulging crotch, or the bedroom eyes of a Rudolph Valentino. Confronted with this argument, men sometimes counter that they wouldn't mind such compliments in the least. They would, though, if sexuality had been considered their only asset for hundreds of years.

Canadian newspapers, even now, daily reinforce these faintly degraded images of women. In 1981, four male colleagues and I—all working at the *Toronto Star*—were honoured with National Newspaper Awards. The *Star* proudly ran a short feature on each of us. The headlines ran this way: for the feature article winner, "Must Go Where the Action Is—Gwyn". For the music critic, "Instant Critics Not Enough". For the editorial writer, a tersely tough "I Call Them As I See Them". For the cartoonist, another tough-guy swagger—"I'm Unfair to Everyone". For me, the first winner of the National Newspaper Award for column-writing, "Feminists Not All Freaks".

For each of the other winners, the newspaper listed previous awards, educational background, and complimentary raves from distinguished observers. We were not told if they were married or had children. For me? No mention of my university degree or my previous awards for journalism, and not even a word about my twenty-year career in Canadian magazines, newspapers, radio, and television. Instead, half the article was devoted to my husband, Stephen Lewis, and minor anecdotes from our shared political past. I was described as "Wife, mother of three, editor, writer". The lack of any mention of my credentials tends to make me sound like a privileged wife who fell into column-writing by virtue of my husband's prominence.

The insult wasn't deliberate. Indeed, the *Star* is the newspaper that hired me to write a daily column from a feminist point of view, rewards me well, and scrupulously refrains from editorial interference. But the article serves to reinforce scarcely conscious attitudes about the unimportance, even the "freakishness", of women writers.

The primitive and unexamined prejudices of some male journalists are a major barrier to women's equality, if only because these men may be in charge of processing and conveying the news. Two senior editors, men who select the news and set the tone of reporting, unzip their pants in a tavern to prove to some startled female reporters which of them has the bigger penis. Another senior editor has a nude poster on his wall; a brilliant photographer carries around doctored photographs of a little boy with an enormous penis. Is there really any chance, given the infantile phallic preoccupations of these men, that news about women's struggle for equality will be dealt with honestly, amply, and without bias?

Most of the men I know are adult, intelligent, and nowadays would rather have egg on their tie or dandruff on their shoulders than let slip a male chauvinist comment. But I get dejected, even discouraged, when I think of the incurable asininity of men in groups.

Consider (if you can bear to) the Winnipeg Press Club, which annually holds a male-only drunk called Beer and Skits. For this entertainment the men put out a special magazine, also called *Beer and Skits*. And for the 1979 edition of the magazine, they solicited ads from Winnipeg's business-men, including such good gray citizens as Eaton's and The Bay, who duly came up with their quota of sniggering sexism.

A local Volvo dealer had a clever pun: "If we sold sex, we'd be known as your VULVA dealer."

"Take the Pepsi Challenge!" crowed another, over a full-page picture of a nude woman squeezing her bare breasts, her nipples covered with Pepsi bottle-caps. "We bottle and distribute nothing but the breast, er, best!"

For sheer squalor, nothing beats the Century 21 Productions ad: In a casting director's office, a woman is lying prone under the desk, presumably performing oral sex on an ecstatic man who burbles into the phone, "Mr Smith, I've found the right girl to sing your commercial."

Great-West Life Assurance Co. elbowed in with its chuckle. A group of naked nymphets adoringly surround a man (he, of course, is modestly under a blanket) under the caption: "Does your group need better coverage? Don't grope around. Come to Great-West Life."

When the Manitoba Action Committee on the Status of Women got hold of this puerile magazine and protested the ads, the press boys, as usual, complained that women have no sense of humour. Funny, there wasn't a single humorous picture of a naked man showing his wares, or submissively baring his bottom, or lying under a desk. That famous male sense of humour that we women are supposed to lack seems a strangely one-sided sort of thing.

The fact is that that sense of humour is both panicky and vindictive. In groups, men act like frightened boys throwing dirt at the things they fear most: women, vulnerability, intimacy. Then, like classic bullies, they want the victim of the besmirching jokes to laugh it off, forgive, and be buddies.

The Winnipeg press boys aren't the only example — though they're the most appalling because these are the same yolts who will be writing the disparaging news stories about the women's movement and dreaming up cutesy put-down headlines. Another example of men-in-groups has been festering in my desk for months. It's the *Toike Oike*, a newspaper printed by the Engineering Society at the University of Toronto, and its so ugly, so squalid, and so unbelievably stunted that I honestly don't know how to deal with it.

Take the long and tortured story of "Stuporman" and judge for yourself. Stuporman bumps into a nun and "punches the living sh-t out of her face" before meeting a woman whom he "pumps furiously" until she bursts into

flames. His "super sperm" burns right through her back and
melts through the furniture. After trailing the woman in the
air "like a used condom", he incinerates her, only to regret
later that he has "ruined the only orifice he had ever known
which could accommodate him."

Then there's a Guest Editorial called "Rape I Love It", in
which a woman supposedly gushes on about the thrill of
being raped by an engineer. And on and on and on the
engineers slobber over their favourite obscenities like little
boys playing with matches.

Sexuality and love must be the most frightening thing
these poor kids have ever dealt with; how else to explain their
obsessive frenzy? And when one of these quivering blobs pries
himself loose from his group, how satisfactory will he be in a
relationship with a real woman?

I wonder what the button-down executives of Eaton's and
The Bay—not to mention James Ham, engineer and president of the University of Toronto—think of their boys now?

The Winnipeg boys backed down; the department stores apologized; the major businesses yanked their ads. It was a temporary
retreat, however; a case of ducking down while the flak was
flying. Within a year, the Winnipeg Press Club had severed its
formal ties with "Beer and Skits", so that the latter could
continue as a separate organization of newsmen with a fifty-year
tradition of "private evenings for gentlemen only".

Toike Oike, despite strong attacks on it by the Dean of Engineering, numerous professors, the campus Status of Women
Committee, the head of the Ontario Human Rights Commission,
and student groups, limps on and on. Some months after I
criticized the paper, I was at the University of Toronto to speak
to a group of women students. To my surprise, a group of female
engineering students were present, in the front row, to carry the
banner for *Toike*. They sat and chewed gum, bored and vacant,
while I spoke. When I'd finished, they jumped up to raise the
question of the engineering newspaper. "It's just good fu-un,"
they whined, drawing out their vowels plaintively. "Whyncha
criticize those libbers who defaced *property* and painted slogans
against *Toike* on our engineering building, eh?" They had drunk

their shrinking-potion, these youngsters, and were proud to be "one of the boys", saving their rancour for feminists.

The most revealing salvo in the whole little skirmish, though, was fired by a woman engineering student who wrote to the *Star* to criticize my criticisms. She proudly claimed that female engineering students, refusing to "march or scream or draw attention" to themselves, really do more for women's rights than other groups because they will "join men in the top wage category", not settling, like other women, for "dead-end jobs". The note of smug conformity and materialism, while saddening, is not uncommon in professional faculties. What is more distressing is the egocentricity. Barely a generation or two ago, feminists had to fight lonely and often bitter battles to gain entry for women into Canadian professional schools and to "join men" in those top wage brackets. Now the callow students take all the credit for themselves. They have so little self-respect that they would rather be the wagging tail on the most chauvinist dog than stand with other women for a little dignity.

If it seems strange that young, well-schooled women in this post-movement era should be so unenlightened, the explanation is not far off. For the past twenty years, young people in North America have been subjected to almost non-stop conditioning in reactionary social attitudes. At the very moment when the women's movement has won significant victories in the courts and in the workplace, the battle is being lost in the living-room: When you turn on the TV tonight for an hour or two of mental browsing, just think: you're plugging into a network of 100 million other North Americans, your nerves flicking to the same stimuli and your brain imprinting the same images. And all of you are getting more sexist, racist, and deluded the longer you watch.

Now wait a minute; don't get mad at me. That's not my conclusion. It's the conclusion of the most respected TV-watcher-watchers in the business — the experts at the Annenberg School of Communications at the University of Pennsylvania, who base those findings on 10 years of research.

On your TV tonight you'll see and believe in a miniature model of our world — but a skewed model, where men form 73 per cent of the population, women are a compliant and adorable minority, and old people don't exist except as cartoons.

The TV men are vigorous, dominant professional types in their 30s or early 40s. In fact, TV is a complete world of 34-year-old men. It's odd how passively we accept that, because, of course, it doesn't reflect anything real except for the "consumer income curve". The men who create TV are creating it for the middle-class men like themselves with money to spend.

Most of the women who flutter and swoop and simper around these TV men are not in their 30s, but in their 20s. "The character population in TV drama," remarks the Annenberg study, dryly, "is structured to provide an abundance of younger women for older men."

One of the most fascinating insights of the study is the way in which "TV women age faster than men." By middle age the women are depicted as old, while the men are still dashing heroes with "romantic possibilities". I hadn't noticed it before, but of course it's true. And when TV women get old, they're automatically frail, accident-prone, and the Character Most Likely To Be Murdered. Victims.

Old age is bad news on TV, of course. So bad that it's practically wiped out of existence: only 2 percent of TV's characters are old (and usually batty), compared with 11 per cent of the real population.

Well, what of it, I hear the restless reader muttering. So what if women are portrayed as overwhelmingly young, attractive, and "benign but powerless", to quote the study? Isn't this more feminist niggling and fussing over trivia? After all, it's just TV.

Yeah. Only TV. The most powerful and pervasive force in our history. (You really think those advertisers would spend billions of dollars if TV didn't sway and mould us?) In fact, what the Annenberg studies spell out is just how massive an influence TV has on us. A couple of years ago, Annenberg told us about the "mean world syndrome" — heavy TV viewers believe that the cities are 10 times more violent than they really are, and have extreme law-and-order ideas to match their TV-shaped world. Now we learn that heavy TV viewers are measurably more sexist. According to Annenberg's 10-year study, combined with national opinion polls,

TV buffs really think that women's place is in the home, that women shouldn't work, that men are more suited "emotionally" for politics. Feminists, gnash your teeth. TV addicts are immune to the movement.

Worse and worse, TV is even more perniciously sexist for children. Men outnumber women more than 5 to 1 on children's programming, and anyone who has watched a morning of cartoons knows how gross are the stereotypes.

True, we're not all heavy viewers and we're not all lobotomized. But even if you count yourself among the enlightened, can you really swear that TV has not affected your idea of female beauty, your concept of a "man's role", or your perception of black and aged people?

It's sinister. The omnipotent story-teller of our time, the one-eyed hypnotist in our living rooms, the enchanter who mesmerizes our children, is telling lies and warping our view of the world.

It's hard to remain optimistic when the voice of feminism sometimes sounds as small as the chirping of crickets in the vast night of misogynist propoganda. The belittling messages are so pervasive, so ingrained in advertising, popular music, newspapers, television, high school curricula, and even our language, that women can almost see their self-worth disappear. After her second or third round of the shrinking-drink, Alice in Wonderland had similar sobering thoughts. "It might end you know," said Alice to herself, "in my going out altogether, like a candle."

SUPERWOMAN CAN'T FLY

EVERYONE WHO WORKS FOR MAGAZINES OR NEWSPAPERS aimed at women lives uneasily with the charge that the media have created a monster. People accuse us of inventing a plastic Superwoman, confidently business-like, elegant, maternal, ambitious, sexy — a mythical Bo Derek who dresses for success and is a dab hand at nouvelle cuisine.

The accusation is true, but a little beside the point. Of course, this 1980s mirage of the perfect woman is one of Himalayan inaccessibility. But why do women fall for it? Why are they goaded to helpless rage by this media-created image, while men seem relatively unharrowed by sports heroes or the multi-orgasmic champs of soft porn? It's worth investigating.

Perhaps men have more antibodies against the infection of inadequacy because, groomed for competition in the world, they are brought up with stouter defences against self-loathing. Every boy is taught to aim for the starring role on the hockey team. Failing that, he learns to swallow his tears and take a reflected pride in the glory of Gretzky. If a man can't score all the goals himself, he can at least take comfort in being part of the masculine team that dominates the league.

Women, on the other hand, are still growing up to compete with each other for the attention and approval of men. There is much more at stake here than there is on the hockey rink; for one thing, there's no comforting embrace of the team to fall back on should you fail to score. At best, only one or two top superwomen will penetrate the male ranks of rulers. Only one will get to marry the prime minister or become the protégé of the president of Bendix Corporation, or win through to solitary womanhood on the benches of the Supreme Court. In the female world, if you are not superwoman, then neither are you a respected member of the team — there is no team. It follows that for women, competition from other women is far more life-threatening than it is for a man. Besides, the competition is fought on more personal and elemental grounds. A boy may fall short of being the top forward on the team and still be valued for his other qualities. A girl who is seen as deficient in her person—a girl with an ugly nose or bad skin—is less favoured even by other women and, cruelly, is considered less warm and less intelligent than prettier girls.

Still, why are women more infuriated by the glamorous career women of *Cosmopolitan* and *Chatelaine* than they are by the silicone sylphs offered up by *Playboy* and the *Edmonton Sun?* Maybe we have internalized the male demand for perfect bodies for so many generations that the ache of inadequacy is as familiar a strain in female life as the monthly cycle. The idea that our bodies must conform to a male-determined standard or else be seen as laughable or worthless has seeped in at the ground-level of consciousness. Superwoman, on the other hand, must seem like the arrogant boast of the new female media types who are themselves Superwomen because of their privileged jobs.

Every one of us who worked at *Chatelaine* in the 1970s was aware of this ironic situation. In promoting the idea of all the choices a modern woman might make and all the new, exciting ways in which she might excel, we were falling into the trap of seeming to espouse an impossible ideal. When we offered a new chocolate-cake recipe in the same issue in which we cheered a new appointment to the provincial bench, our readers sourly concluded that we intended all women to be judges who were gold-medal bakers.

At articles meetings in Doris Anderson's big corner office, we would fidget glumly with our pencils and clipboards when— inevitably—one of our number would propose the idea again: "How about an article on the price that women pay for success?" All of us could hear, immediately, the rattle of skeletons in a dozen famous cupboards. We all knew of the glamorous author who boasted about her childless freedom but who was painfully recovering from yet another secret breakdown. We knew about the millionaire's beautiful wife whose marriage festered in private perversities. We knew about the envied actress whose children were nervous wrecks; we knew about the well-disguised drinking problems, diseases, and even husband-inflicted bruises of some of the female celebrities we wrote about all the time.

The idea would come up, we would debate its merits with malicious but temporary glee, and the idea would sink into oblivion. We didn't do the story — not out of ideology, but out of delicacy and fellow-feeling, not to mention the threat of libel action. Besides, we sensed a gap in the hypothesis. No one wrote about the wife-beating tendencies, alcoholism, or disturbed children of male celebrities — at least, not until the tendencies slipped over the line into criminal action. And who was to say that these human frailties and wounds were the price of success? Might not the woman who failed — or the woman who never tried — also have a brutal husband or a bottle hidden in the broom closet?

It was never our intention to construct yet another perfect image with which women should despairingly compare themselves. But the line between role model and impossible ideal is a fine one, and some of our readers certainly felt belittled rather than inspired.

Writing a column finally gave me the chance to redress the wrong. If journalists couldn't or wouldn't write about the human flaws behind the façades of celebrities, they could certainly afford to be honest about themselves. I was blushingly aware that, from the outside, my life might appear magazine-perfect: cushy, high-profile job; well-known husband; kids; dog; trips to Italy. I hoped that somewhere between a whine and a confession I could strike a note of self-mockery that would be both true and amusingly liberating for my readers. These revelations of chaos and near-disintegration in the life of the working wife proved to be among the most popular pieces I've written. People who never agreed with me about maternity leave or social welfare knew just what I meant about socks, fridges, and department-store dressing-rooms.

The day began badly, with the piano.

The piano shuttles back and forth in our family, as each succeeding generation learns that it is not Glenn Gould. After my crew had had the requisite run at "Swans on the Lake", the piano was due to go back to my mother's house on Monday.

The piano mover said "9 a.m. sharp". I stayed home from work; my mother stayed home from work; the piano mover, apparently, also stayed home from work. At 10 a.m. I knew that it was going to be a bad Monday. I was already an hour behind on a day of scheduled work. The piano movers had just arrived and were guffawing in the living room about the piano they dropped yesterday.

At 10:10 a.m. the phone rang. Espie, my cherished Esperanza, the magic-worker who transforms Monday's dirty laundry into clean, fragrant towers of towels, the creator of order and of dinner, was sick and would not be coming today.

"Kids," I said, "this is how you do the laundry." They followed me to the basement, little soldiers hurling themselves into the breach. I turned on the laundry-room light. The bulb went "ping" and left us in the dark. I put in a new bulb. This time it wasn't "ping", it was more like "be-zat!", along with a shower of sparks.

"Forget the laundry," I said into the dark, and called the electrician.

On my way downtown, I thought about the women who have to get to the office, or the plant or the store, by 9 a.m. or else. Monday was being tiresome, but not as downright rotten as it might have been.

10:45. I have already begun phoning a long list of parents, teachers, and principals for the education article. All, quite sensibly, seem to be on holiday. None is reachable. I am now down to phoning people who might know the home phone numbers of people who might be on holiday in town.

The phone rings. "Mummy, the house painter is here."

Pause.

"The painter? The one who was going to come last year?"

"Yes. He wants to know what colour you want to paint the house."

I remain calm.

"The paint chips are under the hazelnuts in the old wooden salad bowl on the dresser in the dining room."

Pause.

"What are paint chips?"

I begin to feel, subtly, that the day is careening out of control.

Noon. The phone rings. "The roofer is here." Ah yes. The roofer who was going to come three weeks ago. Of course, I picture my house swarming with workmen while my children thrash about with the laundry in the dark.

The phone rings. "Honey," says my husband. "You remember Frank? He's here from Washington and he'll be staying overnight with us."

I phoned home. "Take the Monopoly set off the spare room bed, stuff your old clothes in a closet, and for heaven's sake, wash enough towels for a visitor."

I felt weak, as though my blood were gradually thinning and the oxygen getting scarce. I might have known that the next country to be heard from would be Rosie, the hysterically loyal dog. Rosie's irreproachable devotion can always be counted on to add mayhem to mere havoc. Sure enough: the phone rang. My son, it seems, had gone out to babysit. Rosie had gone out to find my son. First she went to Mike DeCarlo's house, a couple of miles away, in the mistaken belief that my son was visiting Mike.

"Mummy, Mrs. DeCarlo phoned to say that Rosie just opened her screen door and walked into her kitchen."

"Tell Mrs. DeCarlo to be cruel and shove Rosie out the door and yell at her to go home."

"Mrs. DeCarlo says she can't do that because she's Catholic."

Not 10 minutes passed before the phone rang again. "Mummy, you know when the painter took off the screens? Some wasps came into the house and I got bitten and are you coming home soon?"

Any working mother knows how to give instructions over the phone for the settling of bloody battles and the removal of bubble gum from hair, while simultaneously typing, smiling at the boss, and picking up a pencil with her toes. This is routine. But there are days when it all seems to be slipping and sliding away as inexorably as The House of Usher keeling over into the bog.

How good it was, therefore, and how sweet to swirl my day away in a glass of red wine on Monday night and listen to the by-election returns. Piano movers may dally, wasps sting, roofers roof, and dogs act silly; housekeepers may fall by the wayside and working days crumble into rat poop. But on Monday night, the voters looked up from their interest rates and said "NO!" to the government. A Monday's well that ends well.

I don't usually get sentimental over the laundry. It's just that when I unwrapped the shirts from the new cleaner's down at the corner, and I saw that shirt button sewed on so trimly, so firmly, it touched a deep wellspring within me. For four long years, that shirt had been buttonless.

It's not that I'm lazy, Lord knows, I've defrosted fridges and ironed little pleated skirts with the best of them. It's… well… It might as well blurt it out… it's Fear of Sewing.

The trauma dates from the days of Miss R. in Grade 7 home economics. Before that, I was perfectly normal. When I was an innocent, pre-Miss R. child, there was absolutely no symptom of the lifelong disability I was to bear. Oh sure, there were the tiniest warning signs: the time I knitted a doll scarf that started out to be 7 inches wide and wound up a tight little 2-inch scroll. Or the operation I performed to mend my stuffed doll's stomach, which left her looking like a victim of leprosy.

But we never realized I had an actual handicap until the first sewing project in Miss R.'s class. (We had already mastered white sauce, I believe.) Now we were going to make a shirt. The whole class was composed of curly little blonde girls who knew instinctively how to lay out a pattern on a piece of cloth. By the time I'd untangled myself from coils of tissue paper, the others were pinning and stitching and humming along with the kind of starched precision so dear to Miss R.'s heart. Starch was the very essence of Miss R., from her gray perm to her gleaming white uniform to her ironed-flat, crispy-crunchy inflections. "How to cut a pattern?" she echoed me with starchy amazement. "Why, simply cut along the lines."

How the devil was I to know that she didn't mean *all* the lines? The whole business was as profoundly mysterious to me as Stonehenge. It took me all the rest of that year to stitch together the 40 fragments of snipped-up cotton into a dirndl skirt. It didn't help that I was filled with an unreasoning terror of the treadle sewing machine. Or that, when I finally got up the courage to ask about changing the bobbin, Miss R. would snap something that sounded like "Just frong the glamis into the callipers and get on with it."

Meanwhile, the curly little girls went briskly on to churn out aprons, pyjamas, whole assembly lines of "ensembles". By spring, when I had hemmed the skirt for the fourth time (how do you make stitches invisible, anyway, Miss R.?), I had become a personal, overwhelming trial to Miss R. Her face froze into an expression of maddened gloom whenever I loomed up, trailing the by-now-frayed-and-grubby skirt for yet another inspection. Finally, with bleeding fingers, sure at last of Miss R.'s approval, I brought her the fifth and most invisible hem ever. There was a frosty pause for bifocal inspection. "Never mind," she said, with what she must have imagined to be kindly indulgence, "you can always sew up the bottom and use it as a laundry bag."

It's been a long, long trail of safety pins and sticky tape since then. It hasn't been easy. All those paper-clipped Hallowe'en costumes disintegrating around my poor children's ears. All those little corduroy pants rolled up around my toddlers' ankles, ever ready to unroll and trap them. All those shirts and socks stuffed away, holey and buttonless, to be mended mañana.

All by myself, I was the precursor of the disposable generation, cunningly cutting curtains out of felt and sticking up coat hems with "magic sewing glue" that tended to seep through the material in scabrous stains. When needle and thread were unavoidable, my family learned to make wide, cautious detours around me as I sat, clenched and cursing,

temples throbbing, carefully stitching my finger to a sock toe
or the front of a sweater to the back.

My troubles are over now, though. Instead of behaviour
modification, I've discovered wonderful sewing stuff that
looks like cotton candy and cleverly dissolves into rock-line
glue when you iron it between two pieces of fabric. Between
the new cleaner at the corner and the cotton candy, I can
laugh at last at Fear of Sewing. Take that, Miss R.!

How provoking, how mysterious, is the domestic life of the
sock.

Oh, I know, we humans have been almost regally oblivious
to the comings and goings of our little woolly companions.
Lolling smugly at the top of the food chain, we've bashed
baby seals, patronized the pilchard, and totally neglected the
humblest ecosystem of them all: the life cycle of the sock. Now
the socks, after centuries of silent servitude, are taking their
revenge.

There's been palpable tension between me and the sock
world since, as a child, I cursed the scratchy brown lisle
stockings that were my winter nemesis. Knee socks slid down
to form ridged lumps under my instep as I hobbled to school
in rubber boots. Bobby socks stretched, sighed and lapsed
into withered doughnuts around my ankles. I grew into nylon
stockings and knew that, despite all the waist-twisting and
licked-finger-patting in the world, my seams would climb
uncomely zig-zags up the backs of my legs, as wobbly and
embarrassing as novice ski-tracks.

But the true extent of the breakdown didn't occur to me
until about 15 years ago, when I began to be directly responsible for the household socks. It was then that I realized, with
a cold shock, how serious the situation was.

Socks were committing suicide. They were doing a bunk,
going over the hill, divorcing each other, possibly leaping
over cliffs like lemmings. Their family life was a shambles.
From day to day, death and separation took a mounting toll.
Even baby socks were affected. I'd put two pink booties into
the washing machine and know, with sinking heart, that

only one tiny pink bootie would emerge, alone. What happened to that one little vanishee? Did it hurl itself down the washing-machine drain, struggling to reach the rivers that lead to the sea? Did it transubstantiate? Scientists have been unable to find a trace of the billion or more escapees.

In my home, a laundry basket gradually filled with the sombre detritus. Single socks, some shrivelled and some felted, but all ineluctably alone and unmatched, lay tangled in a sullen heap. Navy socks, striped socks, poignant little toddler socks, long outgrown. Sentimentally, I could not bear to throw them out. But only once in a blue moon was there a reunion, when a lost mate would turn up inside the sleeve of a brushed-nylon nightgown, or be rescued from a sleazy masquerade life as a kids' homemade sock puppet with glued-on button eyes.

Homemakers shrugged and bought more socks. Sock factories went into overtime; manufacturers were ecstatic; socks went to $2.50 a pair. Few observers were astute enough to note the social disintegration which underlay this period of economic expansion.

In homes across the nation the merry hours of waking and corn flaking turned slowly into a wrenching battleground. "Where the hell are my socks?" or "Sacre bleu, où sont mes chaussettes?" was snarled in homes from Peggy's Cove to Salt Spring Island. Children, late for school due to lack of socks, have been known to accuse siblings of theft, to ransack their parents' drawers, and to leave (barefoot in their sneakers) bitterly unreconciled and never to return. Sock-snatching has now been shown to surpass loud chewing as a source of family stress. There are few sights more pathetic than the boy slinking to school in his sister's pink-and-mauve Argyles, or a man whose toes are wrung in the tight embrace of socks three sizes too small.

Sociologists have noted a sharp rise in husband and wife abuse, both verbal and physical. There's something in the sight of a drawer full of single socks that triggers an as-yet-unknown chemical combination in the human brain, leading to uncontrollable irritation.

Is it too late to restore the delicate balance of the life cycle of the sock, for so many millennia a model of coupled constancy? Is human-sock compatibility destroyed forever? We don't know. Experts can only tell us that, as we head into a new ice age, with the Persian Gulf ruled by madmen, we're going to need our neglected little friends more than ever. Come home, little footlet. We need you at humanity's bottom end.

Really, it's not that I hate fashion but that I loathe shopping more. I marvel at the women in our fashion photos, balancing Kurly Kate hats on their coiffed heads or smartly discovering spangled acrobat's undies to go with their ammunition belts and sequinned socks. While other women cluck over the sheer outrageous ugliness of square-shouldered suits or black-speckled nose veils, I swoon with admiration for women who can find that much time—and courage—to shop.

You've heard of the Gathering of the Clans? For me, shopping is the Gathering of the Neuroses. Like Stephen Leacock in a bank, I come mentally unstuck as soon as necessity thrusts me into the glittering acreage of a department store. Having wrenched an hour from my schedule to get there in the first place, I find myself lapsing into bovine inattention at the sundries counter. Precious minutes tick by as I linger over cunning little pin cushions shaped like tomatoes, or collapsible travelling shoe horns with attached burglar alarm. Anything to delay the moment of truth in the separates department.

The minute I find myself beside the clothing racks, I begin to skulk. A stern voice seems to boom down at me from the fluorescent heavens above: "You are not a perfect size 10." Even the mannequins, with their 12-inch waists and purple fingernails, leer at me with their empty eyesockets as I surreptitiously flip the tags to find my right (and oh, so wrong) size.

"Can I help you, madam?" I knew it. I knew that someone with bangles, supercilious eyebrows, and a penetrating voice would appear the moment I paused over a teensy Ultrasuede suit.

"Just browsing," I peep, with a conciliatory smile.

"But madam," she laughs piercingly, "this rack is all size 10." All along the aisles, heads turn in mild curiosity.

I flee across miles of carpeting to hide behind a barricade of polyester blazers. I know that I'm doomed to polyester. I know that cotton, silk, and cashmere are reserved for very tiny and perfect millionaires. I know that, finally, I will lurch footsore to the fitting rooms with an armload of nasty, slithery polyester.

"Wanna try 'em on? Only three at a time," a bored prison matron will say as she bars my way to the fitting rooms.

Mental calculations: shall I undress, struggle with increasing clamminess into a series of polyester disasters, dress, come out for the next three monstrosities, undress... "Forget these three; I hate them anyway," I say, relinquishing half my load.

Fitting-room fantasies skitter through my mind. Perhaps they made these door curtains four inches too narrow on purpose? Do department stores spies pace these halls, peering in at half-nude customers to make sure no one is shoving a pair of Sherpa boots into her pocket? Customers of The Room, I hear, get real doors on their fitting rooms. Perhaps rich people are above suspicion.

I anchor the curtain with my purse so that it closes at one side, at least; pile the clothes precariously on the single hook; cower in the least exposed corner; and begin to strip.

"How are we doing, dear?" I knew it. I knew that Needle-Voice would be back, sweeping the curtain gaily aside just as I tried to cram myself into a tube of polyester, with my slip tangling around my ankles and my arms trapped as in a vise.

"Just fine," I snap, trying to sound determinedly private through a mouthful of fabric. Sweaty and panic-stricken (these must be funny-house mirrors), I resolve to buy the first outfit that fits, and sprint for the cash register.

Tap, tap, tap, goes the salesperson, communing mysteriously with her machine. Pitta, patta, goes my heart. What if the lights flash, the bells ring, and I'm summoned to explain to a faceless enforcer on the telephone why I haven't paid my bills? It doesn't matter that I *have* paid my bills. By this time the separates department has reduced me to a state of such abject guilt and inferiority that I'm ready to believe the worst about my own character and financial probity.

Never again, I vow, staggering out into daylight. Not till I'm driven back by the threat of incipient nakedness. High style? Forget it. That day I manage to catch up with last year's "look", I figure it'll be a triumph.

I never knew what liberation really was until I cast off the chains of salon slavery. Beauty salon, that is.

You know the drill: you put it off until your hair is beginning to look like Sasquatch, canvass your friends for recommendations, and blindly make an appointment at Buffoon's or Uni-Snip. It's not so much the culture shock when the receptionist turns out to have mauve nail polish and rhinestone-studded eyelids. It's more the feeling that if you're not ready for a blue rinse, and a mite too old for crinkles or corn rows, you just don't fit in anywhere.

Apparently we're supposed to love the hairdresser's. All that Art Deco, the creamy colours, and the steamy fragrance are meant to whisper that we're being swept into Cleopatra's boudoir for a luscious hour or two of sensuous pampering. So naturally I feel apologetic when I lean back for my hair wash and find my feet dangling ludicrously in the air and a nasty crick in my neck.

Then the moment of truth. A lissome youth trails a few strands of my hair through his finger with a faint air of distaste. "Se-vere damage," he exclaims, peering closer. "Been colouring it for years?" "Never in my life." "Perms?" "Never," I croak.

"Tch, tch. Let me examine it for Ph imbalance under our hairoscope," he urges, hurrying away with an incriminating sample.

I try not to strangle on the towels wrapped like a tourniquet around my neck. Forget the Sasquatch: with all these layers of wrapper, plastic aprons, and linen shrouds, it's more like the Abominable Snowman.

Young and Lovely returns to confirm my worst forebodings. "I really think you'll need one of our special Herbal Ph-balanced Full Body Protein Yogurt treatments to deal with these...ugh...split ends."

I feel myself sinking deeper and deeper into emotional exile. Not only am I undergoing something obscurely medical, with ropes of cotton batting glued to my temples and thick, icy jellies oozing down around my ears, but I seem to have gate-crashed an exclusive club. All around me fly merry witticisms and in-groupy chitter-chatter as the hairdressers snip and curl:

"Did you see the Punk Slash I did for Bibsy? Didn't she look simply too marvy?"

"Alfred says he's going to pop in before the big bash tonight. I simply can't *wait* to see how he'll look à la Travolta."

When they park me under the drier, so the jelly can harden into a crust, the silence is simply too marvy. All I can hear is the hot Sahara wind as it crisps the tops of my ears.

Helpless as an astronaut with an itch, I realize that the ashtray and magazines are one foot beyond my reach and that the orders for coffee are being cheerily taken while I am held incommunicado. Then someone appears before me with their lips moving. "Pardon me?" I cry gladsomely, leaning forward and whacking my forehead painfully on the front edge of the drier.

Young and Lovely tosses his locks and faces up to the challenge of cutting my hair. Possibly to distract himself from the ennui of it all, he takes a few random snips from the skin of my neck on his way to clipping me near-bald.

Bloodied and, yes, bowed, I not only fork over $27 at the end of two miserable hours, but find myself thrusting lavish tips into little envelopes, at the bidding of Rhinestone Eyes.

Nevermore. Last week I broke the sex barrier and nervously lunged into the barber shop "Can you cut my hair?" I blurted (suave is not my style) and two minutes later—no appointment, no wait—found my hair being briskly scrubbed. Five minutes later, it was snip, snip, snip. No hairoscopes, plastic bibs, lotions or potions. No seven-foot photographs of gaunt young women looking morosely accusatory under a mountain of frizz.

Half an hour, ten bucks. And to raise my consciousness still further, I found a neat paperback on my desk, hot from the publishers. *Dr. Zizmor's Brand-Name Guide to Beauty Aids*, among other trenchant exposés of the cosmetic industry, tells you which shampoos will do what for your hair. Example: yogurt, honey, wheat germ, Ph balance, oils and protein conditioners are all either useless or meaningless in shampoos.

In knowledge is strength. Now that's liberation.

Every woman needs a room of her own, and that's why the bathtub was invented.

I first discovered the indispensability of the bathtub when I spent six years at home as the mama of three (successive) infants. Days of delight and coagulated pablum, when I would simultaneously nurse the baby, catch the falling porridge bowl, snatch the scissors from the toddler with the other hand, and all the while try to sound calmly competent to the plumber on the telephone. Each day was like spilling a barrel of Ping-Pong balls on a mountain top and trying to collect them all at the bottom by sunset.

And what does all this have to do with the mystical bond between a woman and her bathtub? Simple. After a day of starting a dozen tasks and being interrupted by 39 others, a woman has to have time to glue body and soul back together again.

It's no use thinking you can do it in the kitchen. If you sit down in the kitchen to read the paper after the little sprouts are in bed, you're sure to notice the sticky rim of raspberry Jello-O around the high-chair tray, and the lost piece of Lego in the sugar bowl, and the tiny shoelace you were hunting for knotted around the table leg. And while you're down on your knees untying the shoelace, you'll notice the kids must have been painting the baseboards with toothpaste while you thought they were learning about dental hygiene....

No, the bathtub is the one private refuge, and the only place a mother can read in peace. Unfortunately, though men don't use bathtubs, they must certainly design them. How else to explain the nightmarish shape of the modern Canadian tub, the drastic lack of ledges on which to keep coffee, ashtray, cigarettes, soap, and dry washcloth (to dry hands before turning pages), and the idiotic design of taps on which it's impossible to spread-eagle a book?

It's obvious that the designers have never considered the centrality of books to the bath ethos. Cleanliness is next to somnolence unless you can let your mind escape to another world. Why not built-in book racks in tubs?

And then the proportions of Canadian tubs are all wrong. A person who settles down for a bathtub read is serious. This is going to take at least 45 minutes, and therefore it's essential that the water be at least neck-deep to prevent goosebumps in the upper hemisphere. The French understand this very well. They have the most delicious deep and narrow tubs, complete with cunning little hand showers. Not only can you poach yourself up to the earlobes, but you are saved the desperate boredom of washing your hair in the shower, where it's impossible to read. Canadian tubs, on the other hand, waste all their space sideways. You sit in a stingy waist-deep puddle with useless water each side of you.

I admit I'm spoiled. I started married life in a flat in the former summer home of Sir Henry (Casa Loma) Pellatt. Now there was a man who knew bathtubs. We not only had a hip bath and a marble fountain-shower, but a six-foot tub where I could do a little elementary backstroking or a dead woman's float when the need for exercise struck.

Later, for a few years, we lived in a house where the bathroom had been planned by a woman: enough floor space for an army of rubber ducks, green plants, a six-foot tub, a telephone with a long cord, and foot-deep ledges everywhere, especially along the side of the tub. Watery bliss was mine.

Now we live in a house that is cursed with a squalid little modern tub (pink, with yellow rubber butterfly stick-ons). No ledge, no book-propping possibilities. I have to sit in an angled crouch to read my book, which wobbles precariously on the side of the tub. My ashtray skates away across the nasty green lino, and I get cold armpits from leaning my arm over the edge for my coffee cup.

How can a woman get her act together if her literary style is cramped this way? Down with stingy modern tubs. Hurrah for the chin-deep soak and all those Victorian tub-building chaps who must have known a thing or two about mother-hood.

"When are you turning 40?"

"I've turned," I answered, as though I were spoiled milk. But the truth is, being 40 isn't the sour descent into the long slide I thought it might be when I was 30 and altogether more pessimistic.

Being 40, it turns out, is a sweet surprise, all the more so because I was far too distracted to notice it when it happened last summer. (It was one of those soft, scented nights on the Mediterranean coast of Italy, and I was so steeped in roses and champagne that the actual numbers on the cake didn't really penetrate my mind.)

Our rich and clever civilization has taken the old sting out of being 40; between the Pill at one end of the fertile years and amniocentesis at the other, the biological boundaries have been blurred. It's possible now to delay motherhood so that a woman in her early 40's may be just settling down to a cosy few years of nest-building after a hectic decade and a half of career.

It's different, of course, for every decade group. A 55-year-old acquaintance told me that when she was 40, she looked at her daughters and realized she would never have their career opportunities or their freedoms. For me, a 40-year-old in 1980, the pattern has been the opposite. I look at my daughters and wonder how they will cope with the revolution of declining expectations. I grew up in a tiny rented duplex in the post-war era of boundless optimism. I knew I would move up in the world. Now my daughters grow up wondering aloud if they'll be able to live in a house at all by the time they're adults. My generation slipped luckily under the wire. We had the career opportunities denied to our grandmothers and the relaxed assurance of material betterment that is lost to our daughters.

Midlife crisis? A distant memory, thanks. More women I know went through that horror of encroaching age and mortality back in their mid-30's. By 40, those "where am I going?" glooms seem to be mostly resolved. And I've never met any 40ish woman who worries about the foreseeable menopause. Men highly overrate that supposed crisis. We may worry about jobs, security, attractiveness, possible widowhood...but end of fertility? Uh-uh.

No, 40 is a time of energy and new beginnings. They say that Thomas Hobbes, the 17th-century philosopher, first read Euclid at 40, became utterly besotted, and even at bedtime kept drawing geometry on his thighs and sheets. I empathize. With the excitement, I mean, not the geometry. Of course, my perspective is distorted. Since I quit smoking at 40, I feel as though climbing Everest would be a mere bagatelle.

But I bet other women share my astonished delight at the freedoms of midlife. I can lock the bathroom door without worrying that an infant will drink Javex while I'm incommunicado; I'm no longer responsible for runny noses and untied shoelaces; I'm even old and smart enough to have given up the wistful yearning for just one more little owner of a runny nose.

I can afford, now, to be sillier and more light-hearted than I was at 30. Images don't count any more; I dare to be as gleefully undignified as I want, and I perfectly understand those middle-aged eccentrics who wear tennis shoes to the opera. Inside my head, I range enjoyably from 12 years old to 90 and back again in the space of an hour. Sooner or later I'll have to take seriously the effects of gravity, as everything south of my eyebrows seems to sag and settle. But right now it amuses me to look out of youthful eyes and see those incongruous gray hairs in the mirror.

Middle-aged women, say the theorists, are more radical than young women: we've already achieved (or rejected) the husbands, children, and homes which are the goals of the anxious young. I don't know about that. I'd say that women of 40 are more radical because we have the energy that comes with the end of exhausting motherhood, the force of knowing who we are, the resilience of being able to grin at our familiar old flaws and foibles. Who's afraid of big bad 40? No me. I love it.

MEN ARE TWO-FIFTHS MORE EQUAL THAN WOMEN

WHAT WE HAVE HERE IN CANADA TODAY IS A SPECTACULAR, massive affirmative-action program, a juggernaut of privilege for one sex only. Special encouragement, education, support, extra pay, opportunity, training, and promotion — all awarded on the basis of sex. Male sex. Consider: a man and a woman, both with the same experience, are working side by side at the same job. On the average in Canada, he will be earning two-fifths more than she will, despite the fact that she is, statistically, better educated and more reliable. What is the difference between them? Privilege, based on owning the right set of reproductive organs.

We like to believe that we are among the most advanced nations in the world. But our national insistence on special privilege for men has put us on the bottom of any index of civilized equality. In 1980, when the international Organization for Economic Cooperation and Development rated nineteen countries for male-female wage disparities, Canada ranked nineteenth. Even when male and female wages are compared with special adjustments to allow for differences in age, seniority, and qualification, there's still an utterly unjustified gap of between ten per cent and twenty-five per cent.

Equal-pay laws would not even up the scales very much. Women are kept in their inferior positions mostly by job segregation. By the simple device of giving different job descriptions to what men and women do, employers from the federal government itself right down to the lowliest nursing-home owner have been able to keep women in the lower-paying category. The only way to overcome the unfairness is through laws enforcing equal pay for work of equal value. Though right-wingers and

41

employers like to argue that the entire country would be plunged into a morass of confusion should such laws be enacted, with armies of bureaucrats trying to compare seamstresses with oil-company managers, this ridiculous accusation is only a smoke-screen. The truth is that equal-pay-for-work-of-equal-value laws, where they exist, make a difference in the fight against grotesque unfairness. Federal librarians (mostly female) were paid less than federal historical researchers (mostly male) until 1981, when it was proven that their education and tasks were equivalent, and the government had to make good the difference. Such laws would offer justice for the mainly female Ontario government switchboard operators. Their situation attracted notice during a recent provincial election campaign when it was revealed that though they need a high school education and a year of expe-rience to qualify for their jobs, they are paid forty dollars less per week than the male parking-lot attendants, who need only grade eight education and no experience.

Affirmative action for women is another topic of furious debate. I have often heard men sneer at affirmative action as the most contemptible of reverse discriminations. "Wouldn't you be ashamed to have it said that you only got your job because of special discrimination?" they often say to me. Why, I wonder, do these men never feel ashamed that *they* almost certainly enjoy their jobs, status, and income because of the overwhelming special privilege given to men? Could they have won and held their jobs so easily if they had had to compete equally with women for those jobs, with no special favours given to men? Of course they could not. If there were real equality of education, opportunity, and promotion, then at least half the men in good jobs today would be way down the ladder, working as cashiers or filing clerks. Unless men want to argue that they are naturally superior in intellect and ability (and no study could bear them out), they would have to admit that their superior success at work is due to unfair sex discrimination. Men hold ninety-seven per cent of the senior executive positions in the federal civil service, and even more than that in business and banking. Even allowing for the relatively later entry of women into the work force, the imbalance reveals a huge favouritism operating for men.

No, it's time to call things by their right name. Men have been enjoying affirmative action all along. Now it is time, not for affirmative action for women, but for the de-privileging of men. We must take away some of the surplus privilege that men take for granted and spread it around a little more democratically.

De-privileging is overwhelmingly supported by the Canadian public, even when it is called by its prejudicial name of "affirmative action for women". A York University study of three thousand Canadians at the end of 1981 showed that ninety per cent agreed "without hesitation" to the right of women to equal pay for work of equal value. Sixty-nine per cent agreed with "affirmative action programmes for women and minorities". However, people who stand to lose their special privileges are not so liberal when the question comes closer to home. Most achievers find that special privilege is so dazzling an experience as to be positively blinding. Even the most mediocre men in top positions are quite sure that they got there on their own merits. They seem unaware that they have won in a race from which half of humanity was barred at the starting line. That's why de-privileging and equal pay for work of equal value must be made law before male affirmative action will end. When the federal government approached seven hundred companies to begin *voluntary* de-privileging programs, only twenty-seven agreed.

The feebleness of the current affirmative action plans can be judged by the limp effort in Ontario, where the provincial government boasted in 1982 that its special efforts had finally resulted in five per cent of women in government services being given an opporunity to improve their skills with a view to future career development. Yes, five per cent.

One of the pioneer researchers into these questions of equality and affirmative action is Dr. Margrit Eichler of the Ontario Institute for Studies in Education. In 1979, she directed a Canada-wide investigation into our attitudes on sexual equality probing the minds of 1,350 Canadians in factories, schools, and boardrooms. The results were, in some cases, jolting. Isn't it just a little frightening to learn that roughly half the male teachers interviewed thought that women should be fired first when there are job cut-backs? Now there, if ever, is the snarl of the cornered man who is defending his own special sex-based privilege. No complaints there about how humiliating it would be to accept a special boost from an affirmative action program, no siree. And doesn't it give one pause to know that more than a quarter of those male teachers think that "boys and girls have different tasks in life and should be educated differently"? Doesn't that seem a little ominous for the prospects of equal opportunity in the classroom?

Don't assume that male teachers are a case unto themselves. All the categories of men who were interviewed, except for the very top decision-makers, agreed with the teachers that women should be fired first. Another wry note was that while most men and women agreed that Canadian women don't have equal access to leadership positions, the most pessimistic of all about changing male domination were the feminists and the top men. Only female factory workers (who have nowhere to go but up) were optimistic about overcoming male supremacy.

And yet... another part of the survey belies this gloomy outlook. Feminists, it seems, are the most politically active members of society. They may be disheartened about the enormous psychic revolution it would take to reverse male chauvinism, and they may be deeply alienated from traditional patriarchal politics, but they are forcefully optimistic about small-scale change in their own neighbourhoods, pouring their energies into women's groups, day-care activism, crisis centres, and such goal-focused campaigns as the Ad Hoc Committee on Women and the Constitution.

This pattern points the way to the future. Feminists may be disenchanted with party politics, but in tackling specific issues they are contributing to small shocks and local earthquakes that will eventually reverberate on a national scale. Two paradigmatic battles have been the perennial struggles to explain the justice of paid maternity leave and the idea of women in combat.

Whew. The postal workers finally won their point about paid maternity leave, and you could almost hear the thump of the boulders as Paleolithic people across the country stomped back into their caves and slammed the doors. Never has there been so much uninformed comment about a relatively simple issue. Let's take it, again, step by step.

No young woman is working as a mail-sorter in the Post Office for glamour, excitement, self-fulfilment, and a second Cadillac. These women are working for the same reason that pushes the majority of Canadian women out the door and into the work place: sheer financial necessity. Women have the same need and the same right to work as men. Disgruntled old-timers may not appreciate that, but it's the law of the land, all the same.

Next step: Should women suffer a loss of income because they are women and therefore the child-bearing sex? Here's where prejudice and muddled thinking have come into play in almost all the public discussion I've seen. Over and over, we hear the insistence that "if women choose to have babies, let them pay the price." This position assumes not only that men have nothing to do with the decision to become a parent, but that motherhood is a totally personal and private affair.

But is it, really? Not in Canada. Motherhood was compulsory for hundreds of thousands of Canadian women until 1968 (unbelievable, isn't it?), when contraception was finally made legal. And just ask any woman who wants an abortion whether becoming a mother in Canada is a matter of personal, private choice. We can't have it both ways. We can't claim that woman's fertility has nothing to do with us when we, through our governments, have asserted the opposite. From tax deductions to baby bonus to unemployment insurance benefits during maternity leave, society has shown it has a stake in supporting the creation of families. Well, of course it has. Look how the slowdown in the birth rate has affected the economy. Ask anyone who can't find cheap labour; ask any redundant school-teacher; ask the childless trendies who will be jolted back in their rocking-chairs when they discover there's no one out there to pay for their pensions. Parenthood is an accepted social good. Should female workers bear the entire cost of it? We've already seen how an earlier generation of women, believing they'd always be "looked after" if they stayed home to raise babies, ended up as Canada's elderly, starving poor. Should we now penalize mothers who try to remain self-supporting?

A favourite fatuity of male editorial writers is this: If women want equality, then they'll take no maternity leave at all, since men don't get any. Or, if women get maternity leave, men should get paternity leave. There's more spite than sense in this approach. No one is arguing men and women are identical and have identical needs. The argument is that it's simply unfair that women should bear the personal and economic hardship every time their needs differ from men's. Paid maternity leave is considered such a shocking demand, such a departure from the rightful norm. But what's the norm anyway? The norm is simply the pattern of society established by men. If insemination took months instead of minutes, you can bet paternity leave would be as normal as coffee breaks.

If we are going to define "equality" as a rigid, narrow inflexibility about gender-specific needs, then let's cancel all those long-term disability plans for heart-attack and stroke victims and those rehab schemes for alcoholics. Those are mostly male illnesses, aren't they?

The fact is that only about 3 per cent of young women workers in their child-bearing years take advantage of maternity leave schemes in Canada anyway. It's a drop in the bucket. Even if it weren't, it's a bill we're going to have to pay because it is right, fair, and socially useful. Of 75 advanced industrial nations in the world, only two (Canada and the United States) are still kicking and whining and dragging their feet on providing paid maternity leave. And that's even more embarrassing than it seems, because only a year ago the Canadian government signed a United Nations document vowing to take steps to enact paid maternity leave in Canada.

Should women go to war? For some military men, them's fightin' words; it's an issue of high emotions, almost tearful anger, and, sometimes, a tempestuous lack of logic.

"I'm very sad," said a retired commandant of the Royal Military College at Kingston when he heard that women would be admitted to the school. "It strikes at the very heart of the special mystique which is provided there."

He's right, you know, as all of us are aware who grew up with the sentimental war movies of the '50s. We learned from them that armies persuade ordinary, vulnerable men to kill without question by an elaborate psychological conditioning: first bully them into a childlike subservience (polish that brass! snap that salute!), unburden them of moral responsibility, and then reward them with the badge of "manliness". If that cold look at the male mystique sounds disparaging, it isn't really meant to be. If men needed that romance of patriotism, gallantry, and male camaraderie to go out and defend us all from the horrors of Hitler, so be it. But those triumphs are past, and so are the social convictions which sustained them.

It's probably true that women are subversive of the rigidly hierarchical structure of the army. Mix up the sexes and suddenly you've got human emotions—sex and love, marriage and the baby carriage—messing up the pecking order. But is this really dangerous? Is Barney Danson, the defence minister, really saying that an army can only fight if it is dehumanized? Why is it more horrible for a woman to be wounded in battle that a man? In life-and-death situations, is sex uppermost in the mind? Soldiers were never so delicate, were they, about the sex of their victims? Anyhow, the gory hand-to-hand combat of Danson's memories seem unlikely now; pushbutton missiles and long-distance electronic slaughter are the more probable style of future wars.

No, what is threatened here is not the safety or sanctity of women but man's fragile sense of himself as the invulnerable defender of the weak. And also, let's face it, the male monopoly of many of the highly trained, specialized, and rewarded jobs in the armed forces. Just last Friday, the National Action Committee on the Status of Women asked the minister of defence to open "all trades and classifications in the armed forces" to women.

The U.S. experience is illuminating. There, the armed forces are willingly opening up to women as the number and quality of male volunteers dwindles drastically. The women who volunteer (because there aren't comparable civilian jobs for them) are smarter, better educated, and more ambitious. At Ontario's Base Borden last summer, a rifle instructor casually remarked to me that female cadets are often better marksmen than males because they're cooler, less emotional, and more accurate.

In the *New York Times Magazine* recently, the anti-feminist author George Gilder made a passionate case against women in combat. Gilder quoted recent Stanford University studies which show that women are biologically less aggressive than men. The U.S. would be sapping its fighting strength by allowing these gentler, weaker creatures into combat roles. But even George Gilder must realize that not all women are less aggressive than all men; presumably, only the stronger, more aggressive types of either sex would choose or qualify for combat duty. Gilder tips his hand when he lets his emotions run away from him. The army's classic role, he argues, is the "socialization and enhancement of young men". Infiltration by women would mean the end of "the warrior mystique, the chivalric traditions, the aggressive glory of the martial style".

Gilder's moist-eyed yearning for the trumpets, drums and The Charge of the Light Brigade shouldn't be allowed to clutter up the debate now brewing in Canada. We have never believed in an army designed to "enhance" young men as warriors. Our army's current and future role is one of peace-keeping, as well as the unstated but very real mandate to provide job security and subsidized higher education to a large number of less affluent youth. If we decide to exclude women from many of these opportunities on the grounds that it would unman the men, let's at least be clear that we're talking about feelings, not facts. Sooner or later, even military men are going to have to confront and discard their thread-bare male mystique.

In 1982, there were clear signs that some members of government were quickly catching up to public opinion. Judy Erola, the Minister of Mines and Resources and also the Minister Responsible for the Status of Women, said she wanted to see mandatory equal-pay laws enacted within a year if industry wouldn't shape up. Backing her was the Canadian Human Rights Commission, which took a beady-eyed look at inequalities in federal civil service pay scales (male storemen, doing inventory and shipping, were earning three dollars an hour more than food and laundry

workers whose equally valuable work required equal or greater
skill) and ruled that the government would have to pay $17
million to 3,300 general-service workers (most of them female) to
make up for blatant discrimination in pay.

Erola's position did not spring full-flown like Venus from the
foam. Her tough declaration on de-privileging owed its genesis
to years of slogging by outspoken women. In fact, Erola wouldn't
have been in the Status of Women portfolio at all if it hadn't been
for an extraordinary chain of events precipitated by a determined
leader and carried forward by an intrepid group of activists.

The story has a satisfying coherent shape, partly because so
much of it centres on the long, vigorous career of Doris Anderson,
an Albertan who came east to serve with distinction as the
editor-in-chief of *Chatelaine* magazine. For fifty years *Chatelaine*
was the one and only national women's magazine, and, as editor
for twenty of those years, Doris was its voice and embodiment.
There was no other magazine like it in the whole of North
America. Doris piloted *Chatelaine* to financial health with a
pragmatic mix of political journalism, budget recipes, home
decor on a shoestring, and middle-of-the-road fashions. Across
Canada, a million women got into the habit of reading Doris's
snappy editorials on equal pay or family-law reform before they
turned to the needle-point-of-the-month. So level-headed and
realistic was Doris's approach that she almost single-handedly
made possible the advance of the feminism in Canada. The most
cautious and conservative women were willing to listen to an
argument for equality when it came wrapped in the reassuring
package of the magazine they could trust.

Anderson would not necessarily have ranked herself as a
feminist leader, but as the foremost enlightened woman in the
popular media, she was crucial. Under her shrewd tutelage, a
whole phalanx of tough female writers got published, developed
their skills, and went on to respected freelance careers. Furthermore, *Chatelaine's* feature articles on women's status more than
once prodded government and women's groups into action.
When Doris retired from *Chatelaine*, frustrated by the company
hierarchy in her legitimate ambition to become the magazine's
publisher, it seemed a logical step for her to move to the presi-
dency of the federal Advisory Council on the Status of Women.

Logical, but not necessarily fruitful. Doris, it was clear, was being rewarded for her long-time Liberal loyalties, and the Council, though it had been set up originally to advise the government on policies affecting women, was definitely seen by government as a safe Liberal pasture for retired female work-horses. There are dozens of such government advisory bodies, but no other is saddled patronizingly with a "minister responsible", as though the Council couldn't fend for itself without a man. It has never enjoyed the prestige lavished on more richly funded bodies such as the Economic Council of Canada, mostly because its members seem to be appointed more for Liberal loyalty than for relevant expertise.

True, the Council seemed to have more verve when it was originally launched in 1973 at the recommendation of the Royal Commission on the Status of Women. But that was almost accidental. Caught short without a list of party faithful to appoint, the first "minister responsible", John Munro, had to fall back on choosing women on the basis of ability. Ironically, the Council's effectiveness began to wane after 1975, when International Women's Year made Council appointments some-thing of a political plum for the first time. By the time Doris arrived, the Council had degenerated to the confusion and somnolence of the Mad Hatter's Tea Party, with faithful but undistinguished Liberal women drowsing behind their teapots. Doris quickly found that all six of her executive members were ardent Liberals, as were at least eighteen of the twenty-six Council members. None of Canada's brilliant woman lawyers, labour leaders, campaigners for native women's equality, or outspoken feminists were on the Council. Doris expressed public doubts about going to Ottawa ("I hope I won't be hollering down an empty pipe") and then she set about getting the Council's budget doubled to $1.4 million, hiring six bright new staff members, and jostling the Council into an ambitious pro-gram of research on women's issues.

The problem of working from within, though, as Doris soon discovered, was that there was no energy for change and no courage for dissent among her new colleagues. A planned con-ference on women and the constitution had already been post-poned once, in the fall of 1980, because of a federal translators' strike. Plans were bubbling ahead nicely for the rescheduled conference to be held on February 14 when, in January, Lloyd Axworthy, the Minister Responsible for the Status of Women, let the Council executive know that the Trudeau government would find it embarrassing to have the women coming to Ottawa to natter away about the constitution just when the parliamentary opposition was attacking Trudeau's constitution across the street in the House. The Council executive, all loyal Liberals and all eager lapdogs for Lloyd, agreed at once to postpone.

In a move that was nothing short of astounding for mealy-mouthed Ottawa, Doris took the disagreement — and the Minister's manipulations — to the public. She accused Axworthy of "sleazy interference" with the Council's independence, and, when the Council hastily met and voted 17 to 10 to go along with the government, Doris resigned in a blaze of public attention. Within the week, eight staff (including five of the six members of the country's strongest women's research team) and six Council members had resigned too.

Women's groups across the country reacted with fury at the government's dismissal of their concern about the Charter of Rights. The furor focused attention on the lack of a women's equality clause in the charter as nothing else could have done. Doris Anderson became a folk hero, and an Ad Hoc feminist lobby group sprang up almost overnight, led by Toronto lawyer Marilou McPhedran, former teacher Linda Ryan-Nye, and Ottawa career counsellor Pat Hacker. Within three weeks they had organized a "counter-conference" to be held in Ottawa on that same fateful day of February 14. To everyone's amazement, 1,300 women arrived from every corner of Canada, mostly at their own expense, to hammer out constitutional proposals that were to have far-reaching effects.

It was a wonderfully fruitful fiasco, the best the country had had in ages. All sides to the dispute revealed their true biases in a way that can only happen in a keyed-up moment of debate. Daily in Parliament the Opposition romped away with the issue while Lloyd Axworthy wriggled like a hooked fish. The *Globe and Mail* showed that when women dare to argue, the *Globe* will call it a cat fight. It headlined its subtly anti-female story "Axworthy Clawed in the Commons for Arm-twisting". Axworthy was

glorious newspaper material. He called the penniless Ad Hoc
feminist group "a bunch of Cadillac feminists", said they were
"tiresome", complained that Doris Anderson had always been
headstrong, tried out a bit of leaden condescension ("I'm happy
to see the women getting together"), and openly sulked about his
wounded leadership ambitions: "It's cast a shadow on my career
... it's hurt me politically and it's unfair," he complained to me
in an interview. Later, he tried to saunter foxily past the sour
grapes. "It's kind of nice to be so totally dismissed," he told
Canadian Press.

Over at the Status of Women offices, the Council and its
executive were in complete disarray. Someone had leaked what
were claimed to be the minutes of their meeting at the office after
Lloyd Axworthy had handed down the word from the Mount.

Win Gardner, vice-president: "My reasons for voting to
cancel the conference has nothing to do with the fact that the
minister is a dear and close friend of mine. I am voting for
cancelling the conference because we looked like fools the last
time and I am not ready... to put our minister in an embarrassing
situation toward his government."

Florence Ievers: "I say it's time we started playing games the
same way the government plays games. We should start being
nice to them. So if this conference is going to be an embarrassment to them, let's play it their way and cancel it."

Lucie Pépin (whom Axworthy later appointed to replace
Anderson): I thought we are doing what we are told. I think it's
about time we learn to do things. We have a minister. We are
supposed to advise him... we have to accept to do things the way
Ottawa wants things to be done. Just because a larger group like
NAC [National Action Committee, a non-government women's
group] knows what's going on, does this mean that the rest of
the women of Canada know things? The government is very well
aware that women don't know everything. I'm voting against
having our meeting in February. We must keep our mouths
shut, no press releases. . . ."

Florence Ievers: "Make sure we all say the same thing about
the reasons for cancelling the conference."

The executive committee of the Status of Women swore an
affidavit that the alleged minutes were false. Shelley-Ann Clark,

the stenographer who took the minutes, sued them for libel. A year later, the suit was still not resolved.

At the constitutional hearing that followed in the weeks after the Advisory Council scandal, the Ad Hoc women gave a brilliantly reasoned accounting of themselves, and won the guarantee of a sexual-equality clause in the proposed constitution. Over the summer lull, Axworthy was quietly replaced—though not before he had restocked the Council's depleted membership with a new batch of Liberal women, one of whom, Diane Harkin, a member of the Ontario Federation of Agriculture, purred, "Lloyd Axworthy is a pussycat. I don't really know what all this hullabaloo is all about." Shucks, honey, don't you bother yore pretty little head.

Feminism's finest hour came the next fall, in November 1981, when, after a year of petty power-tripping and egotistical wrangling, the premiers put together their midnight deal. Amateur chefs Jean Chrétien (Liberal), Roy Romanow (NDP), and Roy McMurtry (Tory) concocted their so-called Kitchen Constitution, and airily left out a key ingredient in the recipe: women's equality would no longer be guaranteed. The hard-won equality clause, along with native rights, would be subject to a "provincial overrride". Though the country seemed exhausted after the protracted constitutional debates, and though further protest seemed futile, the newly vibrant feminist lobby was undaunted. Judy Erola, the new Minister Responsible for the Status of Women, proved a surprise ally: she put her office and long-distance telephone lines at the disposal of the Ad Hoc Committee and an instantaneous national campaign was on.

"Our voices will haunt them through streets, offices, meetings, homes and elections," swore Linda Ryan-Nye of the premiers who had signed the accord. Within two weeks, eight of the ten premiers had capitulated to intense pressure from women's groups. Only Nova Scotia's John Buchanan and Saskatchewan's Allan Blakeney still held out, the latter insisting that entrenched equality rights might jeopardize that province's affirmative-action programs, and also that women shouldn't have equality rights if the native peoples didn't. Buchanan caved in by November 20; by November 24, a shaken Allan Blakeney had to retreat as well. "The women of Canada will give new meaning

to the saying that 'Hell hath no fury like a woman scorned',"
Linda Ryan-Nye had warned, and they had.

It will take years of legal testing before we finally learn what
we really won and lost in the Charter of Rights. But there were
several immediate strong lessons to be drawn from this unprece-
dented victory by and for women. First, the obtuseness of Allan
Blakeney's position was a shock, coming as it did from a civil-
libertarian and a democratic socialist. Activist women found his
stubborn disregard of equality rights almost inexplicable. Then
it was pointed out that there was not a single woman in the
ruling legislative caucus of the NDP in Saskatchewan. And
though I had always argued that being female is no guarantee of
political enlightenment, it was clear that the women in Parliament — of all parties — had led the equality fight, while some
men of the most impeccable egalitarian ideals had utterly
betrayed the idea of women's equality.

At the same time, the compromised position of the Canadian
Advisory Council, stacked with loyal Liberals and on the
government payroll, was now irreversibly stamped on the public
mind. The Council played a minimal role in the constitutional
battles of 1981 (though it sought to take credit in lavish newspaper
interviews), and the mantle of leadership fell on the sturdy
shoulders of the purely voluntary Ad Hoc Committee of Canadian Women, a group that vowed political allegiance to none.
The National Action Committee on the Status of Women, the
largest non-government umbrella group in the country, was
active but not incisive during the constitutional struggle. Long
paralysed by internal ego battles and ideological bitterness, the
group—uneasily representing a million women in 150 widely
disparate organizations—only began to emerge as a more cohe-
sive body after the Charter of Rights furor. Early in 1982, NAC
elected Doris Anderson as its new president. It began to look as
though NAC, too, might become a powerful voice for equality.
Canadian feminism had come of age.

CRUSTS IN THE
LUNCH BUCKET

MEN MAY BE PACKING A SMALLER SANDWICH IN THEIR lunch buckets now that inflation gets the first bite on the family budget, but women workers count themselves lucky to get even a dry crust. Despite their massive post-war move into the paid labour force — about fifty-three per cent of all Canadian women work outside the home, and experts think that will rise to seventy per cent by the turn of the century — and despite all the drumbeating for equality, women still earn far less than men in the same jobs and are denied the most golden opportunities.

If you could take an aerial zoom-lens across Canada, you'd see, in the waters off the coast of Newfoundland, the oil rigs where women are barred from the risky but high-paid employment. A Labrador woman charged Petro-Canada with sex discrimination in a complaint to the Canadian Human Rights Commission. According to a *Globe and Mail* story, the company recruiter told Donna-Lee Hedges, 29, that the oil companies don't want "liquor, drugs, or women" on their rigs. Besides, explained a Petro-Canada spokesman, since workers sleep four to a room, the company would have to hire four women at a time. Surely that shouldn't be an insuperable problem in depressed Maritime Canada?

Pan to Ottawa, where the government is happily spending more than $5 billion in taxes paid annually by Canadian working women. Here civil-service women make up a steadily rising number (81.6 per cent in 1982) of the lowest-paid, most vulnerable clerical work force. Just because women predominate numerically in any one field, though, doesn't mean they match male wages. Even in the category of file clerks, women make only eighty-seven per cent of the male file-clerk wage. In textile

factories, women at their sewing machines earn just over the half
the wage of the men at the neighbouring sewing machines. Same
job, same place, same discrimination there's always been.

Move the aerial camera on west to Hamilton, Ontario, a
thriving industrial city where employers are begging for skilled
tradesmen. Trades*men*, that is. When the Ontario government
hired career counsellor Mary Bray to place women in employer-
sponsored training programs for such desperately needed trades
as machinist, tool-and-die maker and industrial mechanic, Bray
spent a whole year trying to break through the bosses' resistance.
By the end of the year, she'd placed only two women. Bray told
the *Toronto Star* that "I'm convinced nothing short of contract
compliance — mandatory equal-opportunity programs for
women—will change things." Employers, she said, were hostile
to the idea of training women. She heard them state publicly
that they were all in favour of equal opportunity, and then
privately "refuse even to consider the idea of a woman trainee."
That's how governments and anti-women propagandists can
claim that equal opportunities already exist. Any realist knows
it's not true.

Peer down now on Mississauga, suburb of Toronto, where
Phantom Industries Limited, makers of pantyhose, delicately
inquired of a local alderman whether Mississauga would be a
good place to relocate in terms of, ahem, ethnic women.

"Yes," replied the co-operative alderman, there was "a pre-
dominance of Italian, East Indian, and Caribbean sub-communities, and excellent access to [other] ethnic concentrations...."

When the exchange of letters came to light, the company
denied that it had been looking for a pool of cheap immigrant
labour to exploit. Its interest in "ethnic sub-communities" was
solely in the "body type" of said ladies: "We're interested in their
long slender fingers," said Phantom's general manager.

Travel on, moving camera, to Saskatchewan, where the provincial high court ruled that the Catholic school board was quite
within its rights to fire a woman teacher who was living
common-law. Not even the provincial human-rights code protected this woman, because, ruled Justice Clarence Estey, the
Catholic school board is a special religious organization, not a
private employer. And not even the union contract could protect

Elaine Huber, because the contract forbids discrimination on the basis of "marital status" and, astoundingly enough, Mr. Justice Estey ruled that Huber *had* no marital status. There's an Alice in Wonderland quality to the argument: surely the phrase "marital status" includes any or all marital conditions, whether single, married, common-law, divorced, or separated. The judge, however, seems to have fallen for the trendy definition of "status" as meaning "desirable social position" and, on that basis, decided that the only status is the married one.

Over to Calgary, where secretary Laurie Jakab was fired for refusing to make coffee for her fellow employees at Texas Pacific Oil Canada Limited, and where the Alberta Human Rights Commission, such as it is, ruled that this did not constitute discrimination based on sex. The Commission didn't document any cases of men being asked to make coffee or being fired when they refused.

No, Canada is a distinctly thorny paradise for the underpaid woman worker. Even human-rights legislation is relatively meaningless without tough rules and enforcement. The one factor that makes a concrete difference is a union. When women get organized and fight for specific rights and benefits in their contract, they can wrest important changes—changes that become precedents for other women—from the recalcitrant boss. But, as an old union song says, "Ain't nobody here can do it for you." Women have been notoriously lily-livered about getting involved in the gritty adversarial politics of labour-management negotiations. For years, only a tiny handful of women were unionized, and union organizers complained bitterly that even the most oppressed female work force lacked the courage or the conviction to fight.

All that is changing: women have been unionizing at a terrific clip (female membership rising 144 per cent in the decade ending in 1975) and some of the most stirring inch-by-inch battles for decent working conditions have been fought by and for women in recent years.

The first column I ever wrote for the *Toronto Star* was this one:

Bored by women's liberation? Feel your raised consciousness sagging just a bit?

Meet the Fleck women—the 150 who went on strike from their factory jobs making automotive wiring at Fleck Manufacturing Co. in Centralia, Ont. They'll put new fire in your feminism in a single morning: together they're worth a year's subscription to *MS.* magazine and any number of Herstory (women's history) courses. They're spunky, ribald, salt-of-the-earth, riding high on a wave of sisterhood as unaffected as their bright green eye shadow and double negatives. Fifteen of them came to Toronto to testify before the Ontario Labour Relations Board concerning charges their union, the United Auto Workers, has brought against Fleck management and police—charges of intimidation and illegal anti-union activity.

Waiting to testify before the pin-striped board members, they fill the sedate lobby with the slap-slap of cards (euchre and crazy eights) and good-natured banter.

"Guess we're a bunch of country bumpkins," they laugh, poking fun at themselves for not knowing how to operate the 10-cents-a-spray perfume machine in their downtown hotel.

Back in March, the Fleck women struck for decent wages and the right to have union security, a right conceded even by Ontario Labour Minister Bette Stephenson. Many of the strikers are sole-support mothers who were bringing home about $100 a week, far less than the plant's maintenance men were earning. They thought it would be a quick, straightforward little strike, though many were badly scared when the Ontario Provincial Police came into the plant before the strike to lecture them on picket-line behaviour. Many of them got the impression that strikes were illegal, that they might go to jail for five years. They struck anyway.

Union? Strike? They never even thought of such things before they decided to get organized last fall. Once the idea of joining a union was proposed, it ran like wildfire through the plant; in the first week, 82 per cent of the women signed up with the United Auto Workers.

"The management ripped down my notice about the organizing meeting," laughs Sheila Charlton, 35, "so I wrote the notice on my T-shirt with black marker and wore it to work. All the girls were running over to see it."

Girls. All the women call each other "girls". Even inside the hearing room where their sass, ingenuity and gritty determination keep cracking up the lawyers, everyone calls them "girls".

"That first morning of the strike, every one of us was scared to death," says Mary Lou Richard, 30. "I climbed in the car and my legs were shaking. And when they brought out the riot police against our picket line... hundreds of cops, a helicopter... they had these shiny black helmets and big riot sticks. Jeez, it was like the movies!"

"I couldn't believe all that black gear was coming straight at me," chimes in 33-year-old Fran Piercey. "We had to pretend to be a lot braver than we were. You know, most of us are mothers, and we've been bringing up our kids to respect the police. And here we were, walking a picket line, getting shoved around, getting so scared and angry that we were shouting stuff you wouldn't believe."

Intimidation? They've overcome their initial disbelief and fear. "One guy, who didn't go out on strike, he's a big 300-pounder. We were told he'd be coming after us with a baseball bat," says Sheila Charlton. A great whoop of laughter goes up from the crowd of women who are by now listening in to the interview. "There are more of us than him!" shouts one.

Sexual harassment by male supervisors on the job? To hear their stories, these women have put up with more leers, jeers, mauling, grabbing, and sexual insult than any 100 office workers are every likely to encounter. They handle it with their favourite weapon: bawdy, biting humour that slaps down the offender with belittling wit. (Too bad their best one-liners are unprintable.)

Quiet Katherine Kaehn, 26-year-old sole-support mother of two, feels the strike has changed her life. "I'm not afraid to say what I think now. The biggest surprise was how the other unions and locals stuck up for us. They send donations, they help us on the picket line... even nuns and priests and stewardesses picketed with us. It's like the church, the way they treat us like sisters. Even the highest-up guys in the union are down to earth."

Isn't it hard to support a family on the $60-a-week strike
pay from the union? More knee-slapping and laughter. "We
just eat more spaghetti. Lord, if you're used to making do on
$100 a week take-home, $60 ain't no problem."

"I know now who's got the power," says Mary Lou.
"We're fighting for ourselves, and we're doggone proud of
ourselves."

The ultimate proof of their liberation, despite the "girls",
despite the way they stayed up all night on picket duty and
then automatically took on the task of making sandwiches for
hundreds of male picketers who had joined them, was the
way they misinterpreted one of my questions.

"Would all this have happened if you weren't all women?"
I asked, referring to the intransigence and bullying tactics
used against them. "Jeez, no," exclaims Sheila Charlton.
"The men would *never* have had the guts to do what we've
done."

One by one, as the Fleck women are called to testify, they
sail proudly, if nervously, into the hearing room. "Stick to the
truth," is their rallying call to each other. As each one comes
out, she is greeted with cheers and hugs. Sisterhood and
sticking to the truth as they've lived it: two tough and triumphant achievements for the Fleck women.

Fleck was a bitterly fought strike. Down in Centralia, in south-
west Ontario, the Fleck plant rang with the sound of trucks
running the picket lines and the crunch of police batons. In the
legislature, there was a furor when it was revealed that the
Conservative government's Deputy Minister of Industry and
Tourism, James Fleck, was part-owner of the company. When
the provincial police actually massed 500 men near the picket
line of 150 women, the intimidating overkill was duly noted by
the public.

The most interesting thing about the strike was its aftermath.
The women won the right to a compulsory union-dues check-off
and a two-year contract with a twenty-cent-an-hour raise. Nine
months before the contract expired, the union and management
amiably settled on a new one. The *Globe* called the negotiations
"a love-in". So friendly was the signing that Grant Turner, the

burly and aggressive Fleck vice-president who had been a major
source of controversy during the strike, actually admitted that
management-employee relations were better than ever. To celebrate the anniversary of their triumph, Fran Piercey joked to the
press that the "girls" would bake a big cake emblazoned with
"Solidarity Forever". We're going to see how many of the scabs
we can get to have a piece," she laughed.

Things weren't so civilized when a completely different
employer—a southern United States company with a strong
right-wing ideology—set up shop in Barrie, Ontario. Barrie lies
just north of Toronto in the so-called "minimum wage belt"—
the ring of outlying towns and suburbs with a steady supply of
cheap housewife labour.

Two hundred women marched up and down in front of the
Radio Shack warehouse in Barrie yesterday, bundled against
the snow that came stinging down on a raw wind. Behind a
darkened window in the warehouse, Radio Shack employees
filmed their striking co-workers, and across the street, police
kept silent watch from the warmth of their cars. It was a
strange confrontation because there was no one to confront.
The 200 women, from a wide range of Toronto women's
groups and unions, had risen before dawn to get there. There
were celebrating Women's Solidarity Day by walking the line
with the 46 women warehouse workers on strike at Radio
Shack. But management personnel, and workers who have
been crossing the picket lines, had hidden inside the plant by
6 a.m. to avoid meeting them.

Anyway, the real battle is between two clashing sets of
beliefs: the fervent conviction of workers that Ontario law
should protect their right to union security, and the tough,
union-busting philosophy of the Texas-based Tandy Corp.,
which owns Radio Shack.

It's a stand-off. For a year now, since the workers at Radio
Shack won certification as a United Steelworkers local, the
company has blocked and stalled and dragged its feet, and
still there's no first contract. The company has been convicted
by the Ontario Labour Relations Board of unjust firing of
union workers, interfering with the right to organize and

defying board orders. Still no first contract. There may not be one at all, unless the board forces the company to settle.

"We need a union in there," one of the strikers told me, stamping her numbed feet. "They pay zilch benefits…just 40 per cent of OHIP and nothing else. No sick days until after two years. Minimum vacations. A half-hour unpaid lunch break. And the foremen play favourites a lot. Five minutes before quitting time they'll tell you to change shifts the next day. If that means babysitter problems, well, you can always quit. And layoffs? Listen, I've seen foremen pull names from a hat at the end of a shift, and if your name was pulled that was goodbye, no matter how long you worked there."

The company's last offer before the women went on strike in August made its intentions clear. It offered an average 6 per cent raise on a merit basis, no change in overtime, vacation, shift premiums, sick pay, or benefits. And it made outrageous demands, seemingly calculated to block a settlement: an elaborate code of conduct to be made part of the agreement; a refusal of compulsory dues check-off; a clause that would fine the union $10,000 merely for mentioning the company's name outside the plant.

The whole history of the organizing drive is loaded with creepy overtones of deep South union-busting. There's the company security chief, for example, who told the board he's a good friend of the Barrie policeman in charge of maintaining order on the picket line. Testimony by a former company security man that the firm hired spies to infiltrate the union. And company "information sheets" given to workers—among the most scurrilous I've ever read. They slam and distort the positions of both the union and the labour relations board in a frontal attack which the board itself found alarmingly close to "contempt".

The crux of the battle, though, is union security. The women on the picket line have staked their livelihood on it. "Sisters, unite! Stand up and fight!" they shouted on the line yesterday. But union security is being whittled away each day the fight is prolonged, as local housewifes flock to work Radio Shack's special "housewife shift": 9 a.m. to 3 p.m., minimum wage, no security, and summers off if you want.

How can a company get away with stalling on a first contract, even though the union has won its right to bargain? Simple. Ontario, unlike some other provinces, has no law insisting that the companies come to terms with a newly formed union. If the company can hang on long enough — and Tandy, with its annual sales of more than $1 billion and its boast that no union has ever got a foot in the door, can hang on — then there's a good chance that it can break the union. You can't live forever on strike pay. And there are no laws in Ontario to give a union the compulsory dues check-off it needs to survive. Way back in 1946, Justice Ivan Rand ruled, in an historic decision, that "the organization of labour must in a civilized manner be elaborated and strengthened for its essential function in an economy of free enterprise....

"I consider it perfectly equitable that employees should be required to shoulder their portion of the burden of expense.... they must take the burden along with the benefit."

On the windy picket line, the women weigh their chances against the Texas cowboys, and pray that the Ontario Labour Relations Board will see it their way.

The Ontario Labour Relations Board most emphatically did see it their way. In December 1979, Board Chairman George Adams ruled that the company was guilty of bargaining in bad faith, "pervasive unlawful conduct", a "persistent and flagrant campaign of unfair labour practices", threatening to move the plant out, illegal firings, photographing union meetings, hiring spies to infiltrate the local, and rigidly sticking to inflammatory contract offers. Adams capped his long list of Radio Shack transgressions with an historic order. The company was to pay the union's "extraordinary" strike expenses and to reimburse strikers for wages lost owing to the company's illegal behaviour and anti-union coercion. And the company was to present a contract offer complete with union security.

That spring, the union and Radio Shack signed a collective agreement including a compulsory dues check-off. By March 1981 harmony reigned at the Radio Shack, Barrie, warehouse. Despite the company's red-neck cussedness, despite its boast that no Radio Shack employee around the world had ever been unionized or ever would be, the settlement turned out to be mutually agreeable. A second agreement, with improved vacations and benefits and an 18.8 per cent raise over two years, was peacefully signed in March 1981, and the next fall the company paid between $100 and $600 to each of its employees as compensation for its illegal union-busting. A further $200,000 went into the union coffers. The union local told the press that the settlement was acceptable to both sides and "results from a mutual desire to conclude old differences and continue a co-operative working relationship."

Even Texas cowboys can learn new lessons, it seems.

What most of us would consider the minimum decencies of the work place simply don't exist for many pink- or blue-collar workers. Even with a strong, active union, some skirmishes go on and on, as workers pit their dignity against an employer's push for efficiency. Shortly after a new president came to roost at the Canada Packers plant in west-end Toronto, a time-honoured work pattern ended and the washroom wars began.

This is Em's job: for 8½ hours Monday to Thursday and six hours on Friday, Em stands by a conveyor belt in a steady 6-degree (42°F.) chill, trimming the fat off pork necks. The pieces of 4,700 hogs pass by her flashing knife every day. Em, 39, is about the size of a skinny 12-year-old kid, and her hands are all twisted and swollen at the joints from 23 years of handling cold, wet meat at Canada Packers on St. Clair Ave. West. Em is stubbornly proud of her perfect work record. Perfect, that is, until this fall when she was hit with a one-day suspension for using the washroom too often. That cost her $82 and an outraged sense of injustice. "They called me up to the office," she told me. "I felt like crying but I held on to it; I wouldn't cry where they could see."

Em is proud and a bit shy, which makes it all the more embarrassing for her to be caught in the middle of the great Washroom Wars. It happened this way. Last winter, just about the time that Canada Packers realized it was going to lose about $3 million this year in the Pork Cutting Room where Em and 180 others work, it also dawned on it that some workers were taking advantage of the easy washroom privileges. The company decided to get tough about washroom visits. No more regular relief men coming around three times a day to let assembly line workers "go". Instead, workers were urged to cut down their washroom breaks to no more than one a day. Most workers did cut down the length of their visits—but not the frequency.

"They tell us we got to go during our two 10-minute breaks or our half-hour lunch," explained Elsie, another long-time worker. "But we can't; there are nine toilets, with two or three of them always out of order, for 22 of us girls."

The women have to go down a hallway where the floors are often coated with sheet ice, walk through a tunnel, wash off the fat and sometimes blood from their stiff, nearly frozen hands, line up for a cubicle...the 10-minute break is over. Lunch is equally hectic. "From the moment that buzzer shrieks, you have to run."

The company wasn't satisfied with these explanations. For three months in the fall, a sub-foreman sat at a desk outside the washroom door, marking the punch-card number and the time of entry and exit of each washroom user. A worker with more than one daily visit would be reprimanded and then suspended.

"They told us they'd make exceptions for a lady who had her time of month," Cheryl, another worker, told me. "Well, hell will freeze over before I tell the foreman when I have my monthlies!"

There's no longer a man posted at the toilet door. But now the women have to run upstairs to ask the foreman's permission to go to the washroom. "It's humiliating," Cheryl said. "And I hate it when he says, 'What, again?'"

In November, a provincial arbitrator ruled that the company had the right to impose "reasonable" restrictions on the use of the washrooms. Okay. But what's reasonable? One break a day might be reasonable for office workers. But assembly-line workers in hard, unpleasant conditions, who start work at 7 a.m. and are on their feet all day in cold rooms where fat and blood and water mingle on the floors, may have different physical needs.

Em, for one, had a doctor's letter saying that she has chronic cystitis. "The foreman says he doesn't remember seeing the letter before he gave me the suspension," Em says. She has launched a grievance and maybe she'll get her money back. What really worries her, though, is her record. "I hope they'll wipe my record clean," she says. "I feel terrible about this."

Norm Alexander, president of Local 114 of the United Food and Commercial Workers, stresses that the company isn't a bad employer. The pay is pretty good—an average of $9 to $10 and hour—and the company gives you 25 silver dollars and a banquet if you make 25 years. It also donates 600 ice-cream bars to the union picnic, and Christmas hampers for all the workers. But 23-year loyalties have turned sour in the Washroom Wars. People like Em have had their dignity wounded. That's a hard thing to forgive when you don't have much else.

And another thing. All the women I spoke to were so frightened that they insisted I disguise their identities. And all they were doing was telling me about how it feels to have to ask permission to "go".

The washroom wars are still dragging on, with each case being brought before an arbitration board to determine whether the employer had overstepped its rights. Meanwhile, several other companies in Toronto began a washroom monitoring policy— again, aimed solely at women. A few years earlier, one food-packing plant actually had closed-circuit television cameras aimed at the door of the women's washroom to record their entrances and exits, but an arbitrator ruled the company out of order, and the cameras had to come down. Since these cases of washroom watching and besetting are directed mostly at female employees, can we deduce a pattern of harassment and intimidation? The question isn't frivolous. According to a University of Michigan study, women work longer and harder than men. The average man uses fifty-two minutes a day for coffee breaks, relaxing, and extra lunch time; women, who use only thirty-five minutes a day for these purposes, accordingly put in an effort equal to 112 per cent of that by the men. So why is it women who are subject to washroom badgering? Why, at Block Drug Company in East York, do the twenty-three women workers have to punch a time clock when they go to the toilet—their total washroom time not to exceed ten minutes a day—while the twenty-six male employees go unmonitored?

Perhaps some companies push around the employees who they think won't resist, just to show who's boss. This autocratic style of management was very much in evidence at a long and unpleasant strike in 1981 at a toy company plant in Toronto. Owner Arnold Irwin seemed determined to run his company as the lord of the castle, with no interference from uppity workers.

Let me introduce you to some of the folks who bring you the Rubik's Cube, Slinky, Strawberry Shortcake Dolls, Jim-Dandy swing sets, Turco Barbecues, Star War models, and Atari Space Invaders.

They aren't Santa's little helpers, I can tell you that. And Arnold Irwin, president of Irwin Toys, which imports, assembles, and sells all those toys, is nobody's Santa Claus, either. Especially not to his workers, some of whom are still out on the picket line four months after failing to get a first contract. President Irwin was unavailable for comment when I called him. Mac Irwin, the vice-president, told me he had no comment. But I met the Irwin strikers in a black, drenching downpour outside the gates of the Etobicoke plant at 7 o'clock one morning.

Marg O'Brien is picket captain, a red toque pulled down over her hair, her glasses streaming with rain, but still cheerful. All the "girls", who are much younger, call her "Ma".

"Most of our women are assemblers and their average wage last June was $3.33. We got us a union last February, and Irwin offered us 5 cents above the minimum wage. His final offer was 10 cents. Well, that's just an insult. We got no benefits. Mind you, they were very nice when I was sick last winter; they didn't fire me. But I didn't get sick pay, neither."

Initially, the union asked for a raise of $1.25 an hour. But most of all they wanted a less arbitrary system. Irwin has 31 different pay rates for only 114 workers, making it very difficult to compare salaries fairly.

After two years, you're lucky to get $230 every two weeks in your Irwin pay envelope. Says Velma, who is very young and has a cherub's face and long blonde pigtails: "The guys get paid a quarter more an hour that we do, but when they're not around, we do their work anyway, don't we, girls? We lift those heavy barbecues off the line same as the guys."

If the pay is miserly, the working conditions match. This is pint-sized Sherry speaking: "I work in the paint room. When the heat got up to 145 degrees last summer, I fainted, but they wouldn't let us go home. I wish they'd put in a fan."

Donna says: "The lunch room has no sink. So the girl who cooks the macaroni has to run to the bathroom to get water."

Inside the vast, gray concrete plant, there are lights on and people looking out at the pickets huddled in the rain. In the four long months of the strike more and more of the strikers have drifted away to other jobs. Strikebreakers have been hired. Of the 114 workers at Irwin's Etobicoke plant, only 30 are left doing regular picket duty. However, they joke about the rotten weather, and about the possibility that Irwin will keep on ignoring them and they'll still be there when the snow flies. "We'll wear snowsuits, eh girls?" But they won't settle for that contemptuous, unbudging 10-cent offer.

The law of Ontario says that workers have the right to form a union and that both sides are supposed to bargain in good faith. But Irwin has stonewalled, possibly in the hope that if the strike drags on long enough, union support will be whittled away. The Ontario government is concerned enough that it has appointed a two-man Disputes Advisory Board to look into the situation.

Someone produces a plastic sheet and, to form a little shelter from the downpour, we fasten it to the barbed wire at the top of the seven-foot fence that surrounds the sprawling plant. The fence and the barbed wire went up just before the strike, and probably cost Irwin a lot of nickels and dimes. But then, according to his report to shareholders, he happily anticipates 1982 sales of $100 million, up from $63 million in 1981.

Think of the barbed wire, and women trying to live on $3.33 an hour for heavy, dirty work ("You get black as coal from the oil coating on the steel," Donna says. "I take it off my skin with Comet.") when you decide whether to buy one of those Mustang horses or cute little Strawberry Shortcake dolls for Christmas. Better still, let's submit an idea to Irwin. At his last Junior Shareholders' meeting, he challenged the kids to come up with a new game that "will reflect Irwin Toy's activities". Okay. How about "Mr. Scrooge, An Exciting Game of Union-Busting! Do not pass the barbed wire. Do not collect a fair wage."

The impending strains of Noël did not soften Scrooge's heart. The provincial disputes advisory committee proposed a barely adequate $3.70 an hour, and the hungry Steelworker local, by now reduced to twenty-six strikers on the picket line, accepted. But Irwin, smelling possible victory, flatly refused. Christmas came and went, and finally, facing charges of bad-faith bargaining at the Ontario Labour Relations Board, Irwin agreed to settle—for the same old $3.70 minimum. Weary, broke, and dispirited (it's hard to see your boss and your colleagues treat you like dirt), the twenty-six women waited to be called back to work.

But a funny thing happened. Just as Irwin had earlier threatened, he had quietly been reorganizing his furniture assembly line behind the fence and concrete walls. Even after the strike ended, most of the women were never recalled to work. With a bare handful of union members back inside the plant, Irwin had only to bide his time for a few more months till a full year had passed. At that time, as they would then legally be allowed to do, the scabs who had crossed the picket lines would be only too eager to vote against having a union in the plant... and the long painful, and costly battle will have been won by Irwin by default.

Women workers in Canada have yet to learn the basic lesson that many men absorbed in the earlier union battles of the century: the only weapon of the wage worker is solidarity. Every woman who crosses the picket line, every woman who drifts away to another job, tries to tell herself that her actions are neutral. She's a private individual getting on with the job. In truth, she is the silent (and unrewarded) ally of the boss. One by one, such women help the employer to beat the union down.

PAYING THE PRICE
OF MYTHOLOGY

DREAMS, WISHES, AND MYTHOLOGIES MAY SEEM TO DRIFT in and out of our mind as freely as air, but they are costlier than we realize. Myths may—and do—underpin our laws, reinforce cultural patterns, and receive for generations the unquestioning adherence that even established religions are no longer able to command.

In North America we are paying compound interest for one of our favourite myths, that of "the little woman". It's years, of course, since men called their wives "the little woman", and probably none of them intended by it that their widows should end up starving, but the idea of the diminutive wife—adorably fragile, adoringly dependent—is still alive in our mythology-based economic structure. One of the prices we pay is that women are the poor of Canada. Forty-one per cent of all female-led families live in that grey and pinched region known as "below the poverty line", compared to 7 per cent of male-led families. And 38.1 per cent of single women are poor. To look at it from a different angle, if all the poor people in Canada massed together in one huge throng, two out of every three faces in that crowd would be women's faces. Only now are we beginning to wake up out of the long dream and realize how it happened that women are poor.

We were conned. We were willing dupes. We grew up believing that marriage, not work, would keep us safe and warm. And now we wake up to realize that although ninety-four of every hundred women marry, only twenty-six can expect to live with their husbands until death. Most of us will be widows one day, and, as the National Council on Welfare hammered home in its 1979 report, two out of every three widows in Canada are living in soul-shrivelling poverty.

I've always known, intellectually, the statistics on older women and poverty; I've known it less abstractly, too. When I was a young newlywed, my husband and I helped to rescue an old woman who was quietly, politely, genteelly starving to death while bureaucrats squabbled over her meagre pension. And who hasn't seen the old women in supermarkets sorting through the packets of giblets and soup bones to find the smallest and cheapest?

But it wasn't until I read the Women and Poverty report that it all clicked together for me. "Poverty in Canada is overwhelmingly a female phenomenon," said the report. One and a quarter million Canadian women are scrabbling for existence below the poverty line. Women who live alone are five times more likely to be poor... and most of us will live alone at some time in our adult lives.

The report isn't talking about the "inherited poverty" of the slum-dweller, either. The overwhelming majority of widows and single mothers who are poor come from respectable, non-welfare families. "The majority of Canadian women," says the report, "whatever their backgrounds, are very vulnerable to becoming poor overnight."

Working women won't be spared the humiliation, the slow erosion of dignity, the panic, and the scrimping. Not at all. Most minimum-wage earners are women. So are the non-unionized, the part-timers, the marginal and seasonal workers. Contributions to the Canada Pension are low, and are whittled away still more by time out for child-bearing. Ever know a waitress or cashier who retired with a nice fat pension? No, she retires to penny-watching, anxious, long years, struggling desperately to support and look after herself—if she's lucky, in her own home.

At first, talking to Mabel, it seems that the house means everything to her. She sits in the dark middle room, her swollen feet planted squarely on the floor, and by her side the exquisite pastel baby clothes she knits for charity.

Three narrow rooms in a narrow semi-detached house in the respectable east end. The upstairs is rented out; the garden is unreachable because she can't negotiate the steps. A neighbour mows the lawn. Last year, the TV aerial blew down, and it cost $600 to replace it and repair the chimney. One more such blow and the rest of her savings will be wiped out.

"I'll be finished then," she says. We exchange a long look. We each think about nursing homes, where old women, full of years and work and the dignity of their experiences, are scolded like naughty children.

Mabel is 86. She has cataracts and a heart condition. It is no wonder that the big, gentle women who still has a Norwich lilt in her voice turns a little stubborn when she vows to stay in her house. It is the first secure home of her own that she has ever known. She was born in an English village, Lowestoft. Her policeman father and baby sister died in the same week, when Mabel was 2. Her young mother kept body and soul together by stitching the leather uppers of shoes.

"Don't worry, Mum," Mabel used to console her exhausted mother. "When I get 18, we'll travel around the world."

But her mother died when Mabel was 12. For two or three years, Mabel had been labouring at the treadle machine in her ailing mother's place. Now she was shuttled around to relatives, finished school at 16, and was apprenticed to a London florist. The four-room cottage where she was born was pulled down.

Mabel did travel. She travelled the world as an almost unpaid companion to a wealthy family seeking the sun to cure their tubercular infant in Madeira, South Africa, South America, and the United States. The family washed up in Canada in 1936, and Mabel went back to florist work.

She worked for about 20 years, first with Munro Florists and then with Percy Waters Florists on the Danforth. She does not have any pension from either the family she worked for or her florist employers. She still loves flowers ("anything artistic," she says wistfully) but all she can afford now is a bowl of plastic roses on the hall table. She sniffs deprecatingly at them.

Mabel lives on her Old Age Security and Guaranteed Income Supplement, which comes to $340 a month. She was married once, in her middle age, but the man died after only two years of married life in rented rooms. It was after that that Mabel scrimped and saved to buy her house. She finally paid it off two years ago, when she was 84.

Mabel thinks she has been lucky. She clings to two of her mother's maxims ("They can't put you out if you own your own home." and "If you've only got sixpence, and it's honestly earned, you can look anyone in the eye") and feels that God has been good to her, and that people have been wonderfully kind.

Her life is terribly circumscribed. She used to be friends with the woman next door, but she is bedridden on the second floor now, and Mabel can't get up to see her. Mabel has had to give up attendance at one seniors' club because she can't climb the streetcar steps to get there, but she gets a ride to WoodGreen Community Centre every Friday night when she helps with registration at the door. Sometimes she meets a friend and they sit in the nearby park.

Mabel has practically nothing, by most standards. But she has her own house, her soft-spoken dignity, and her privacy. And the knitting and WoodGreen give her that life-sustaining glow that she is worth something to her community.

There are more than a million single or widowed women over 65 in Canada, most of them poor because we would rather let them starve than have to think about them. We don't like their lumpy, troublesome bodies. We are embarrassed by the hair on their faces or their clumsy hands, thickened by arthritis. Old people aren't trendy. They don't disco or jog or sip amusing milkshakes at Mr. Greenjeans.

Slowly, though, we are being forced to think about them, by the sheer force of their rising numbers. It has dawned on us that if we continue to shovel old people into institutions at our current 8 per cent rate, we in Ontario alone will have to provide 1,900 new beds a year at an annual cost of $50 million. We have just twigged that it would cost a tiny fraction of that (not even 10 per cent) to keep old people happily at home with services like Meals on Wheels, Visiting Homemakers and public health nursing. After all, 45 per cent of the people in nursing homes, exiles from life, could be fully self-sufficient. So now economics have finally caught up with the ideas of the humanists who have fought furiously for the elderly all along.

This year, the Ontario government will bring in a $500 property grant for pensioners like Mabel. It's no exaggeration to say that it will mean the difference between life and death: I'd wager the whole $500 that if Mabel were driven out of her house and into a nursing home, she would die.

It's odd how ideas materialize into the iron laws of the land and begin to shape us instead of our shaping them. Consider: if this were a matriarchy, in all likelihood the housewives and mothers of the land would be amply rewarded—fat salaries, pensions, bonuses, and tax credits would shower down upon them. Doctors, on the other hand, might be expected to work all their lives as volunteers, providing healing and solace to the community out of sheer love and Hippocratic duty. Any discussion of pay for doctors might elicit righteous little yelps from brain surgeons and radiologists: "I'm insulted at the idea of being paid! I care for my patients out of love, and consider myself fortunate to be loved in return. That's all the pay I need."

We are so deeply conditioned to expect women to work as mothers and housekeepers for nothing but their room and board, while non-family work is thought of as financially valuable to the society, that this inversion strikes us as ridiculous. And so it is, of course: anyone whose work benefits the larger community earns a material reward in our economic system. Why aren't women rewarded, then, for the housewifery and motherhood that are so sentimentally exalted in the mythology of "the little woman"? Why is poverty the most likely lot in life for women who have devoted themselves solely to these sanctified tasks? The answer is simple. Her worth is defined only in relation to man. The whole world beams upon her devoted motherhood until her husband leaves her. Then what avails her secret brownie recipe, her gleaming floor? She has no skills worth selling in the outside world, and so must become that most despised and impoverished of all humans in Canada, the welfare mother. Now her motherhood has something tainted about it; intimations of filth and degradation surround her. The shudder we once reserved for illegitimacy is now awarded to the women unlucky enough to have children but no longer any man to serve.

If her husband dies, she is rudely evicted from the sheltering arms of the state and shoved into the frost of penniless old age with a pittance of his Canada Pension. Now we see how deeply society valued her work all those years, when her cooking and cleaning and devoted care enabled him to be a productive citizen. Now she must be extremely lucky in the bureaucratic lottery to qualify even for her percentage of the Canada Pension—does she have her own pension? income? dependants? If divorced, did she remember to apply within a three-year limit for pension-splitting? And as for private pensions, three out of four Canadian widows will be painfully startled to learn that they collect not a cent of their husband's pension after he is gone.

Canadian sociologist Margrit Eichler has compared the assistance offered by various nations to their female citizens. "As a society, Canada treats its children and their mothers extremely poorly," she writes. In Sweden, a "parenthood insurance plan" guarantees that employed parents can decide whether mother or father will use a full nine months of "child leave" at 93 per cent of income. Hungary gives 20 to 25 weeks of fully paid maternity leave, reduced working hours during the breast-feeding period, and up to 60 paid days of leave a year to care for sick children. Spain, France, Norway—all have variations of generous paid maternity leave. Only Canada and the United States lag far behind.

Our entire economic system in North America hinges on the wispy premise that women have babies out of whimsical private indulgence, and that men will always be the stalwarts to pay for them. Massive job discrimination is excused or justified by governments (remember Jean Chrétien arguing that women are only "secondary wage-earners"?) on the basis that women's primary task is one of wifedom and motherhood. Well, society can no longer have it both ways. If our primary task is as wives and mothers, and if this task is vital, as logically it must be, to the future of the nation, then the state cannot assert that it is entirely up to each woman privately to find or force some man to pay for her children or otherwise go hungry.

That is not an easy task; most men do not support the children they leave behind: fewer than one-third of Canadian fathers make their court-ordered child-support payments. But when the father defaults and leaves his children penniless, the onus falls on the mother as an individual to pursue him to claim the unpaid support money. Society does not lift a finger on her or the children's behalf. And motherhood is unrecognized as a social utility even in our tax and pension systems. A divorced father can claim tax deductions for his payments to children; the mother who must care for the children pays income tax on these payments. His money counts; her labour doesn't. When the divorced husband dies, the wife and mother can claim a small portion of his pension only for those years she served him as a live-in wife, but not for the years and years in which she alone raised their children. If a woman receives welfare, even the presence in her house of a man who contributes nothing to the family income will mean that she loses some mother's benefits, so powerfully rooted is our irrational belief that any woman who cohabits with a man is automatically his economic dependant.

It is these mythologies, which are based on the unpaid and even unacknowledged work of the woman as mother, house-keeper, and servant of man, that guarantee the poverty of so many Canadian women and children.

One proposal that would cut economics loose from mythologies is the Child Care Tax Credit outlined by sociologist Eichler. The somewhat ambiguously named Tax Credit (it would really be a taxable cash payment) would at last dispense with the old assumption that child-rearing should be the exclusive burden of women. Each at-home parent would receive a monthly payment, equal to the average cost of a day-care space, for each preschool child in his or her care at home. After the child reaches school age, the monthly payment would be scaled down to cover the cost of lunchtime, after-school, and holiday care. Payments would be made through the existing Family Allowance structure, so that they would most benefit the poorest children, and would be taxed back from the more affluent.

With one stroke, the state would rescue the one-quarter of all Canadian children who now live in destitution. Who can say how many of those would also be saved from emotional trauma, simply by having access at last to a good day-care centre, a hot lunch, and the perspicacious eye of a public health nurse?

Mothers would be freed to work outside the home or not, as they chose. Those best suited to stay home to mother full-time would be able to use the Credit for food, shelter, clothes, and recreation for the family. Those who work outside could afford safe and decent child care.

At the same time, every person in Canada would come into the Canada Pension Plan. The public would pay the contributions for each adult who stayed home to care for dependent persons (either children or bed-ridden adults). But if someone stayed home simply to keep house for a working spouse, without having the care of dependent children at home, the employed partner would be obliged to make the monthly pension contributions.

Eichler suggests that the Child Care Tax Credit would replace all state subsidies to day care, the day-care deduction, the married exemption, the refundable child tax credit, the equivalent-to-married exemption, and the transfer of deductions between spouses. Further savings would surely come from reduced burdens on the school system, chronic-care hospitals, and publicly subsidized nursing homes. Still, the substantial remaining cost would have to come from income tax, that is, the transfer of money from the childless and the affluent.

But the rewards in rational betterment would be enormous. With one splendid move, we would at last acknowledge the dignity and worth of child care and housework as full-time occupations. We would at last annihilate the poisonous myth of the little woman who had to depend on her man, whether or not his devotion burned with a gem-like flame. We would remove child support and care from the gender wars. We would ensure the dignity of older persons, male and female. If the women's movement achieved only this, it would achieve more than enough, because it has been the helplessness and vulnerability of the mother, her dependence on the good will and earnings of a man, that have trapped generations of women into lives of poverty and suffocating mythology.

Reactionaries may have their own reasons for wanting to keep women barefoot and insolvent in the kitchen. But how can we explain the women themselves, the housewives and mothers who are so often the first to shrill against new proposals for tax changes and family support that would defend them and their children from sudden, ruinous poverty? You would think the icy facts would be enough to make ardent feminists of us all. But somehow we don't make the connections. We coast along in a cocoon of ignorance — it's too painful to think of the day we'll be left alone. Besides, weren't we all brought up to believe that marriage was "happily ever after", the end of the story, the ticket to everlasting security? And though most of our daughters are growing up with the same myths, many women still think it's "extreme" or "silly" to take action against sexist TV commercials, to set up women's studies courses in the high schools, or to battle for pension reform or job equality. Unless we wrench ourselves into awareness, our daughters, too, may one day be lingering by the meat counter with empty shopping baskets, picking over the soup bones.

Mud-wrestling is the latest titillation in suburban taverns across Canada; a minority taste, but revealing. The thrill of it is to see lightly dressed women grapple and smear each other with gluey brown mud. The pleasure must lie in the mild perversity: just when commercials nag women to become ever more dainty and deodorized, filth becomes exciting. If you really believe in a goddess, I suppose it may be reassuring to know that she sometimes loves to grovel about in mud.

Well, if naughty boys exorcise their shames this way, what's the harm? And if some women are desperate enough to earn a living by pandering to a taste for kindergarten degradations, that's nothing new either. But middle-class women should take care not to sneer. Some of them have their own version of mud-wrestling. They abuse and degrade other women in public, not to earn a dollar, but to justify themselves before their uneasy consciences and to pander to the prejudices of their men.

Feminist-baiting is what I mean. Not the mud-slinging from the extreme right, not the insults the men who fear equality, not the pathetic silliness of the Total Women in their whipped-cream bras, but the casual verbal abuse dispensed daily by middle-of-the-road women. You can see it any day in the newspaper. A bridal consultant blames "feminism" for women who want to wear white at their second weddings. A writer who was never a feminist and who never married blames her "decision not to have children" on the feminist movement. A woman writes a letter to the editor to complain that since "women's libbers" came along, men don't give her their seats on streetcars.

Feminism is blamed for the rise in rape, the fall in the birth rate, the escalating number of divorces, the destruction of the family, the gonorrhoea epidemic, and the increase in homosexuality. Drifts in society and paths that we took blindly and that now turn out to be prickly, these distresses we now lay at the door of the feminist movement like disowned babies.

In fact, though the movement can take credit for impressing many profound insights on the public mind, the great shifts in the structure of marriage and child-rearing pre-date the rise of modern feminism. The shift began during the First World War when thousands of women abandoned the home and domestic labour for work in the factories. By the time of the Second World War, it was no longer only servant girls who surged into the work place. Although a massive anti-feminist repression took place in the 1950's, when women were forced by public opinion to retreat to their Hollywood kitchens, baby showers, Tupperware parties, cinch belts, pointed shoes, and other cramping accoutrements of subservience, the pattern was already set. The birth-control pill had unleashed choice upon the world, and now any woman could control her own procreation. The rigid structure of the patriarchal family, based on the woman's helpless dependency, was doomed. Those who had always been unhappy in the family now had a way out, and took it. And once the flush of prosperity receded a little from the pudgy cheeks of the McCarthy era, women remembered the exhilaration of wartime financial independence and went back into the work place. Crinolines and constricted attitudes ("ladies never whistle") were useless on the factory floor, and were cheerfully abandoned. Economic reality and birth control were the twin levers of the social avalanche — not, much as we might wish to take credit, the feminist movement.

Recently, an article in *Maclean's* magazine entitled "Housewives Are People Too!" argued that housewives have become "the lepers of society. The women's movement and glossy fashion magazines accuse loyal wives of living vicariously and of not conforming to the correct image of the Dream Woman."

Right away, the author has a serious confusion on her hands. She lumps together the Virginia Slims lady in the glossy ads with the ideologues of the women's movement. This seems like unnecessarily sloppy thinking. Does she really think that all career women are feminists? That fashion magazines represent the aims of feminism? Slick career women who smoke Virginia Slims are an invention of capitalists eager to exploit a new market. It is the ad men who concocted this shiny "Dream Woman". Feminists, on the other hand, have struggled to destroy false images and to free all women from stereotypes. The "Dream Woman" is a nightmare to a feminist, who knows how it feels to be trapped in someone else's fantasy. It is feminists who have worked so hard to dignify the work of women in the home, writing about the economic value of housework, the freedom of choice that women must have between kitchen or career, the importance of child-rearing, and the housewife's need for financial security protected by pensions. Feminists have laboured for family-law reform, women's clinics, shelters for battered wives, co-op day care, counselling services—all the "safety net" services that back up the woman in the home.

There is something dangerously soft-minded about all this whimpering and blaming feminists for feeling blamed. Just who is the victim? Women who work outside their homes, according to a 1982 National Welfare Council report that made front-page news, are saving their families from poverty. Indeed, the ten per cent drop in the number of poverty families in Canada is accounted for solely by the rise in working wives. So who are the victimized women who love housewifery and are being guilted? They are the affluent and middle-class women who can afford the luxury of staying home to raise a family while their husbands earn enough for both of them. Some victims.

The author says, as anti-feminists say everywhere, "Don't misunderstand me—I'm not against equal rights for women." But the argument sounds disingenuous to me. If she's *for* equal rights for women, why is she attacking feminists, who are the only ones fighting for those equal rights? Why is she attacking feminists for crimes they never committed? Could it possibly be that it's simply safer to attack other women than to blame the ones who really do denigrate woman's work...the men in government? After all, it is male governments that have consistently put down women's work in the home by leaving it out of the economic reckoning of the Gross National Product, by refusing to reward it with pensions, and, until the feminists did battle, by not even acknowledging women's contribution to marriage when dividing property during divorce.

Paranoia is always a symptom of projected anger. In my opinion, many housewifes in these hard times are struggling with their own guilt about relying on their husbands to pay the bills. It's easier to displace some of the uneasiness onto feminists than to demand more support, help, and respect from the man who is paying the mortgage and leaving his wet towels on the bathroom floor.

The threatened or resentful housewife ought to be told that most working women are housewives too. They also clean bathtubs. They also love and listen to their children. They are working to help keep their families above the poverty line, and their double lives are not meant as a reproach to anyone.

The women's movement rose up partly in answer to conditions that refused women not only rights but even the most limited of choices. Since the 1950s, we have become accustomed to women being quoted, as they step into high management positions, as saying, "Of course, I'm not a women's libber." We've become accustomed to women, protesting against some injustice that has struck home, saying, "Of course, I'm not one of those bra-burners…" And we've become accustomed to the defensive whine from some women who have chosen not to work outside the home, who blame their uneasy feelings of guilt and worthlessness on women who have made different choices, instead of on the male-dominated society which regards their work as valueless.

This subservient chorus of women's voices is perhaps the most disheartening drag on the energies of feminists. Every "Of course I'm not…" woman is riding on the skirts of the activists. But meanwhile she perpetuates an ignorant stereotype of feminists that serves male supremacist ideology. I call it mud-wrestling. I think it beneath the dignity and duty of any woman, whether she works in or out of the home—or whether, like almost all of us, she does both.

THE HEAVY FIST

BY 1978, THE PHRASE "BATTERED WIVES" HAD ALREADY become the brussels sprouts of women's journalism, something you chewed obediently and gulped down without much passion or scrutiny, a standby idea that had lost its freshness without ever having been fully tasted.

I was prodded out of this mental inertia when a downtown shelter for battered wives asked me to interview the women and write about their not very glamorous problems. One of those surprising small journalistic earthquakes happened: "Alice" 's humanness struck me so forcibly that battering stopped being a catch-phrase.

We get very cosy in the narrow rut of our lives: back and forth to work and home, grumbling about taxes, taking our blessings for granted, wearing the rut deeper and deeper until we can barely see over the edge into other people's lives. So it was good for me to meet Alice at Interval House the other day. Alice, 29, with that self-deprecating Maritime verbal shrug in her voice, is so thin that the light almost shines through her. There's a transparent honesty in her face, too. Her frailty sparks a protective tenderness in people she meets. But not in Jimmy, who gave her that scar under her eyebrow when he smashed her glasses into her face during one of his beatings.

You might wonder why a decent, bright woman like Alice would stay for five years with a man who terrorized her with his fists and boots. You might think she was a fool or a masochist. But you would be wrong. When a Jimmy gets battered in his childhood, he learns to batter others. When an Alice gets battered, emotionally, she grows up blaming herself. She takes her "punishment" mutely, believing that somehow she deserves it, or that she's not worthy of reaching out for something better. Even now, after she has finally wrenched free from Jimmy, she has to fight off the pangs of remorse and guilt when he comes to Interval House crying that he needs her, that he's losing weight without her.

Alice grew up in a coldly respectable Nova Scotia family, country Baptists who "weren't used to showing affection". Just before her final exams in Grade 10, the family skeleton came rattling out of the closet: Alice's "mum" was really her grandmother. The woman she thought was her older sister was really her mother. Everyone...father, brothers, nieces... was something other than what she had always thought. The whole shaky house of cards that was her family came tumbling down around her. Alice's grandparents tersely admitted the truth and closed the discussion. "I had all these feelings and no one to talk to," remembers Alice, not blaming but sad. Her "father" drove her to the local mental hospital and she was left there for a month and a half. She never went back to school after that.

No one to talk to. That's really the story of Alice's life. Her family disapproved of Jimmy, so she could never tell them how there was no food for the baby, or how Jimmy beat her up when she tried to get a job. Alice felt alone, weak, helpless...and hated herself for it. Jimmy fitted exactly into the pattern of Alice's family: he was never emotionally available to her when she needed him. Her half-brother, the one she was close to, was killed in a car accident. "I took it hard," whispers Alice. Jimmy took off for three days and nights.

Jimmy is a jazz drummer with long hair and a Genghis Khan moustache. "He's so talented. I would sit in some club and just fill up with pride when he played," Alice says, looking at the floor so I won't see that her eyes are brimming. But the glorious moments were few. "He didn't let me come with him often. He said his appeal was to female audiences and I spoiled it for him."

Usually, Jimmy was too "drug out" from partying and dope to hold a regular job. They took welfare, drifting from one furnished room to another. He choked her, punched her, kicked her with his boots on when she was pregnant. Later, their toddler clung to her leg, trembling, when Jimmy was in a rage. It was only when Halifax welfare ran out and they migrated to Toronto with their 19-month-old baby that Alice found Interval House and a way of breaking free. They're helping her with the red tape of getting custody of the baby so Jimmy can't snatch him, finding a cheap room and day care, and applying for a Manpower training course.

Alice's face lights up, tentatively. "I've always been so shy, so inward. But since I got here, I haven't stopped talking."

Alice cradles her blond baby passionately against her thin shoulder and tells me, "I'm not going to let David grow up the way Jimmy did. I'm going to make it on my own. I'm going to start liking myself now."

If it's any help, Alice, I liked you a lot.

Alice's fragility, and her wobbly determination to make a life for herself, broke through the stereotype of the rye-soaked slattern who almost deserves to be beaten by her drunken husband. It was my first experience with the impulsive generosity of newspaper readers. Within hours after the column appeared, the switchboard lit up: older women offered rooms in their now-empty homes; baby clothes and furniture began to pile up beside my desk; envelopes of money rained down on me; a separated schoolteacher sent Alice a year's worth of monthly $100 post-dated cheques (I've been beaten, too"). A day-care centre came through with a subsidized space for the baby and the prospect of a supermarket cashier's job shimmered on the horizon. A basement flat was found and furnished for a dazzled Alice. Bell Telephone broke its rules to install a telephone for a mother still on welfare, because it sympathized with Alice's terror that Jimmy might find her and try to do her harm.

A week later, the real-life Jimmy called. He put all the cocky swagger at his command into his voice, bragging that he recognized himself in my column, despite the pseudonym, and could easily have me sued. "Please do so," I urged him politely. He backed off: "Look, all I want is for you to print my side of the story," he wheedled. "Alice told you a pack of lies."

I heard from Alice about a month later. She was lonely, out there in her suburban basement apartment, and frightened to be on her own for the first time in her life, but she thought she was "making it". She had started work at a terrific factory job.

Six months later, Jimmy called. "Just thought you'd want to know that Alice and I are back together again," he purred. He put just a hint of menace into his voice: "She promised she won't be telling no more of those lies about me, neither."

I didn't have the courage to break the news to readers who had so urgently wanted to help get Alice back on her feet. Besides, I couldn't be sure that Jimmy's boast was true, or that the reunion would stay glued for long. Most battered wives, I had learned in the interim, are so demoralized and dispirited by their dependence on brutal men that they need several tries to break off the relationship.

But the incident provoked me into re-examining the subject. In the half-hour after Jimmy's second phone call, I had felt and thought every crude stereotype about battered wives that it's possible to imagine. I'd mentally pushed Alice at arm's length from me with critical recollections of her social class, lack of education, and weak ego. If I, who had met and been touched by her, could so easily reduce her to a cardboard cliché, what about those for whom the phrase "battered wife" was still an irritating bore? A film about a man called David Fox and his wife Jeannie helped put things back into human perspective:

David Fox looks right into the camera, crooking his strong eyebrows in bewilderment. He's 40ish, with a sensitive mouth and the pleasantly blunt look and lilt of a north-of-England man.

"I don't see myself as a violent man," he says. "If I'm pressured out in the workaday world, you know, I'd...uh... run away. I'm timid, really." He leans across the half-door of the barn, earnestly groping with clarity. "But it's like with a child. You have to, well, administer, uh, discipline. You do it," and his inflection turns up with genuine warmth, "because you love them."

David is the enigmatic star of *Loved, Honoured and Bruised*. The half-hour documentary film tells the true story of David and his wife, Jeannie, a fresh-faced, gentle woman in her late 30s who took their five little daughters and walked out one day when she thought he was going to kill her. As she edged past him to reach the children's suitcase, he clouted her so hard that he perforated her eardrum.

I went to see this small and honest film by Canadian Gail
Singer because I was uneasy about a spate of letters reacting
to my column several weeks ago about Marianne, the beaten
wife. Marianne, an articulate, middle-class wife not unlike
Jeannie, had told me about her agonized terror of her husband. Most of the women who wrote expressed sympathetic
anger on Marianne's behalf. Most of the men who wrote said
that Marianne must "seek tyranny", "have rocks in her
head", "enjoy punishment". Their chorus, above all, was
"Why the hell doesn't she get out?"

Just for a moment, I found myself sharing their impatience.
It sounds as though they're blaming the victim, but I believe
it isn't as simple as that. Theirs was a howl of anguish, too.
They hated to read about a woman being smashed and
kicked by her husband. If it were them, they'd hit back, get
out, do something. Fervently, they wish Marianne would act
more like a man.

I arranged for a screening of *Loved, Honoured and Bruised* to
clear my head of simple-minded solutions. It did.

Jeannie and David are likeable, decent people who grew
up in ordinary, non-violent homes. They do not use alcohol
or drugs. They loved each other; the film-maker says there
was a palpable physical attraction between them, even after
16 years of marriage, and 13 savage beatings—about one a
year, starting after the first baby was born.

Jeannie was devastated when he first threw a scalding
teapot at her and the baby. "I managed, though, to put it
aside," she says of her shock and outrage.

That's the crux of it. When people say, "Why doesn't she
just get out?", they're imagining a marriage of unending
squalor—drunkenness, beatings, hatred. It isn't usually like
that. Alas, like all of human life, it's complicated. Yes, there
were bruises, welts, dislocated bones. There were also long
stretches of peace, animated conversation, working the farm
together, playing with the children, plans, hopes, intimacies.

Do you snatch your baby daughters away from their
father because of an annual tantrum? Which is the real
David, the good father or the batterer? Is it just an aberration,
the kind that good wives shove to a back corner of their

minds? Or maybe it was meant to be ("Love me, hurt me,"
moans the disco singer); or maybe, maybe Jeannie really
deserved it?

Watching her, you know that's not true. She's not weak or
a nag or a whiner. Gentle, maybe. Used to the man being the
strong one who makes the decisions. Willing to please, to try
harder. "He called me stupid so many times I began to think
it was true," she says, blushing. "After one of his rages, I'd be
walking on eggs, trying so hard to anticipate his wishes so I
wouldn't provoke him. Yet when people malign him, something in me springs to his defence."

Jeannie didn't leave sooner because women cling to the
familiar four walls when the babies are small. And because
women are raised to doubt themselves before they doubt the
man; and also because it was an eight-mile walk to the nearest
bus stop and she had absolutely nowhere to go with five little
ones. If, finally, there hadn't been a women's shelter in the
nearest prairie city, Jeannie never would have managed to
get out. But there was. Now she is a waitress, living on her
own, raising the children. It's hard and she's lonely and you
can't tell if she's happier now. Even a battering husband does
not batter all the time.

In the long run, "getting out" is no big solution to the
problem of men who hurt their wives. We're beginning to
know why women put up with it so long before they "get
out". Now, let's start asking the tougher question: "Why does
he hit?"

As it happens, crowds of cheering bystanders did not rush
forward to debate my question about "why men hit". Even the
copy editor who wrote the headline switched the onus back onto
the wife when he titled the column "When Men Hit, Why Do
Women Stay?" No, the public focus, and mine, stayed gloomily
on the subject of women as victims. That's a pity, for several
reasons. After all, it is amply clear by now *why* women are
victims: centuries of economic discrimination, social conditioning
to passivity and dependence, and lesser physical size and strength.
But the more interesting question—why do men hit?—has been
shrugged off as a given of human life. Zoologists who dwell on

man's aggressive legacy from prehistory have not been able to explain why neolithic impulses of violence should still be present, and even encouraged by society, in an environment strikingly devoid of sabre-tooth tigers.

Most of society lifts one shoulder in a lazy shrug when it hears about the violation of women's bodies. According to a University of British Columbia professor, Donald Dutton, who has been researching domestic violence for more than a decade, "Of every 10,000 [domestic] assaults on Canadian women every year, only two men are ever convicted." Dutton told a House of Commons committee that about 9,200 wife assaults go unreported each year and that police respond reluctantly to only half of the reported 800. Furthermore, when they do respond, they "often witness an emotionally distraught woman and an apparently rational, if somewhat agitated, man," Dutton was quoted by Canadian Press. "They often draw unwarranted inferences about what has preceded their arrival, give incorrect legalistic advice to the woman, are not knowledgeable about transition-house services, and don't collect evidence to aid a prosecution. A case can certainly be made that the criminal justice system appears to tacitly condone wife assault."

As we now know to our grief, it is not only the criminal justice system that appears to condone wife-beating. Soon after Dutton's testimony, the two most powerful bodies in Canada, the House of Commons and the Supreme Court, both of them overwhelmingly male, made their views known. In 1981, the Supreme Court reduced the power of provincial courts to protect women from violent husbands. The Supreme Court ruled that provincial judges had no right to order an abusive husband to stay away from his wife and to stop harassing or beating her.

This astounding decision, weakening the already flimsy recourse available to the beaten wife, was typical of a misogynist drift in Supreme Court decisions, going right back to the Persons Case in 1930, when women were declared to be "not persons". This ludicrous mid-twentieth-century piece of bias was followed, in the 1970s, by a litany of injustices from the justices. Irene Murdoch was told, after years of litigation, that she was not entitled to any share of the farm that she and her husband had bought and worked together, simply because it was in her husband's name. The Pappajohn decision made available to accused rapists, and only to rapists, the defence of "an honest belief, even without reasonable grounds for that belief", that the woman consented to be raped. Imagine if the Supreme Court allowed a man to plead not guilty to beating his neighbour because he honestly believed, despite the neighbour's screams and struggles that he enjoyed being attacked! Then the Supreme Court ruled that Stella Bliss was not being discriminated against on grounds of sex when she was denied unemployment insurance after being fired because she was pregnant. "If section 46 treats unemployed pregnant women differently from other unemployed persons, be they male or female, it is, it seems to me, because they are pregnant and not because they are women," wrote Mr. Justice Pratte, with syntax as tortured as the reasoning.

Male laughter recently accompanied one of the most revealing moments in the history of the House of Commons. When the committee before which Professor Dutton had testified finally made its report in May 1982, it wrote: "We have found that wife battering is not a matter of slaps and flying crockery. Battered women are choked, kicked, bitten, punched, subjected to sexual assault, threatened and assailed with weapons.... such behaviour is far too common.... We have been given good reason to believe that every year in Canada one-tenth of the women who live with men as a couple are battered."

This grim and jolting report was greeted in the House of Commons by braying laughter, jeers, catcalls and a boorish male barrage of witticisms, mostly from the Conservative caucus, when NDP MP Margaret Mitchell (Vancouver East) rose to discuss it. The television cameras picked up the laughter on the soundtrack but didn't show us the faces of the men who laughed. Fellow MPs were equally discreet in shielding the identity of the hecklers. It took two days and two attempts before the Members of Parliament would give unanimous assent to a "motherhood" motion that affirmed the Commons' concern about wife-beating. There were actually men who voted against such a motion, though Hansard does not record their names.

Beatings hurt; quite often they maim, or even kill. I wonder how beaten women reacted as their MPs hooted with laughter at their plight. I wonder how many of the male MPs beat their wives; statistically, at least twenty of them.

The incident of laughing louts alerted Canadians, both men

and women, to the nonchalance with which our law-makers view assaults on women. Still, although the spotlight briefly shifted away from the beaten women and shone instead on the men who think it's all a joke, the emphasis generally remains on woman the victim, not man the aggressor.

Feminists have struggled unavailingly with this problem. The more we talk about the ways in which women are victimized and oppressed, the more we alienate the many young women who very naturally scorn to identify themselves as underdogs. I would even go so far as to guess that many confident young achievers, when they heard of the uproar in the House of Commons, preferred to identify with those relaxed and confidently laughing men than with the cringing and powerless beaten women described in the report. Every reformist ideology, from socialism to Social Credit, suffers from this structural handicap: the very individuals whose wrongs are to be exposed and sufferings relieved would much rather see themselves, thank you very much, as winners, not losers. Happily deluded that they themselves are invulnerable, they reject the critique along with the sackcloth and ashes.

All the same, feminism can't shirk its task of bringing bad news to reluctant public attention. The last twenty years have shown us that each new layer of encrusted prejudice uncovered by feminists is greeted first by groans of irritation by the unconvinced majority, who would rather not be disturbed; then by a flurry of grudging but stirred-up attention; then, gradually and painfully, by concessions and reforms; finally, casual acceptance of achieved change. There is not a step along the way that is not painful and unwelcome to some.

A couple of years ago, when a book called *Father's Days: A True Story About Incest* came across my desk, I avoided reading it for three weeks. When the author, Katherine Brady, came to town and an insistent public-relations person set up an interview for me, I dreaded meeting her, as though she carried some obnoxious plague. Rarely have I dragged myself to an interview with more shrinking revulsion...and rarely have I come away afterwards more touched and more galvanized. My little gavotte of abhorrence but eventual empathy was utterly typical. We all keep ugly stories at bay, often by blaming the victim for causing the whole mess. And for all of us, feminism is one long, continuing exercise in confronting and cutting through such cowardly reflexes.

When I met Katherine Brady, I discovered a likeable and attractive woman of thirty-six who had bravely been "saying the unsayable" all across North America. She was determined to crash through what child experts call "the last frontier" to make incest as widely recognized a crime as child abuse. Ten years ago, don't forget, even Children's Aid workers and welfare officials denied the allegations of investigative reporters who said child abuse was a widespread crime. Further back, in 1963, when I suggested to my editors at the *Globe and Mail* that I do a story on incest, I was told in the strongest terms that I was off-base, that incest was merely a weird and extremely rare aberration. Well, now we know otherwise. In May 1982, for example, one suburban Toronto distress centre alone reported an upsurge in desperate calls from incest victims—up to fifty of them a year. Some of them are very young.

Katherine Brady (a pseudonym) was eight years old when her father, a prison guard and ex-Marine, soothed her fear during a thunderstorm one night by taking her into his bed. Mummy was a timid, emotionally pallid women, working as a nightshift nurse. From fondling, coaxing, caressing, and flattering, Brady gradually led his small daughter to repeated sessions of mutual masturbation. Always he lured her with promises of love and tantalized her with a barely understood sexual excitement for which she felt morbidly guilty and ashamed.

"You can't leave me this way, Kathy," he'd whine, or "Your mother doesn't give me enough." Horrified, but sexually teased, the child would give in, partly in a desperate belief that she was somehow helping to save her parents' marriage.

There's no isolation quite so profound as the isolation of a child with a guilty secret, and this may be the ultimate crime of the sexually exploitive father. Sinking deeper and deeper into a choked passivity, Katherine never found the courage to tell anyone or to get away—until she married the town's rich boy, a carbon copy of her cold, domineering father, when she was 18.

She finally fled from her predictably rotten marriage into the arms of a woman, and still feels "more comfortable in the company of women". She won custody of her two small girls, aged six and nine, in a landmark court battle in which the experts all praised her warm mothering and stressed that "it is heterosexuals who bring up homosexuals." Could any evidence be more pointed than the presence in court of Katherine's father?

Bright, funny, and bouncing with the energy of one who has moved physically and intellectually from a small mid-western town to New York, Katherine Brady has even, after years of psychoanalysis, forgiven her father. What she cannot forgive is the furtive, hush-hush attitude of society. "One in ten little girls is a victim of incest," she told me, her blue eyes snapping. "After I appear on TV, I get flooded with letters from ten- and eleven-year-old girls with 'Help' scrawled on the envelope. Many say they have told their mothers and teachers and not been believed. The public agencies aren't much better. The usual reaction is to subject the child to a pelvic examination—can you believe it?—to see if she is lying, or to throw the father in jail and put the kid in a foster home."

Incest is the most unreported crime, because the crime itself silences the young victims. The child is stranded. The adults in her family have betrayed her by "not knowing" what's going on; she is too guilty to ask for help; she's driven into a growing dependency on a narrowing little world of sickly love that her father offers her; and finally, if she ever finds the courage to tell someone, she may well be accused of lying.

A perfect trap. And despite our latter-day enlightenment about this crime, a new, improved trap has lately been placed in the path. Some theorists now declare that incest may not be so terrible after all; there are even avant-garde American men who advocate incest as a "liberating" experience for the child, and male movie-makers, in a fantasy that neatly reverses the human reality, present their audiences with a whole succession of

Lolitas—nubile little girls who cunningly seduce their innocent fathers and uncles.

No wonder that swinging young urbanites commonly mouth the hip new cliché that incest isn't so traumatic. Not traumatic? No screams and scars, perhaps. Just years and years, a lifetime, of twisting self-hatred that can make normal love in adulthood impossible. When incest victims speak for themselves, most tell of years of pain and incalculable damage.

All these men—the laughing MPs, the pro-incest lobbyists, and, yes, even the moviemakers with their lies about seductive children—all must take responsibility for the cruel twist by which little girls and grown women who are sexually assaulted are then blamed for their crime. Consider these cases of almost pathological injustice: in 1981, a Wisconsin judge exonerated a rapist because the five-year-old girl whom he had raped was, in the judge's words, "sexually promiscuous". In 1981 in Windsor, Ontario, a Children's Aid Society declined to move a ten-year-old girl from a foster home where the father had several times sexually molested her *while she slept*, because, according to the CAS worker, the child was "sexually provocative" and would probably be molested in any foster home. And in Britain, in the same year, a judge set a confessed rapist free with only a fine, because the teenage rape victim was guilty of "contributory negligence" in that she hitched a ride—a judicial decision as crazy as exonerating a burglar because the jeweller displayed gold rings in the window.

With violence against women and sexual exploitation of children so deeply accepted by so many, what hope is there that we will ever reach a point when such attitudes will bring an automatic shudder? Will we ever take the next step forward from the state of minority awareness and feminist agitation?

Given the surge of pornography, as omnipresent and insistent in our culture as industrial pollution, there is room for doubt. Despite the feminist outcry over pornography in recent years, despite what seems to be its obvious fascination with female degradation and pain, the attitude of most Canadians to pornography remains one of hesitant, embarrassed liberalism. Tugged between the arguments for "freedom of expression" and a muddled 1960s cliché that "hey, bodies are beautiful", most people avoid looking straight into the disturbing face of modern porn.

Many women bolster their indifference to the issue with the placid assumption that the men they know and admire share their revulsion for "hard-core" stuff. Their assumption is wrong. What we all need to recognize is that pornography is no longer the harmless stuff of fantasy, as reviewers often claim. Perhaps in the more innocent days of air-brushed nudity and clumsily simulated intercourse, porn could be seen as an erotic stimulant and nothing more. By the early seventies, though, organized crime had become deeply involved in what is known as the skin trade. In their unscrupulous efforts to expand the market, mobsters have provided ever more intense and grotesque thrills to stimulate the wilted ganglia of the audience.

Today there are very few pornographic films or even magazines that show only naked men and women enjoying mutual sex. In fact, there is no mutuality; the unspoken but constantly reinforced message of almost all pornography, from the mildest to the most horrifying, is male dominance and female submission. At its most refined level, in magazines like *Playboy*, pornography wears a middle-class face, but still, its content is the crowing triumph of men over women. At the more extreme end of the spectrum, here are some scenes scissored out of recent films by the Ontario Film Classification Board:

- a naked woman, eyes closed in moaning rapture, masturbating a horse;

- a young girl, elaborately costumed, handcuffed, and strapped to a table to be raped while her mother looks on happily, waiting her turn;

- a group of women streaming blood from whip wounds, with bits forced into their mouths;

- women trussed up like butchered pork loins, with meat hooks jammed into their private parts;

- women strapped to operating tables, spurting blood from unanaesthetized amputations, while men gleefully spray semen into their faces.

According to Ontario censors, the brutal, sadistic kind of pornography comprises about half of all the pornographic films made. Many men dispute these figures; since most hard-core is illegal, proper statistics aren't available in any case. What is indisputable is that once-unthinkable images are now a marketplace cliché. Teenage record albums frequently display chained and tortured women —or various parts of them — and the bound, bleeding woman is a dime a dozen on the paperback racks. Artists and intellectuals have always argued passionately and with great justice against the practice of censorship; such libertarian views are now extremely popular. Maxine Sidran, for example, a journalist writing in *Quest* magazine, argued that pornography is "a valid commodity", especially for the lonely and the handicapped. In a culture in which everything is reduced to a commodity, that may be partly true. But take heed: the Mafia may be your friendly local sex grocer, and what may seem only titillating may turn out to be a time bomb that explodes in our faces. It is no longer artistically courageous and admirable to argue for total freedom and to ignore the consequences. Since popular pornography of even the most tepid variety is now utterly without affection (love or erotic tenderness in an ordinary men's magazine would seem absolutely startling), we must consider the effect of this cold, mechanistic domination-sex on a whole growing generation.

Eroticism, after all, is conditioned by culture. The Chinese learned to be sexually aroused by tiny bound feet. Isn't it possible that our own adolescents may be learning, through the all-pervasive images of female bondage, that sadism is luscious? The advent of home videotape machines has meant that in large Canadian cities a video store has sprouted on every corner. Most of them, by their own admission, sell hard-core porn tapes under the counter. This means that in the 1980s, thousands upon thousands of homes will be running hard-core brutality in their living rooms, where passing toddlers and enthralled primary school kids will have surreptitious or even free access to profoundly warped images of female degradation.

It is useless for porn-users to protest, as they always do, that "it's only fantasy". Real fantasy exists in the mind. Modern pornography uses and abuses millions of very real women and children photographed by its cameras to embody the crude mechanistic fantasies of mass marketeers, manipulators who turn up the heat to make more bucks. The horror is that you can't make kiddie porn without real live kiddies. For them, it is not a harmless daydream.

So far, porn apologists have taken the offensive. When the Ontario Film Classification Board banned *Pretty Baby*, the "romantic" Louis Malle film in which a twelve-year-old's virginity is auctioned to the highest bidder in a "kindly" whorehouse, the critics had a wonderful time sneering at the censors. But *Pretty Baby*, like *Taxi Driver*, *Lolita*, and *Beau Père*, actively changed the public's perception of prepubescent girls. Little girls became legitimately eroticized; not only was their unspoiled flesh tempting, but they themselves were depicted as the temptresses hot with desire and unscrupulous in their pursuit of men.

Now it's time for the lordly defenders of *Pretty Baby*, who have never bothered to consider the effects of such middlebrow male daydreams, to defend themselves. Waves of child-murder have swept over the continent in the last few years. In Atlanta, in Chicago, in Texas, and in British Columbia, there have been gruesome cases of mass rape and multiple sexual murders, all of children. Such evil is not unrelated to the explosion of material depicting eroticized childhood in our local movie theatres and on the milk-store magazine racks. Is it art, fantasy, a harmless "commodity", or a dangerous destruction of society's taboos? If censorship is abandoned, are the porn apologists ready to tolerate the social fallout from what they call art? Is it acceptable to them that incidences of rape, wife-beating, and child murder should increase in the name of movie and magazine freedom?

Bonnie Klein, director of the National Film Board documentary *Not a Love Story*, used movie freedom to pose this question and others. In the clamour of male fury that followed, it was clear that a woman's freedom of expression to show men at their most degraded is not as acceptable in our society as men's freedom to show the opposite.

I was rocked by the vitriolic tone of the reviews, coming as they did from usually placid reviewers who manage to find civil things to say about the most suppurating Hollywood trash. I was surprised to read that Canadian feminists in the movie were talking like "fascists" and calling for censorship. Could a new radical right-wing form of feminism have sprung into being while I catnapped at my typewriter? Piqued, I rushed off to the National Film Board offices to see this perverse bit of filmed demagoguery. I sat through it in mounting astonishment. Far from the ideological rampage the men claimed to have seen, *Not a Love Story* was a remarkably polite depiction of the multi-billion dollar porn industry in Canada and the United States. The camera follows two women, a hip young stripper, Linda Lee Tracey, and middle-class mama Bonnie Klein, as they explore the kingdom of porn, from corner-store sex magazines to New York peep-shows and "adult" movies.

In a sense, the bitter male unanimity about the film is the most interesting thing about it. The emotional bias of the women in the documentary is no surprise, although the lugubrious tone favoured by Bonnie Klein as on-camera narrator-interviewer is offset by the tart bravado of stripper Linda Lee, who boasts of her sense of power when ringside gogglers hotly thrust money at her naked, undulating body. It's a foregone conclusion that Bonnie Klein will find her worst fears about porn confirmed in the course of her research, and that Linda Lee, drawn into the exploration in a way that shreds some of her self-delusions, will have a change of heart. But what a shock awaited us in the reaction of men whom we had previously considered enlightened, tolerant, and allies of the raised female consciousness. Sid Adilman of the *Toronto Star* wrote, "An offensive belch, a one-sided tract of outrage that only feminists and the Moral Majority will take to their bosoms." Jay Scott, an award-winning film reviewer whose admiration had previously stretched to campy Grade-B, male-bonding war movies, suddenly revealed the limits of his tolerance. "Bourgeois fascist feminism," he raged after seeing *Not a Love Story*. "A dangerous attempt to police reality and censor fantasy…Puritan prejudice…a film that supports censorship…whining naïveté."

There must have been something in *Not a Love Story* to sting the men to such extremes of excited ire. (Could it have been the natural defensiveness of the scolded boy-child caught red-handed with dirty magazines?) Are movie reviewers so incapable of distance from subjects that reflect badly on their gender? How tolerant, in retrospect, all females reviewers have been, endlessly praising films in which women have rarely escaped from the roles of lewd tart, dumpy housewife, evil schemer, dumb blonde, or bosomy mattress.

Three Toronto reviewers saved their most scathing contempt for the scene in the movie in which Robin Morgan, the feminist writer, weeps while discussing pornography. Their criticism implied that Morgan was self-pityingly melodramatic ("bawling" said Scott). Their reaction was a rare and perfect revelation of how little empathy they have for the female viewpoint. Many women have wept during screenings of *Not a Love Story*, which has achieved the status of a hit film, touring the country to packed audiences. They weep because any woman who looks into the pornography industry must react eventually with pain, anger, and tears to the brutal ugliness that allegedly "turns men on": all those hundreds and hundreds of young women, spreading their vulvas or anuses open for the camera in an attitude of almost doglike submission; the girl who smiles ecstatically into *Chic* magazine's cameras as she thrusts a kitchen knife into her vagina and the blood gushes out; the girl whose rump and legs are sticking up out of a giant meat-grinder on the cover of *Hustler* magazine, the rest of her having been converted into a tidy pile of red ground meat.

To talk about these things and our reaction to them, as only feminists have done so far, is a vital first step. Underneath, our polite lives, as far-reaching and intricate as the sewer systems beneath our cities, the pornography industry spreads its images and its influence. Until now, most of the women I know have chosen not to hear, see, or talk about it. They do not have strong views about pornography. Why? Because they don't know what's out there. Furthermore, they don't want to know. Watch the women avert their eyes at the local milk store as they sidle past the men standing transfixed at the porn-magazine rack. If women don't look, don't know, and don't feel anything about it, they can defend themselves from falling into an embarrassingly unliberal state of rage.

Between men and women, pornography presents a sometimes unbridgeable gulf. The men are baffled that anyone should question the existence of porn or their delight in it, tranquilly certain that they embody an enlightened sophistication, an almost artistic élan, as they browse through Marquis de Sade or *Chic* magazine. Men are not accustomed to having any of their pleasures questioned. When challenged, they are liable to lash out as tempestuously and irrationally as the men who reviewed *Not a Love Story*. Rather than confront either the arrogance or the fury, women would prefer not to know. Rather that be sneered at as "prudish" (is there a worse insult among the enlightened middle classes?), women would rather not talk about it. How effectively these anti-censorship men censor the anti-pornography faction!

There is no simple answer to pervasive pornography. It may take several generations before our new perceptions of male and female roles make the domination ethic of porn as repulsive to men as it is to women. The 1980s are the first decade in our history, after all, when enlightened and sexually sophisticated women have dared to object to harmful male fantasies. Most of us are still afraid to protest when husbands, lovers, or sons use sadistic pornography to amuse themselves; we've been trained to consider male sexuality as a delicate flower that might wither at the faintest breath of reproof. Though men are conditioned to admire other men who (in fantasy or reality, depending mostly on social class) actually brutalize women, we women are conditioned to despise as a "ball-breaker" any female who spoils the fun by raising her voice against the brutality. The starkness of the double standard is only now becoming obvious. What would happen if we raised our sons to despise "women-breakers"? Would they really lose their manhood; would they be robbed of sexual potency if we told them that rape was the daydream of pathetic wimps, not of real men? If such statements already seem tediously self-evident, consult the popular culture, from rock music to movies, to see that the rapist ideal is still alive and thriving. Two generations from now, such infantile longings to assert one's will regardless of the other may seem as unimaginably prehistoric as Neanderthal man seems to us now.

Meanwhile, it is not with controls but with consciousness that we must fight the corrosive power of pornography. The more we articulate our rejection of pornography's values, the more we provoke pornography's users into self-revealing defensiveness.

No one allows chemical dumping into fresh streams without a stiff fight nowadays; cultural dumping will soon be seen clearly as an environmental offence. We don't legislate the nickel mines of Sudbury out of existence, but we try to keep its byproducts from stunting the surrounding life forms. In the same way, we should support local bylaws to keep shaved vulvas and whipping-posts out of the sight of passing five-year-olds. If and when police fight organized crime, we should remember that pornography is one of the fungi growing on that dung-heap. The new Canadian law against the sexual exploitation of children ought to help limit the sale of fresh young bodies for kiddie porn. And when advertisers use chic bestiality to promote their perfumes or blue jeans, we ought to let them hear from us as endlessly and irritatingly as possible.

There may always be people who need commercial pornography—packaged women—for their lonely sexual release. It is not the intention of any feminist to regulate these private dreams. But to let the theme of female degradation permeate our popular culture is another question, and to stand idly by while real women and children are used as meat for the mass marketing of sex is unthinkable. Some day, those who "need" pornography will be driven back on the use of print. They will have to supply their own pictures out of their own imaginations. And boys will be raised to think that erotic passion has more to do with human love than with power, mastery, and dominance.

NOT TAKING NO FOR
AN ANSWER

IT'S ODD TO LOOK BACK ON MY CHILDHOOD AND TO reflect that despite all the grown men who secretly fondled, snickered, or flashed their way into my startled awareness, I managed to grow up without hating men. Partly I managed it through "sleight of mind", a mental juggling trick that many girls of my generation perfected early on. Quite simply, we kept a separate and sealed compartment of our minds for "bad men", a compartment that was kept segregated from normal daylight thoughts. And partly I managed, like many other properly brought-up little girls in the 1940's, by believing that these nasty secrets must be my own fault. To believe that adults could be bad and wrong was to shatter the world order as I knew it.

Psychologists are familiar with this phenomenon of internalized guilt. Rape and incest victims do it all the time, blaming themselves instead of their attackers. How does such a crazy inversion of the truth ever get started? I think it must have been a habit positively endemic among the freshly pinafored little girls of my era, with our nightly baths, the gentle order of our days, and our untroubled belief in the kindly perfection of our adults. Sexual feelings were never mentioned, fondling uncles and flashing strangers never explained. So we had to teach ourselves to believe in the lie that sexuality must be our own lonely invention.

What an important lie this was, as dangerous and hidden as a swallowed safety pin. We grew up falsely guilty because of the false naïveté of our environment; if only adults had admitted the universality of sexual impulses, perhaps a whole generation of women would not have nurtured an unconscious conviction of personal guilt that, by extension, tainted all other women.

My first tumble from paradisical innocence into guilt is as

fresh in my mind today as the evening when it happened. I was four years old, lying cosily in bed with the sheet up to my chin and waiting for my goodnight kiss. My hands were tucked comfortably between my thighs. My adored mother came in, perfumed and luminous. A warm sweetness came with her, as always. She leaned over to kiss me and, just as she leaned, noticed that both my hands were under the covers. "What are you doing?" she asked quickly, with a tiny worried edge to her voice, "Nothing," I said with equal haste. Her brow smoothed, her lips touched my cheek.

That was all. But my heart was thudding with a painful discovery. That touching, that good feeling, must be dreadfully wrong if it made my mother look worried. I know now, of course, that I was an oversensitive child deducing far more than was actually there; my mother could never had wished on me such a ferocious punishment. But from that moment, I harboured the guilty secret that I alone in the world had invented sexual feeling, and that it was wrong.

In one way or another, the majority of girls of my class and generation decoded the same message from the silences, pauses, and omissions of our prudish age. Silently, we decided that the unaccountable and never-discussed behaviour of adult men must be brought upon us because of some guilt of our own. My mother warned me against strangers who gave candy, for example, but never mentioned the flashers in dusky doorways as I came home from skating in the park, waiting to fling back their coats as I approached to show me something sickly white, something that looked foolish and obscene at the same time. Why didn't Mother warn me about these men? Could it be that she didn't know? Could it be that these men waited only for *bad* eight-year-olds like me, who had touched themselves between the legs? Frightened laughter caught in my throat. I sped for home, my skates bumping on my back, and never told.

Confused guilt choked my protest when, at age nine, I sat in the Saturday movie matinee in frozen panic as the stranger at my side began to slide his hand up my thigh. Trembling with fright and astonishment, I racked my brains to discover if this was something ordinary that grown-ups did, if it was perhaps an accidental straying on his part — perhaps my imagination had conjured up something wrong in an accidental brushing of a hand against a leg?—and agonized whether to cry out or blunder out of my chair.

I must have felt this way at twelve, a nubile and almost ludicrously innocent twelve-year-old, when a beer-bellied camp director took me into his parlour to "treat" a fractured breastbone by insisting that I take off my shirt and let him stroke liniment onto my chest. I stared in alarm at the oil paintings on the wall—nude portraits he had painted of his wife—and flinched back in ghastly embarrassment while he crooned, "My, what lovely big breasts you have... no, no, stay still, I tell you, I'm just like a doctor. Tell me, does your mother have such nice big breasts too?" I never told anyone about his constant pursuit of me; lonely and mortified, I learned to hide in the girl's bathroom when I saw him coming near.

When I was a seventeen-year-old camp counsellor, and yet another, more sophisticated camp director (a New York psychologist) spent the summer trying to persuade me that I was a naïve fool not to let him "relieve" me of my virginity, I kept that a secret, too. Numbly I sat through special late-night meetings in his cabin, summoned there ostensibly to discuss camp programs; always, wearily, prepared to fend him off, always convinced that my awkward clumsiness and stubbornness made a fool of me. And *I* was considered an articulate, aggressively argumentative, and "unladylike" teenager!

It wasn't until I began to write about rape in my columns that some of these long-buried incidents in my past came knocking at my consciousness and asking to be re-examined. The first jolt came in the form of the Ontario Provincial Police report on rape in January 1979. By now, the women's movement had shed ample light on the mythologies about rape. Without much self-examination, I had thoroughly accepted the liberated analysis. Furthermore, I confidently assumed that most of the civilized world shared the modern view that rape is a random act of violence and hatred, and has no more to do with its victims' sexual appeal or loose behaviour than robbery has to do with its victims' carelessness.

The OPP report was a startling kick in the midriff to these assumptions. Here, clothed in all the authority of our provincial police force, was the bland assertion that, based on a statistical study, seventy-one per cent of all rapes are provoked by the promiscuous behaviour of the victim.

For a day or two, so ingrained is the habit of female self-doubt on this issue, I was rattled. Could feminists like me have been distorting the issue all along? Wasn't there some glimmer of truth here, that sleazy Goodbar types picked up men, took them home, and got into trouble when things got out of hand?

Then I read the report itself. I learned that it was prepared by two statisticians who pulled rape facts from a file: they hadn't interviewed victims or attackers, nor had they consulted any of the considerable scholarship on the subject. Simply by noting the locale of the attack, the police felt they were able to assign blame. All rapes that occurred in certain situations—"home environment, social occasion (dating, swimming, picnic), accepting a ride, hitch-hiking or runaways"—were deemed to be "provoked" rapes. All others (twenty-nine per cent) were listed in the report as "unprovoked".

Flabbergasted, I called Staff Superintendent Neil Chaddock, head of the OPP research branch that prepared the report.

"How did you conclude that seventy-one per cent of the rape victims were promiscuous?" I asked.

"Listen, according to Webster's Dictionary, that word 'promiscuous' means 'indiscriminate'. That's all we're saying—these girls were indiscriminate."

"Do you mean that they slept around with a lot of different boys?" I asked.

"No. Indiscriminate means indiscreet. We didn't ask these girls any questions about their sex lives. This report was compiled from statistics. Taking a ride from a stranger is indiscriminate."

"Then taking a ride from a stranger is promiscuous?"

"Yes, Indiscriminate."

Taking a ride or going on a picnic is indiscreet, indiscreet is indiscriminate, indiscriminate is promiscuous, and that's how in 1979 we had headlines stating that the "Ontario Provincial Police Say Rape Victims are Promiscuous". When I pointed out to Chaddock that major police studies from the United States show only 4.4 per cent of rapes can be called "provoked", as opposed to 22 per cent of homicides and 10.7 per cent of armed robberies, he was unmoved. In his opinion, the report would help to prevent rape by showing young girls (he was a father himself) the error of their ways.

Chaddock's stubborn insistence that any young girl who takes a ride is "promiscuous" forced me to remember an episode I had long since blocked away in my mind. I was eighteen, and like one of Chaddock's "indiscreet" teenagers I accepted a ride. I was seven thousand miles from home, on an Israeli kibbutz, plodding across miles of ploughed fields under a hot sun on my way to the nearest post office, when the watchman of our kibbutz cantered up on his horse, his holstered pistol slapping at his side. Happily I accepted his offer of a lift to the village, feeling it was an adventure to ride bareback behind him on the horse. Innocently—"promiscuously"?—I thought of him as an adult whose job it was to protect me.

In the village he was hailed at every second Arab house and invited to drink a glass of arak, the potent local vodka-like drink. Dutifully I joined him in sipping at one glass of arak after another because he hissed at me under his breath that our Arab hosts would be mortally insulted if I didn't. To me, it was all colourful and quaint. I had never drunk liquor before, and I was a politely brought-up girl. I visited the post office, and we rode back across the baking fields. Half-way there, my head whirling from arak, I fainted and fell from the horse. As I hit the ground and simultaneously came to, the man attacked.

I won't ever forget my stunned surprise, our long, squalid struggle as I fought back and he tore at my clothing, the bruising press of his pistol on my thigh, or the way I lay exhausted and retching on the ground long after I had scared him off at last with my frenzied screams.

As shocked as I was, rage didn't come until the next day when I shakily told the story to my Canadian friends on the kibbutz. I expected consolation, moral support, and maybe even protection from future attack—particularly as the watchman's cabin and mine faced each other cross a patch of grass, isolated from the rest of the kibbutz, and we washed each morning at the same standpipe between the two cabins. The only other girl in our group of Canadian students was aloofly silent, her reticence a judgement on my morals. The boys were convulsed with laughter.

"Great fantasy life you have!" they shouted. "Don't you just wish!'' They slapped each other's backs in shared mirth and derision.

A moment like that puts iron in your soul; the humiliation you feel is nothing compared with the frustration of trying to batter through those contemptuous assumptions. It was years and years till I risked ridicule by telling the story again. But then a strange thing happened: the story was like a touchstone. Friends, colleagues, women of every kind would suddenly unlock their own memories. The uncle or camp counsellor who secretly fondled them when they were children; the fear of "telling" on an adult and being accused of complicity; the rape and attempted rape of boyfriends, neighbours, landlords, a husband's buddy. Always this story was told with gritting rage, not just against the criminal, but against all those who refuse to hear how it happened and what it felt like.

The OPP's report may have breathed new life into the old libel for many of the public, but for me its stupidity was salutary. Not until I heard the policeman smugly labelling rape victims as "promiscuous" did my own long-buried story click into focus for me. For years I had carried around a rage against the young men who refused to believe me, who thought I was fantasizing some wished-for rape. Now I realized that while I had rejected that slander, I had accepted a deeper one—the sense that I was somehow shamefully complicit in the attack on me. The shame was the real reason I hadn't told.

My insight deepened when I researched a series of articles on sexual assault and learned the hard way that anyone who talks about rape risks learning more about her dinner-party companions that she might want to know:

> Drop the subject of rape into a group and it ticks like a time bomb. Sooner or later, it blows a gaping chasm in the conversation. On one side, there are always a few—defensive and exasperated—who say, "C'mon. She was no innocent; she should never had gone with him; she had it coming." More and more, there are those on the other side who insist, "Whoever she was, whatever she had done before, she had a right to say 'no'."
>
> "It's the Great Divide," a rape counsellor told me. "Men

are shocked and nauseated when they see the man being raped in the movie *Deliverance*. But some just can't identify with a woman's anguish the same way."

A porcelain-pretty lawyer blushed but fixed me with a level glance when she said, "My husband is also a lawyer and we just cannot discuss rape any more. We no longer talk about it."

Anyone who deals with the subject of rape has to confront, at some point, this duality. On the one hand, every informed person knows that rape is never an act of love and almost never an act of sexual passion. Rape is, by the testimony of convicted rapists themselves, an act of aggression and the will to dominate. Most rapists have wives or girlfriends for regular sexual release and, in any case, are not particularly potent. Their victims are not sexy flirts, but the first female (infant or aged) who comes to hand. We know all this and yet, on the other hand, we keep hearing the leering jibes about slutty women who lead a man on and then cry rape.

Why is this myth so persistent? Perhaps there are the occasional careless women who want to cover their tracks. They are not, however, the ones who take the painful, drawn-out, and public step of lodging a rape complaint. Even according to the U.S. Federal Bureau of Investigation (not your average feminist lobby group), 98 per cent of reported rapes really did take place. A detailed Canadian study in 1977, by criminologists Lorenne Clark and Debra Lewis, found that 94 per cent of rape reports in Toronto in a given year were valid.

Cry rape? The exact opposite is true. So successfully have we pushed the propaganda that the rape victim is tainted with guilt that the victims themselves believe it. They choke on the violence that has been done to them, they swallow it in silence, they sicken from it, but an estimated 90 per cent of them never report the crime at all.

How can a myth have such a stranglehold that it manages to skew our entire police and legal system against the victim? Our helter-skelter times must take part of the blame. Now that the lines have been blurred between "good" girls (untouchable) and "bad" girls (up for grabs), men must often be confused about how to interpret the signals. After all, it has been only a blink of historical time since women were sexual chattels.

And partly, the confusion springs from the central lie of our popular culture: the lie that women enjoy being violated. It's a fantasy all-pervasive from locker room to fashion magazines. Photographers from *Vogue* pose their wet-lipped, blank-eyed models on toilet floors, in handcuffs, or even being savaged by Doberman pinschers. A film like *The Postman Always Rings Twice* is billed as "the erotic sizzler of the decade" and features a woman who is aroused to passion by slaps and blows. In *Dressed to Kill*, women are trussed in leather porn gear, semi-nude, begging for rape, dripping with blood. The movie-going public gets the message: women "want it". Macho violence "turns them on".

Now we have chilling proof that the deluge of brutal rape images has the power to condition men to be more sadistic. In a series of careful experiments at the University of Manitoba, psychologist Neil Malamuth learned that glamorously violent films and popular pornography could make men measurably more callous to women's pain. Male students who watched *Swept Away*, a film in which a woman is first humiliated, starved, and injured, and then grovels adoringly at the feet of her gloating rapist, were aroused by her excitement and indifferent to her suffering. Indeed, these normal students showed a preference for women in porn films to suffer pain along with their orgasms. This appetite for cruelty, Malamuth wrote, "revealed a pattern that bears a striking similarity to the callous attitudes held by convicted rapists."

The creepiest finding of all was that after just one reading of a sado-masochistic story based on a *Penthouse* magazine feature, *more than half* the young men said they might themselves commit a rape if they could be sure of not being caught. (In other university surveys, between one-third and one-half of the men approved of using force to get sex from a girlfriend.)

Women are by no means immune to this media brain-washing. Though the female students in Malamuth's study were repelled at the thought of being raped, a substantial number thought that *other* women might like it.

It's an easy flip of the stereotype from woman as masochist to woman as bitch-temptress. And it's a subtle, sickly influence, this projection of vice onto the stranger or the "other" woman. The distortions have spread throughout our system to make the treatment of rape in Canada a national disgrace.

One out of every five Canadian women is sexually assaulted against her will, according to the 1979 Winnipeg Rape Incidence Survey and the federal Advisory Council on the Status of Women. That includes grabbing, fondling, clothes ripped, attempted rape. One out of every seventeen is forcibly raped.

Yet ninety-four per cent of sexual criminals walk free, never to be arrested, say the same studies. Only two per cent of all rapists will ever stand in court and hear themselves pronounced guilty. And for those two per cent, the average sentence will be 2½ to 3½ years, though many are let off with a warning or a fine. For comparison's sake, note that in the winter of 1981 a man in Toronto held up a grocery store, stole fifty dollars and a carton of cigarettes, and was sentenced to nine years in jail. Another man lured two sixteen-year-old boys to his hotel room with a promise of free liquor, sexually attacked them, and was also sentenced to nine years in jail. But what about a man who had ten previous criminal convictions, four of them for armed sexual attack? Early one morning he grabbed an innocent fourteen-year-old paper-delivery girl, dragged her at knifepoint to a park, raped her, forced her to commit fellatio, and got five years. Was his crime so much less serious than stealing fifty dollars and a carton of cigarettes? (In 1982, the Crown won an appeal and the sentence was raised to nine years.) Or consider the Toronto man who had forty-five previous criminal convictions. A fifteen-year-old girl, who met him through a friend of he family, took a ride with him. He raped her and dumped her on the highway, far from home, at 3 a.m. The judge lectured the girl to "use better judgement in future," and sentenced the man to 2½ years.

I don't argue that longer sentences are the cure for crime. But to compare the relative seriousness with which courts view these different crimes reveals that the legal system is a monstrous sick joke, a joke of which women are the butt. Defence lawyers ranted to me about rape charges as though the rapists are the aggrieved victims. And in weeks of interviews, at least ten experts, ranging from psychologists to lawyers, made the same telltale slip of the tongue: they referred to the raped woman as "the accused". It's an upside-down world created by men, in which male-written laws and male judges sit in judgement on their fellow men, and the raped woman, who is nothing more than a witness at the trial of her attacker, is subtly turned into "the accused" in the eyes of too many of the participants in the charade.

Despite angry denials by defence lawyers, who specialize in angry denials, the conviction rates tell the story. In 1979 in Toronto, for example, 207 alleged rapes were reported, but only 87 men were actually charged by police, 16 of them were brought to trial, and 12 were finally convicted of rape or a lesser charge. On the basis of those two last figures — 12 out of 16 — Toronto law officials slyly claim a 75 per cent conviction rate. But what of the estimated 88 per cent to 90 per cent of rapes that the federal Advisory Council on the Status of Women says are never reported? What of the hundreds of rape reports that are never investigated by the police because they felt the evidence might not be strong enough to stand up in court? What of all the cases that somehow evaporate between charge and trial?

No on seems to be able to clarify the confusion of rape statistics. Indeed, the chaos of crime and court records and the absolute dearth of judicial, police, and provincial co-ordination mean that we are all groping in the dark about this hateful crime. In part, the chaos is a real function of anti-woman prejudice. Though a number of rape victims and their counsellors from rape crisis centres had told me that individual police officers were helpful and enlightened, I found that at higher levels police attitudes were revoltingly ignorant.

I arranged to interview two Toronto police officers, described to me by their superiors as top Toronto spokesmen on rape. Sergeant John Luby and his superior, Staff Sergeant Malcolm Dufty, both of the Investigative Support Squad, sat across a cafeteria table from me, bristling with wary defensiveness. I began by asking Dufty about the "unfounded" rate in Metro Toronto. This police term is worth explaining. The public tends to assume that an "unfounded report of rape" means that no rape took place. In reality, as Canadian criminologists Lorenne Clark and Debra Lewis demonstrated in their book *Rape: The Price of Coercive Sexuality*, the term "unfounded" usually means that the police choose not to believe the complainant or not to pursue the case because they think there isn't the kind of evidence on which a jury could convict.

Statistical analysis shows that even if there is no question that a sexual assault took place, police tend to write off as "unfounded" all those complaints in which the victim had been drinking, knew her assailant previously, was on welfare, or waited more than twenty-four hours to report the crime. None of those factors come into play when it's a robbery being reported, of course — one reason why only three per cent of robbery reports are deemed "unfounded", compared with thirty-five per cent to fifty per cent of all rape complaints. If you are a young, middle-class student living at home with your parents, police are more likely to take you seriously when you report a rape. This pre-judging of criminal cases may save the courts a lot of work, but the public is entitled to ask whether our police have been empowered to make binding legal judgments of this sort.

So when I asked Dufty about unfounded rapes, I expected him to explain some of these factors, perhaps to justify police assumptions. Not at all. He was more blatant than that. He simply insisted, unblinkingly, that "unfounded" means no rape took place. Furthermore, he was adamant that there are no statistics on unfoundedness in Toronto.

"And he should know," said Luby, "because he's the officer in charge of rape statistics."

Flummoxed, I decided to switch my jargon. "Well, what about false rape reports?" I asked Dufty. A moment earlier, he had claimed to have no statistics on "unfoundedness". Now he rose to the bait of the word "false".

"Oh, false reports," he said confidently. "We call those unfounded. Oh yeah, easily fifty per cent of rape reports are false. You know, women who are mad because their boyfriend left them, or teenage kids who come in late and they're scared their dad will be mad so they make up a story that some guy raped them."

I told Dufty that Clark and Lewis, examining police files, had found a maximum of six per cent that could be deemed false reports, and that the FBI puts it even lower, at two per cent, the same as for all other crimes. But Dufty stood by his flat contention that half of all rape reports are trivial lies.

He also quarrelled with the usual estimate of forensic experts that only ten per cent of rapes are reported to the police. "I mean, how would they know?" he asked. This, from the officer in charge of statistics. So I told him about population studies, polls, surveys, and rape crisis centre logbooks. "Oh no," he said placidly. "I think we pretty well hear about all rapes."

Dufty and Luby went on, oblivious to my astonished reaction, to blame a lot of rapes on women who walk at night in seamy downtown parks and prostitution districts, or who pick up men in bars and then "the men just can't control themselves." But let's get it clear: the majority of rapes take place in the victim's home, where she is attacked either by a previously trusted acquaintance or by an intruder. The men who "can't control themselves" are a figment of police imagination. A high proportion of rapists have planned the attack ahead of time and the victim is selected at random.

Luby and Dufty, hand-picked representatives of Toronto's finest, chilled me by their placid allegiance to misogynist myth. When I asked them about sadomasochistic pornography, they jumped to the subject of the disgraceful provocation offered by women who breast-feed their babies in public. When I asked them about any rise in violence, they suddenly began talking (indeed, giggling) about a European case in which a woman purportedly raped a man. Like the people who call the rape victim "the accused", these officers seemed to be standing the world on its head in order to blame women for the crime that is committed only by men.

In a recent anti-rape campaign, the United States Army sternly warned its commanding officers: "One need not be a rapist to be part of the problem. Repeating myths about rape, either seriously or in jest, is a form of psychological sexism that can actually encourage rape." After talking to Toronto police, I believe those words should be carved in stone over the doorways of every police station in the country. While the views I heard may have been predictable as the views of an uninformed or inarticulate minority, I was frightened by the fact that I heard them from two men who hold key positions in the control of rape statistics and investigation.

Clearly, more education on the subject is needed in Canada, and one step in the right direction is the National Film Board documentary *Why Men Rape*.

Patrick Watson looked levelly into the camera and said "Most rape is just guys who won't stop. Most rape is…not taking 'no' for an answer."

Staring right back into Watson's eyes, and squirming a bit, will be thousands of teenage boys who are going to see *Why Men Rape* in their high school or college classes in the next few years. Watson's summing up is perhaps the most effective moment in an entirely effective film, because it asks male viewers to wrestle with everything they've learned about macho sex.

Most of the film consisted of interviews with 10 convicted rapists in Canadian prisons. Yet these shadowy criminals ("Good-looking young men, mostly," producer-director Doug Jackson told me, "and some with university educations") are only a small part of the film's point. True, they were horrifying. True, they proved in their own words what feminists have been arguing for years: that rape is a crime of aggression and rage, not of "uncontrollable" sexual attraction.

"When I saw the fear in her eyes, the sex was just nothing… what I got off on was the old power-trip," said one rapist.

"I hate to admit it but I hated women," said the teacher who had raped 20 women. "I felt inferior…I wanted to control someone else," said another.

And there was the classic criminal, a 16-year-old boy, beaten and rejected by his parents, his grandmother who had loved him now dead, forced into sexual perversions by an uncle at age 11. One winter day when he was 16, he ran up behind a 9-year-old girl and held a knife to her throat and forced her to perform fellatio. Later, he kicked and strangled and stabbed her: "She was crying and I saw myself in her and I hated myself even more."

Over and over, the rapists told the same stories: Lovelessness. Feeling like nobody. Being afraid of asking a woman out. Retreating into violent fantasy, fed and fanned by sadistic pornography. A strict, repressive and often religious upbringing, where sex was unmentionably muffled up in guilt.

As ugly as all of this was, the film's most chilling moments for me were provided by the non-criminals, the normal men interviewed in singles bars, their offices, or the classroom. "Listen," argued a man with a slick pompadour, à la Elvis, "when a woman leads me on, eh, and physically I'm all built up, well I'm not going to take no for an answer. I mean, she says no but she means yes."

"We went out on the street and interviewed businessmen," Doug Jackson told me, "and we told them we were doing a film on rape, and yet at least one-third of these men actually said that if a woman 'led them on', they were entitled to have sex with her, even if she said no," Jackson thinks this male view of being entitled to take sexual pleasure is responsible for the vast majority of rapes—what he calls "the date rape" and what Patrick Watson called "not taking 'no' for an answer".

"We deliberately cut a lot of shockingly violent material out of the film because when we tested the film on college groups, young men would say, 'Oh well, that's a psychopath, that's not me.' We want them to understand that the psychopaths make up a very small minority of rapes," Jackson said.

What makes men think they have a right to infringe on someone else's body in order to satisfy their own? Is it the way they're brought up? The porn image of man as conquistador and woman as willing slave? Or the whole "might is right" tenor of our society? I think that young men believe and act that way because until now, it's been the majority view in our society. In Jackson's film, a defence lawyer from Montreal, Frank Shoofey, who has successfully defended 100 men from charges of rape, looked into the camera and played his game:

"If a woman leads a man on," he purred, "what's a man to do?" And, with his carefully coiffed curls tumbling around his head and his eyes sparkling with superior amusement, he went on to sympathize with men whose "uncontrollable sexual urges" are kindled by wanton women.

Shoofey's views are revolting. They are a lie. But they are

> prevalent. As long as there are any young men who think that
> way, we'd better rush Jackson's excellent and thought-
> provoking film into every school in the country. These young
> people have a lot to learn about human rights, and the right
> of a woman to say no whenever and however she wants.

That right applies to all women, and their sexual relations with
any man.

In the last week of 1978 my eye was caught by a newspaper
picture of John Rideout, 21, smirking with insufferable conceit
and triumph as he strolled out of an Oregon court-room, a free
man. He had been charged with raping his estranged wife, and
he had been acquitted. (Before the Rideout affair was over, this
pathetic pair was to have a much-publicized reconciliation and
another violent break-up.)

I wrote in my column that "John Rideout was right to smirk.
His acquittal was a triumph for all those who believe that a man
has a God-given right to his wife's body. But was it a triumph for
justice? Rideout freely admitted tampering with his wife's car in
advance so that she could not flee, chasing her into a public park
where he allegedly threatened to beat and rape her in public,
dragging her back to the apartment, and having intercourse. He
denied that it was rape. 'I told her I was sorry,' he said."

Greta Rideout, 23, testified that Rideout repeatedly slapped
her, demanding, "Are you going to co-operate?" While he
punched her, tore off her jeans, and choked her, Greta could
hear their two-year-old daughter, Jenny, who was in the room,
crying "Mummy, mummy." Rideout ordered the child to leave,
but throughout the alleged rape, Greta could hear her crying
and calling in the kitchen. Afterward, Greta testified, Rideout
forced her to look at her bruised and swollen face in the mirror
and told her, "That's what you get when you don't co-operate."
Neighbours testified that they heard screams, thuds, and muffled
choking during the incident. They saw Greta rush distraught
from the apartment to call the police. A doctor and a nurse who
treated Greta at hospital testified that she had a black eye,
bruises, and physical symptoms of forced intercourse. Police
officers testified that Rideout swaggered at the police station,
boasting that "If I had done it properly, she [Greta] wouldn't be

here to complain." He also asked if it were true that a man could be charged with raping his wife...before the police had mentioned the word "rape" to him.

During Rideout's trial, the judge ruled that Greta's previous sexual experience was "relevant testimony". So the court heard how she and her husband had extra-marital affairs, heard about her two abortions, and, most crucially, heard how she had once lied to her husband in claiming to have lesbian fantasies. It's interesting how this kind of evidence works against the victim of the crime. Two men who had read the same news stories as I told me at the time that "Greta was a bit of a lesbie and liked to get knocked around a bit before sex."

So much for the "relevance" of sexual evidence. How could Greta's fabrication about lesbian fantasies have any bearing on whether her husband did or did not beat her into forced submission? It was completely irrelevant, of course. But it was part of the clever reinforcement of prejudices which was woven by Rideout's lawyer, and which must have had tremendous impact on the jury. The turning-point in the case, observers told me, came when Rideout's lawyer, Philip Kelley, attacked the law as "unfair to men", since it protected only women. It gave the state a chance to regulate marital sex, he said. And it gave the balance of power in marriage to the woman, since she now had the legal right to say "no" to sex.

When I asked one of the prosecution lawyers how on earth Rideout got off, despite the powerful evidence against him, there was an incredulous pause, as though he couldn't believe I hadn't got the message. "Why, he got off because he was her husband," said the lawyer at last. "There's a strong feeling in this community that the law is wrong, that a man has conjugal rights."

Even the judge, in his charge to the jury, appeared to be asking for a clear conviction of first-degree rape. But the jury listened to Kelley's last plea: "Are you ready to have this man called a rapist for the rest of his life?" And they were not ready. A woman's pain, a woman's right to her own body, do not weigh so heavily in the scales of justice as a man's reputation.

If the case itself was a bitter revelation of United States attitudes, the aftermath was even more shocking to me. In the following week, one man after another—old news-desk hands, middle-rank editors, seasoned reporters—dawdled by my desk as though by accident, and stayed to vent their anger about what I had written. "Dammit, a man has *rights*," gritted one gentle soul. Another banged my desk so hard that the papers jumped: "Every damned tease in the country will be running to cry rape on her husband if you feminists get your way," he yelled. "You're crazy!"

The status of women as hunks of property was borne in on me that week as never before. I refuse to believe that every man is, at heart, a rapist. But that week it certainly seemed as though many a married man wanted to believe that he had the right to be a rapist when the mood struck him. "You are undermining the sanctity of the marriage bond," one man wrote to me. How could a man like that not see that to insist on his right to rape his wife was an insult to his own dignity as a man? What kind of person would believe that he could enjoy his wife's sexual favours only if the law permitted him to use force? What sort of husbands really could imagine that, if Rideout were found guilty, wives would instantly rush out to make false rape accusations against their husbands? And, of course, it was a revelation to me—a sickening one—to hear men insist that they owned their wives' vaginas the same way they owned their cars and television sets.

The theme of rape is destined not to vanish. Normally, once I've written about a subject, I shuffle it to the back of my mental file. But rape keeps happening, keeps being reported, keeps demanding an excessive emotional response from any woman who follows the news. Betty Friedan, in her new book *The Second Stage*, testily reproved the rape crisis volunteers for "wallowing" in the rape victim's misery and anger. There is a sense in which Friedan is right: when you contemplate the savagery and intimate brutality of rape, and the casual indifference with which much of male society treats this crime, you can slip into a drowning blackness of rage that can only be self-destructive. Once the OPP rape report had revived my scorching memories of the fury I felt, as a betrayed eighteen-year-old in Israel, I had continually to protect myself from slipping into unreason.

But Friedan is wrong, too, because most women are *not* in danger of wallowing in that strangling fury of the helpless victim. Most women protect themselves from such a state by denying that rape can happen to them, or by keeping it at arm's length by the convenient belief that it can only happen to "other" women, "bad" women, "silly" women, women who live in "unsafe areas". The need to believe in that illusory safety is perhaps the only way we can keep functioning in a city where our mothers and our daughters are continually exposed to danger. But no matter how alert, brave, and resourceful a woman may be, she can still become the victim of a sexual assault through no fault of her own.

Take the case of Becky, a twenty-five-year-old private secretary who still lives at home and combines a dark, lush beauty with a soft air of vulnerability. If you read the few terse sentences in the news report ("The victim met the accused in a bar...") you might dismiss Becky with a scornful shrug. You would never be so reckless, would you?

I interviewed Becky in a midtown restaurant, where she told me of her story, backed up by court transcripts:

Becky's friend didn't show up that evening as planned, to listen to a favourite band in one of those asparagus-fern-and-stained-glass taverns beloved of Toronto singles. So Becky sat down to wait and to sip a diet soda. It would have seemed silly...over-reacting, maybe...to object when the two attractive young men sat down at her table. Besides, they looked familiar, and it turned out that Becky and one of the men had a mutual friend in a church drama club. They spent the evening in affable chatter. One of the young men was excited about opening his own little French restaurant after working for his dad's catering business. When the two men gave Becky a lift "to make sure she got home safely", they coaxed her to pop in and admire the restaurant.

They must have had it planned all along. The minute Becky was alone with one of the men, he leaned across and grabbed her by the throat, cruelling squeezing her breast with his other hand and snarling: "We're gonna kill you like we killed the other whores." The other man came back grinning, undressed. Both of them violated her in a grotesque series of acts. She was knocked to the floor; she struggled; they burned her with cigarettes. Their hatred and violence were white-hot, and the whole time she was nearly strangling with terror.

Despite all that, despite their frenzied brutishness and hoarse threats, she kept her wits about her enough so that, in a desperate moment when one of them had drawn back, she was able to break away and dash out into the street, half-dressed, battered, and sobbing for help.

The police were decent; the judge was fair and would not let the defence attorney smear her with questions about her sexual history. Both men were convicted—sentenced to eighteen months in reformatory. Becky's sentence was longer. After two years, she still looks down silently, struggling with her emotions, when you ask her for details. The morning after the attack she phoned the Toronto Rape Crisis Centre. "I just wanted to know if I was guilty or not," she say softly, with absolutely no irony.

It took Becky well over a year to get over her fear, her corrosive self-doubt and shame and shaken self-confidence. "I must have spoken to the Rape Crisis women every day for a year," she says. "They were incredibly wonderful." They counselled her, buoyed her ego, backed her decision to press charges, accompanied her faithfully to court, and gave her the courage to go on with her life when the ugly memories threatened to overwhelm her.

"A rape is a violation of the envelope of the self," said a U.S. crisis expert. The violation is so extreme, the total loss of control so humiliating, that one U.S. study says that half of all rape victim's marriages break up within the year. Toronto Rape Crisis Centre volunteers agree that it takes a least a year to heal the emotional wounds.

It would be rubbing salt in those wounds to pretend that "rape avoidance" research can lead the way for every woman to escape sexual assault. For one thing, rape-avoidance techniques seem to work best with strangers, and most studies show that between fifty per cent and seventy per cent of assailants are known to their victims to some degree. Still, studies on U.S. women who managed to avoid a rape attack are tremendously illuminating. Colorado psychologist James Selkin has long argued that rapists follow a clear pattern of testing the victim's compliance ("Where is Yonge St?"), her willingness to help ("Can you show me how to get there?"), and her vulnerability to threat ("Don't scream and you won't get hurt"). There are ghastly ironies here: a woman may smile and smile, just as she has been taught to do, and still be a victim. In fact, it is her conditioning to be helpful and polite, and to avoid making a fuss. Selkin says that one-quarter of Denver rapes were committed against women who responded to a request for help. In another city, a rapist used a fake cast on his arm to lure women into "helping" him.

At the very first approach, coolly and clearly and without any ambiguity, a woman must refuse to be drawn in, to help or be helped by a stranger, says Selkin. A rapist wants as little commotion as possible. Prompt refusal to co-operate is the first, best defence. Two 1980 studies done for the U.S. National Institute for Mental Health back this approach. One of them, a study by Dr. Pauline Bart of the University of Illinois, shows that sixty-eight per cent of the women who tried physical resistance managed to avoid getting raped. It was also found that "rape avoiders" were more job-oriented, more self-confident, more likely to have played a contact sport in childhood, and less likely to have been punished for fighting with siblings in childhood.

Screaming, running away, strong verbal aggression, and physical struggling were all successful in fending off rape. But what about the risk of being badly injured? It's true that rape resisters risked a slightly higher incidence of minor injury. But, as these researchers point out, the news media have unnecessarily terrified women by reporting mainly those rapes involving grisly violence. Actually, only a tiny percentage of rapes (the FBI estimates two per cent) are committed by a psychopathically violent man. A woman must rely on her own quick judgement of whether to fight back. Selkin, for one, urges women to take the chance, since risk of serious injury is relatively small (unless the man is armed), and since even docile, submissive victims get hurt by crazy rapists. One thing is sure: in both recent studies, crying, reasoning, begging, or pretending to be pregnant or to have venereal disease did no good at all. In fact, they may enhance the rapist's determination to subjugate his victim. In Bart's study, flight was the best technique and pleading was the worst. Of ninety-four women, only five tried no form of resistance whatever. All five were raped and two were hurt.

It is clear that although the thought of rape may overwhelm us with its peculiar psychological terrorism, we owe it to ourselves and all women we know to shake off passivity. There *are* positive steps to be taken.

Women are fighting back, not only when physically threatened but when their right to dignity, privacy, and full recognition of the violence they have suffered, is threatened by male lawyers and judges. But progress has been slow, and many purportedly progressive changes in the law have backfired in our faces. The option of a publication ban on a rape victim's name and her evidence during a rape trial, for example, has led to a succession of news stories in which only the accused rapist's biased and distorted version of the incident is read by the public. The ban, designed to protect the victim, gives her the balm of anonymity but reinforces anti-woman stereotypes. No wonder that some feminists working in rape crisis centres now reject the entire masculine police-hospital-court axis. I empathize with their rage, but I think they are wrong to despair. By 1982-83, after nearly ten years of dogged effort by Canadian women's groups, Parliament will be discussing Bill C-53, an act to amend the Criminal Code "in relation to sexual offences and the protection of young persons".

The bill is a bold effort to erase some of the sexual prejudice that underlies many of our laws. It proposes an end to husbands' immunity from rape charges, and stresses every individual's right to personal inviolability, rather than focusing on the emotional-laden sexual aspects of rape. The very word "rape" is abandoned, so that the new "sexual assault" laws will closely parallel the already existent non-sexual-assault laws.

It's a two-edged sword, of course. A rape is so deep and personal a violation, so much more shattering to the ego's integrity than a beating or a blow, that many women's instinctive response to the new law will be to insist on retaining the word "rape" and the current penalty of life imprisonment. But the harsher penalty for rape now in the Criminal Code is illusory. The life sentence applies only if it can be proved that the rapist's penis penetrated the woman's vagina. Proof is so elusive that the ferocity of the law works to the criminal's benefit. Juries are reluctant to convict. And if proof of vaginal penetration can't be found, the importance of the attack is so diminished in the eyes of the law that no matter what terror was experienced, no matter how prolonged or ugly the nature of the attack, from forced fellatio to jamming objects into the woman's orifices, the maximum sentence under the law is five years. Of course, if the attack was committed against a man, the maximum sentence is ten years.

How much better the new law will be will depend largely on how well the legislators listen to the women's lobby groups. Almost all the major women's organizations, from the National Action Committee on the Status of Women to the National Association of Women and the Law, agree that there should be three levels of sexual-assault charges, instead of the two now proposed. The first would be punishable by up to five years in jail, with a judge able to use his discretion in punishing lesser offences like grabbing. The second level would be sexual assault while armed with a weapon or that results in bodily harm. It could be punished by a maximum of fourteen years. This category seems an enormous improvement on the present law, under which a woman can be brutally harmed and sexually coerced and yet, if no actual penis-vagina penetration occurred, the attacker is liable to a maximum of five years. The third level (sexual assault with intent to wound, maim, or disfigure, or to endanger the life of any person) would be subject to life imprisonment.

These changes in the law may slowly begin to tilt the balance toward justice for women. Until now, there has been such a massive weight of bias and injustice in our courts that Canadian women could only stand by, sickened, as a parade of rapists strolled through our criminal-justice system and came out winners. Even when they're found guilty of the most insanely cruel crimes—raping a women immobilized by two broken ankles in a hospital bed, or holding a baby by one leg, upside down, over a high-rise balcony, so a buddy can rape the baby's mother—these men escape with three-or four-year sentences, ensuring that they will be out on the streets again in a matter of two or three years.

No wonder that some radical feminists have turned their backs on such a travesty of a justice system. Their angry rhetoric may antagonize some male reporters, but I am grateful to them. Even when I most disagree with them, I applaud them and acknowledge the debt we owe to women who go out on a limb. Ten years ago, or even five years ago, rape was talked of as a joke, an occasion for women to be embarrassed and defensive. Now the tone has begun to change. Soon, social attitudes will shove the law forward. None of this could have happened without the boldness of radical feminists who shook us all out of our fixed attitudes with their "unreasonable" howls of outrage.

OUR BODIES, MEN'S RULES

SEVERAL YEARS AGO, WHEN THE ONTARIO STATUS OF Women Council produced a research report on women's health, it ended up asking some acerbic questions that women don't ask for themselves. Why is it, asked the report, that no sooner did the hysterectomy rate level off, after it was shown how many of these operations were unnecessary, than the Caesarian rate shot up to a horrifying fifty per cent in some hospitals? Why, in 1982, are there only 38 beds for women addicts in Ontario's detoxification centres, compared to 313 beds for men, even though female alcoholism is rising and women are twice as susceptible as men to cirrhosis of the liver? Why do unnecessary operations on women seem to go so faithfully hand in hand with changes in health insurance coverage, or the special equipment or training of the doctor in question?

What the Council didn't spell out was its clear conviction that women often receive inadequate or inappropriate medical care because most doctors are men. Medicine, of course, is no more exempt from popular culture than any other discipline. Doctors are bombarded with ads in medical journals convincing them that every known mood and phase of a woman's life, from childhood fears to adult anger, is a cranky neurosis that should be kept under control by mood-altering drugs. Gynaecology textbooks still peddle the most medieval nonsense about "hysterical" female emotions. Medical and surgical equipment has a high-tech glamour for many of the mechanical whiz-kids who become doctors: those who have access to electronic foetal monitoring, for example, insist on using this dangerous and sometimes lethal new system on every woman in labour, regardless of whether or not there are any indications that it may be needed — just as an earlier generation of doctors recklessly damaged babies with newfangled forceps.

124

Worst of all, as Dr. Robert Mendelsohn points out in his book *Male Practice*, it is the sheer *otherness* of women that make them particularly prey to what he calls "medical and surgical overkill". Doctors who would go to any lengths to save a male patient's genital functions and organs will slice out a woman's womb or cut off a breast almost without a second thought. One small example he uses is the episiotomy operation, the cutting open of the woman's perineum during labour in order to widen the vaginal opening for the baby to emerge. North American doctors perform this surgical routine almost universally, with the excuse that "surgical cutting will prevent accidental rips." Doctors in countries like Holland use an episiotomy in only about eight per cent of all childbirths. A normal woman, especially one who is not forced to lie unnaturally on her back during childbirth, doesn't necessarily need an episiotomy; the perineum is remarkably elastic. But surgeons are so anxious to practise their hard-earned skills that they do the episiotomy anyway, even knowing that it may cause post-partum infections. Episiotomies are responsible, says Mendelsohn, for about twenty per cent of maternal deaths; the anaesthetic needle has been know to pierce the baby's brain and kill him; botched episiotomies have later caused endless excretory and sexual problems for women; and, to top it all off, even a tear would rarely require as many stitches or risk as much damage as the episiotomy.

Is it only male doctors who intervene so gratuitously and sometimes ruinously? No, but women doctors, trained in all-male institutions, can hardly help blotting up the predominant male attitudes. Until a change in conventional thinking comes about, the male view of women will continue to rule the practice of medicine. Although more women are enrolling in medical schools (more than fifty per cent of McMaster University's medical students are female), male students still outnumber females by a daunting two to one across Canada, and three to one at the post-graduate level, so that the profession will be heavily male-dominated for years to come. Since physicians, as numerous studies have shown, are mostly drawn from a rather conservative middle-class background, they are rarely in the vanguard of social enlightenment. A nay-sayer like Dr. Mendelsohn is as rare a creature as the boy who saw that the Emperor had no clothes.

It would be wrong to imply that male doctors are evil necro-mancers, performing their wicked deeds on helpless victims. The passive female patient, conditioned to a proper state of humble deference in the doctor's office, is the other half of the equation. Very few ever question a diagnosis or prescription that doesn't seem right to them. As the Status of Women Council report stressed, women have agreed to be hypnotized by the snake-charmer's spell. Hence the need for a growing new field: female therapy.

"Female therapy recognizes the role of a woman's social and physical reality perhaps more than traditional psychiatry does. The female events, like rape or menstruation, *invade* us psychologically. Even the possibility of rape is a lifetime threat. So women are used to feelings of powerlessness, of chronic rage and dependency," explains Dr. Elaine Borins, director of the new Women's Clinic at Toronto Western Hospital. "Also, women are genuinely under-privileged. Female therapy takes into account the psychological realities of a woman who has to walk to the supermarket with two babies in tow and who does not have enough money to pay for the food."

The Women's Clinic has an all-female staff of five, ranging from social workers to psychiatric nurses. "It's a necessity. Women now prefer to be seen by women. In the U.S., male psychiatrists are looking for patients but women psychiatrists have long waiting lists," Dr. Borins says.

It's not a question of female chauvinism but of the almost inevitable dominance relationship when the doctor is male and the patient female: "Women spend most of their lives emotionally adapting to men. They don't want to do it any more when they come for help."

"There's an overwhelming pervasiveness of male attitudes in medicine," says Elaine Borins. "I really became aware of it when I went back to medical school to study psychiatry for four years. In several thousand hours of training, I had precisely four hours of supervision by a female." Fledgling psychiatrists may later decide to devote their attention to specialized corners of their territory (child psychiatry, sexual deviation) but only a page or two of their texts will refer to the emotional lives of women. And the same student psychiatrist may go right through his training without ever having to consider what specific traumas like incest might do to a woman.

This extraordinary gap in the doctors' and psychiatrists' training is all the more disturbing when you look at the facts of women's lives. As Margaret Mead demonstrated, marriage is demonstrably bad for women's health. The rates of mental illness and physical ailment skyrocket for married women, while married men benefit hugely on all scales of physical and emotional well-being. That, say some recent experts, is because when women enter marriage, they enter a legalized position of subordination, which is bad for one's health. "Conditions of subordination set the stage for extraordinary events that may heighten vulnerability to mental illness," write Drs. Carmen, Russo, and Miller in the *American Journal of Psychiatry* (October 1981). "The frequency with which incest, rape and marital violence occur suggests that such events might well be considered normative developmental crises for women."

Translated, that means that incidents of personal violation may be as "normal" in the lives of young women as team sports and growth spurts may be for young men. If such traumatic upsets are par for the course for women, is it any wonder that twice as many women as men are clinically depressed? And is it any wonder that this fact is misinterpreted, because the men who write the stress charts simply leave out all the high-voltage incidents in any woman's life—abortion, childbirth, rape, or dysmenorrhea—so that it looks as though men suffer more stress?

The curious inversion by which women deride and downplay their own discomforts is nowhere more clearly at work than in the subject of menstruation. When, in the mid-1970s, I wrote a magazine article about "the curse", I was not surprised to learn that women still accepted a set of taboos and a sense of shame that go back to prehistory. "There is no other normal bodily function that has cast half the adult population, in almost every society in every age, in the dark shadow of a stigma," I wrote then. "If future historians were restricted to the study of just one phenomenon, menstruation, they would have a perfectly complete history of male chauvinism...and of how deeply women have accepted male evaluations of female functions."

Young girls told me about secrecy, shaming taunts from brothers, agony in the drugstore, feelings of disgust, a whole litany of male insult-names ranging from "riding the rag" to "back in the saddle". There is just no parallel. It's unthinkable, for example, that boys would talk about ejaculated semen with the same self-loathing. Given the universal negativity toward this normal and useful function, it's not surprising that doctors have, until very recently, treated menstrual pain as yet another neurotic symptom.

The teenager lay in a New York hospital room and the doctors trooped in to admire her incredible bravery. For two weeks, the girl with a broken back had walked around and attended school after initial X-rays had missed her injury. Yet, despite the searing pain, she hadn't screamed, fainted or complained

She was mildly surprised at the doctors' compliments. "I've been in training for years to endure pain," she said afterwards. I was used to coping through a haze of nauseating pain every month, without fail, when my period came."

Menstrual cramps aren't usually as agonizing as a broken back. But as Dr. Penny Budoff makes clear in her terrific book *No More Menstrual Cramps and Other Good News*, the young woman's pain may have been out of the ordinary but her treatment by others was not. Mother was sympathetic at first, then increasingly impatient with the monthly writhing and weeping, then coldly rejecting. Teachers and the school nurse were kindly once or twice, then brusquely dismissive. The gym teacher was furious. Later, in her early adulthood, the young woman heard these words of wisdom from various gynecologists: Have a baby. Have a hysterectomy. Have an operation to sever the nerve endings. Kneel on your hands and knees for 15 minutes a day. Stop faking; no such menstrual pain exists. Take Demerol. Don't take Demerol; it's all psychological.

If you've ever given or heard advice like this, you'll be as riveted as I was by this statement in Dr. Budoff's book:

"The pain of dysmenorrhea [menstrual cramps] is analogous to the pain experienced during a heart attack. There is a chemical basis for menstrual pain, and women who suffer from it are neither neurotic nor weak."

In fact, the same chemicals are at work during an attack of angina and a bout of menstrual cramps: prostaglandins. They are the chemicals which control the tone of our smooth muscles, like the uterus, the intestines, the blood vessels, and the heart. Too many of the wrong kind of prostaglandins (and the 50 per cent of all women who suffer have five times as many prostaglandins as the non-sufferers) will contract the uterus so violently that blood vessels are clamped off. The resulting spasm—the lack of oxygen and the crushing pain—are just what happens to the heart during an angina attack.

Have men ever been told that they should suffer the pain of angina in silence because it's their biological destiny, or that they should do push-ups, or that it's all in their heads? Uh-uh. But it took a woman doctor like Penny Budoff, a Long Island family physician, to snoop through the medical journals, piece together the pathetically scanty research, conclude that prostaglandins were the culprit, and conduct tests using simple, available anti-prostaglandin drugs, which are closely related to Aspirin.

Presto. More than 85 per cent of the women she treated with Ponstel (Ponstan in Canada) got excellent relief from menstrual pain.

"It's simple, it's effective, it has no side effects if you take it with food or milk. And you need only a few pills a month, instead of taking birth-control hormones all the time as millions of women now do to control their cramps," Dr. Budoff told me in a phone interview. (Of course, a physician has to prescribe Ponstan or other anti-prostaglandins for you, and you should follow Dr. Budoff's advice for timing the doses.)

Simple, isn't it? For centuries, women who suffered were blamed and guilted by those who did not. Then the women's movement made the discussion of dysmenorrhea taboo, an admission of womanly weakness. No more. Budoff's book is a sensible, forthright, highly readable guide to what's wrong and how to cure it. The almost hysterically grateful reception Dr. Budoff is getting—NBC's switchboard was jammed for days—is a testament of how badly women needed to hear her good news.

It's clear that better health for women will depend on more women asking more questions and pressing for new solutions. But will Canadian women find that energy and focus within themselves? So far, no. Women have not been galvanized by the startling thirty per cent annual jump in teenage pregnancies, for example. Though desperately needed sex education is still an incredibly random, hit-and-miss affair in Canadian schools, the only active groups speaking out on this issue are the reactionary and narrow-minded. Not even the revelations that female workers are being exposed to hazards in the environment and the work place, hazards like lead, pesticides, solvents, anaesthetic gases, ionizing radiation, and methyl mercury—a chemical soup that could hurt women and their unborn children, has aroused women's protest.

Then along came the first woman's health story to provoke a sharp public reaction—toxic-shock syndrome.

What was your reaction to the recent stories about toxic shock syndrome?

Did you, like me, tch-tch nervously over the reports that 350 U.S. women had suffered and 29 had died from an illness caused by tampon use? Did you, like me, think with some distaste, "Oh, well, those women couldn't have changed their tampons often enough"?

Actually, news reports offered two other, equally plausible explanations—a new strain of bacteria, or dangerous new materials in the Rely tampons—but how quick we all were to blame other women for their misfortune. It wasn't until much later, when I had done some investigation, that I suddenly recognized that our reactions and the toxic shock syndrome are both part of an old, old pattern.

First, I called some tampon manufacturers. Richard Innis, president of Playtex Ltd., talked willingly about the "sanpro industry" (sanpro means sanitary products). Then I asked him about the ingredients in the deodorant tampon. "Oh, no, we don't reveal that information at all," he said with finality. I asked him what government standards or regulations his product had to meet. "None whatever." We women are supposed to buy and use, in the costly millions, a product which we insert in our bodies, but we are not to ask what it is we are using.

I called some doctors. Gynecologist Dr. Dawne Jubb, of Women's College Hospital, said tampons were only part of the story. "Vaginal sprays, deodorants, and douches serve no real purpose and are a common source of irritation, rash, infection, and actual chemical burn," she said. A general practitioner laughed in cynical resignation. "Go ahead. Ask the government what labelling requirements they demand."

So I started to call government offices, Dr. Ajit DasGupta, head of the medical devices bureau of the Health Protection Branch, spoke to me, impatiently, about tampons.

"No, we don't test them. Tampons have not caused us any concern until now. We respond to priorities, and they have not been a priority."

I was interested to learn that none of the hundreds of intimate products used by women is a priority. But the one intimate product used by men, the condom, is "a very high priority indeed," said Dr. DasGupta, "especially as it is a protection from disease."

Condoms are tested "rigorously" by our federal government. Strict standards are set, Dr. DasGupta said, for safety and efficacy of materials, and for dimensions, strength, and pinholes.

The nearest female equivalent I could think of was contraceptive diaphragms. Are they tested? "No," Dr. DasGupta said, somewhat imperiously. "We can hardly test all 250,000 medical devices on the market, from dentures to diaphragms."

I see. The pattern is getting clearer. Though condoms are used for a few minutes and discarded, and diaphragms are used for years, and may remain inside a woman's body for hours at a time, condoms are a priority and diaphragms are not. Toxic shock syndrome, I began to realize, was not just another commercial exploitation and unfortunate accident. It is part of an old pattern of government indifference to women's health. Our own secretive shame about our bodily functions, our own guilty eagerness to blame ourselves and each other, are an essential part of this pattern.

Remember the morning-sickness drug thalidomide, and its heartbreaking parade of deformed victims? And then there was DES, taken by millions of women to prevent miscarriage and paid for in suffering (vaginal cancer, deaths, stillbirths, sterility) even unto the third generation. Remember the birth control pill revelations, and the banning, too late, of certain lethal types? Then the Dalkon Shield intra-uterine device, which lacerated its users, killing some and damaging infant brains, before it was yanked off the market?

Toxic shock syndrome is just one more betrayal of women's well-being that we can add to the list. And perhaps we were right, in some measure, to blame women. The tampon companies can honestly say that they never receive questions or challenges about tampon ingredients. The only letters they get are from women who are ashamed to see sanitary napkins advertised on television.

The toxic-shock furor had one tangible result. Ottawa now requires all manufacturers of tampons to submit ingredient information and test results to the government before *new* brands can be introduced, but the government does no independent testing. Diaphragms, menstrual pads, and "other feminine hygiene products" don't even need to clear this tiny hurdle to get on the market. The manufacturer need only notify the Bureau of Medical Devices that a new product is about to be sold, and be prepared to show its in-house testing results to the government *if asked*. Is it enough protection for women to have pharmaceutical companies test their own products?

The toxic-shock controversy, though, was a mere sideshow to the larger drama of women's bodies being governed by men's rules. Far more central to our self-respect, our health, our autonomy, and our dignity as human persons, is the question of abortion.

Encouraged by fundamentalist successes south of the border, Canadian extremists have stepped up the campaign to prevent all Canadian women from having abortions. An early ominous note was struck in a March 1981 provincial election in Ontario, when an anti-abortion group calling itself Campaign Life used the technique known as targeting to help defeat two Toronto New Democratic Party MPPs and significantly reduce the winning margin of another.

Victorious and feeling its oats, the organization then whinnied its way into the news with a new alarm: the Charter of Rights, it declared, was a threat to Canadian morals. The Charter would lead to abortion on demand; just as bad, perhaps, "women would lose preferential auto rates...would lose the right to financial support for their children...women would have to participate in army combat duty...and even share night patrols in police departments...."

By now, even Cardinal Carter of Toronto and other anti-abortion parties were mortified by the Moral Megalomaniac tone of these warnings. In a remarkable move, the Cardinal publicly rebuked Campaign Life and declared that the Charter was in fact neutral on the question of abortion. Even more outspoken was the Coalition for Life, another Catholic anti-abortion group. "Their tactics are hysterical," Coalition spokeswoman Mary Clark told me. "And our group doesn't believe in political targeting. We did it once to Andrew Brewin in Greenwood and then felt terrible when he won by just one hundred votes....After all, he was a good man in Parliament and there are other issues besides abortion."

Unfortunately, few other anti-abortion campaigners share this moderate viewpoint. The next ominous move in the abortion wars took place in the winter of 1982, when the Supreme Court of Canada ruled that a Saskatchewan health-food-store owner, Joe Borowski, had a legal standing as a concerned citizen to challenge Canada's therapeutic-abortion laws. (Borowski, a bizarre and controversial former NDP highways minister in Manitoba, last year conducted an eighty-day hunger strike to protest abortion.) The Court not only gave him the right to challenge the abortion laws, but even awarded him court costs of $70,000. The pro-choice Canadian Abortion Rights Action League estimates that legal costs to oppose Borowski's action will be at least $100,000.

Of course, it is fatally easy to mock the extremists of the far

right and to overlook their menace. As a journalist, I've seen just
how far the anti-abortionists have warped the democratic process
with their monotone shrilling. Whatever one might say about
their motives or their goals, their tactics are thoroughly repre-
hensible. They specialize in misleading images: one never sees a
poster defending the "right to life" of a fuzzy little blob of tissue.
Anti-abortion posters and ads have successfully planted the
unconscious image of all aborted foetuses as cute little shmoo-like
creatures, brutally torn from their cosy womb-homes. Yet the
huge majority of abortions take place when the so-called foetus is
so embryonic that it could in no sense be called a person. In fact,
even the word "foetus" is misleading. While the anti-abortionists
fight for the rights of the unborn, we forget that we are not
talking about babies but about zygotes—simple two-celled
organisms. To the anti-abortion crusaders, the rights of that
two-celled organism far outweigh the human rights of the adult
woman in whose body the zygote rests.

The warped perspective is symptomatic, I think, of the way
the extremists have robbed us all of the right to discuss abortion
in a calm and reasoned atmosphere. They've even hijacked the
vocabulary and appropriated all the benign words for themselves. After all, I'm as "pro-life" as anyone; I'm in favour of
happy marriages, families, children, and mothers. I don't wish
any living creature to die. I'm even anti-abortion, in the sense
that no sane person actually *likes* that procedure. But I also
think, along with the great majority of Canadian people (sixty-
nine per cent, says a Gallup poll), that a woman has the right to
make that decision, in privacy with her doctor, and without the
interference of religious vigilantes.

Our abortion laws are far from perfect, but steady and shrill
pressure from the right-wing minority has successfully forestalled
any formal parliamentary debate on reform of the laws. Just as
effectively, they have silenced much public debate. Reporters
and magazines writers shy away even from using the word
"abortion", because they know that no matter how oblique or
neutral the reference, they will be inundated with sick, vicious,
hysterical hate mail. Just venture out of hiding with a bit of
useful information—like the fact that Britain has a much lower
abortion rate than ours, despite freer laws, because of widely

available birth control and sex education—and the anti-abortion crowd gallops across the trail with its reliable red herrings.

They claim that women want "abortion on demand" to use as birth control instead of "using self-restraint". This clever wording immediately makes the unreflective bystander think of licentious harlots, copulating in the streets and aborting their poor wee babes into the gutter in a final gesture of obscene immorality. Indeed, one cannot separate the strong undertone of punitive anti-female sexual repression from the entire anti-abortion crusade. The fact is, I've never met anyone who speaks of abortion on demand, and the only people who would use abortion as birth control are those pathetic, stunted creatures who aren't deterred by laws anyway. The anti-choice minority has done a grave disservice to free speech by these techniques of intimidation and distortion.

Women's feelings about abortion are far more subtle, complex, and sophisticated than the extremists would like us to believe. Most reasonable women would argue that, although they have strong emotional impulses to treasure the awakening life within them (depending, of course, on their life circumstances), they do not feel that the potential life of a two-celled organism takes precedence over their own.

My conviction that women have not been bamboozled by the horror pictures of tortured foetuses and the inflammatory rhetoric of the Borowskis was borne out by a *Life* magazine poll in 1981. *Life* learned from a study of 1,000 women that, astonishingly, a clear majority of all groups—including Catholic, rural, conservative, old, young, and urban—would support a woman's right to have a legal abortion if she decided it was necessary. Despite the fact that more than half the women polled thought that abortion was morally wrong, 92 per cent would favour an abortion if a woman's health were at risk, 88 per cent if the woman had been raped, 87 per cent if the foetus had a severe genetic defect, 72 per cent if the mother was an unmarried teenager, and 67 per cent on any grounds, simply because they feel the woman has the right to make the choice. Furthermore, as voters, the women were not willing to be stampeded by the moral cowboys. Most did not think that a politician should be judged simply by his stand on abortion, and 70 per cent expressed anger that male courts and male legislators now have the right to rule over women's intimate lives.

All this demonstrates a remarkably sophisticated political view, one that can tolerate a high level of ambiguity and uncertainty. It remains to be seen in Canada whether such pragmatic women can be roused to fight against the moral tyrants who want to bend us all to their will.

I respect the person who chooses never to have an abortion. I respect the right to religious belief. I would fight strongly to defend the rights of anti-abortionists (even Joe Borowski) to have as many babies as they want. But for religious fanatics and arrogant male supremacists to assume the right to rule our bodies and our lives is an affront to human freedom and good sense. When all is said and done, we may debate about the real beginning of human life for years to come, since there is absolutely no scientific unanimity on this mysterious point. The arbitrary, superstitious and magical belief that life starts at the moment when two cells meet is just that: a piece of religious doctrine that has nothing to do with me. And that is the crux of the conflict. The anti-abortion campaign is fuelled by the unacceptable determination of a minority to force its religious beliefs and practices on the rest of us.

BUT IF IT'S MY BODY, WHY AM I DOING THESE AWFUL THINGS TO IT?

WHILE I WAS WRITING ABOUT WOMEN'S BODIES AND MEN'S rules, I was gradually sinking into a modern heresy of my own — a state of health that would not have been envied by an Egyptian mummy. After a year and a half of column-writing, I realized that there was not much point to ranting on about what men's rules do to women's bodies if I were single-handedly going to destroy my own through wilful neglect. Column-writing has its egotistical rewards, heaven knows, but it can exact a gruesome price. For the first year of my job at the *Toronto Star*, I was churning out five columns a week, without benefit of secretary, clerk, or researcher. I often spent six hours a day just answering phone calls and mail, then another six researching a story, and then another four to six writing it. In the leisure moments between, I shopped and cooked for three children under the age of twelve, ran to parent-teacher nights, showed up at school concerts, talked philosophy with questing young minds while my own nerve-endings screamed for sleep, snapped their innocent heads off when they dared interrupt the staccato of my typewriter, and generally acted like a fever-eyed maniac under extreme conditions of front-line stress. By the time I took off for the Pritikin Longevity Center in California, I was smoking close to one hundred cigarettes a day and felt as though I were about to perish.

My situation and my solution were both extreme, but they were right for the times. Women (and men) everywhere were frazzled by juggling two to three jobs and guilty because they weren't jogging, squashing, or otherwise lurching about in the service of cardiac sufficiency and muscular splendour. The

137

demand of any information about any self-help program was so
insatiable that, within a couple of weeks of my return from
Pritikin, the *Toronto Star* had reprinted and sold twelve thousand
copies of the series giving an embarrassingly honest account of
my trip. In another era, day-dreamers yearned over the girl from
the little mining town in the west who married an English lord.
In the eighties, we all day-dream about personal transformation
from fatties to thinnies, sloth to vigour, blob-like mortality to
eternally elastic youth. My California diary reads like an X-ray
of the wishful soul:

November 26. — By the time you read this I'll be landing in
California, land of kooky dreams, to confront a hard reality.
Can an all-too-ample 40-year-old, with a 25-year nicotine
habit, whose most vigorous exercises are coughing and treading
water, go cold turkey? Can a slothful foodaholic turn her life
around?

For the last week, I've been racing around buying track
shoes, reading diet books, and getting ready for what feels like
a moon launch. And let's not fudge it (aaah, fudge), having
Last Lunches, Last Dinners, and Last Snacks. There was the
Last Buttered Toast, the Last Stuffed Capon...

But why go on? For the next 26 days I'll be at the Pritikin
Longevity Center in Santa Monica, eating 600-calories-a-
day-worth of whole grains and vegetables, and learning, I
hope, to love a brisk walk more than I love lounging in a hot
bath. And (groan) at the same time I'll be giving up coffee
and cigarettes, my two main props at the typewriter. If I can
make it, if a walking compendium of urban vices like me can
change in midstream, it should give heart to every overweight
huffer and puffer in earshot. So far not even the fitness fad,
the fear of cancer, my graduated wardrobe, or the concern of
those who love me, have budged me from my ruinous habits.

This isn't a question of leaping into a rainbow-coloured
sweat suit and jogging off to the spa to firm up a few tummy
muscles. No, I'm one of your hard-core High Risk cases, the
original human yo-yo. The 60 pounds I lost a few years ago
found me again in no time; so did the next 20 I lost, and the
next 30. The combination of stress and overweight finally

earned me a nasty encounter with arthritis. My cigarette addiction is so extreme that I wake at night in terror of the Big C, automatically reaching for a cigarette to soothe away the panic.

Then along came my friend Beryl Fox. She had just finished producing her latest movie, *Surfacing*, and wanted to immerse herself in Pritikin's enormously popular health regimen. Would I come along? My doctor, family, and friends all said it was a great chance to buy time for myself. Given my priorities (it's always more important and more fun to help a child with Latin homework, dash away for a family outing, or stay up late reading, than it is to go jogging), my physical state of total wreckage seemed inevitable. Just getting *started* on changing any of my rotten health patterns demanded more energy than I could summon.

So here I go, hopping down the Bunny Trail, lettuce to the left of me and lettuce to the right. (Maybe I'll furtively roll some of that lunch lettuce into an illicit smoke...)

It is only thin people, usually thin male doctors, who actually like naked salad, who talk about "will power"—a smug phrase dreamed up by skinny non-smokers to describe whatever comes naturally and easily to them. Then there are the nutritionists, who in all innocence tempt me to murder whenever they prattle about "learning what foods to eat". O naturally bony ladies, fat people know more about diets, calories, carbohydrates, and the natural benefits of bran than you will ever know, having been obsessed all their lives by all things edible.

No, it's the inner demons that call the shots. My own personal demon was born when I was 4 years old, shivering in my undershirt in the office of Dr. Alan Brown, a top pediatrician of the day and co-inventor of Pablum. He looked into my brown eyes, surveyed my sturdy little Mediterranean-type body (no, not fat), and then shocked me with a sudden cruel yank on one of my braids. "Hi, fatso," he said. He advised my alarmed parents to put me on a rigid "preventive" diet. I can still see the pale blue mimeographed list pasted to the fridge door.

I learned a lot in Dr. Alan Brown's office. I learned that

my secret and dreaded name was Fatso. Other people told me I was pretty; I earned money as a child model and a professional actress; later still I was courted and loved. Still, as my weight see-sawed up and down, as I slunk past mirrors, as I surreptitiously weighed myself with the weight on my left foot only in the forlorn hope that it would make the needle go down, I was being the 4-year-old Fatso that Dr. Brown had invented.

People keep asking me, with maddening good cheer, if I'm looking forward to my Pritikin month. Well, no. Actually, I'm scared silly. I'm scared I won't be able to write without the habitual cigarette stuck between my fingers. For 25 years I haven't answered a phone, opened a book, or written a word without first patting my pockets for my nicotine equipment.

I'm scared I'll be hungry and miserable. I've even fantasized about hiding a cache of Callard and Bowser butterscotch in my suitcase for moments of total food panic. (Ever since Dr. Brown, I've cast a wary glance at every new situation to make sure there will be enough food.)

I'm scared I'll be the last person limping and puffing around the track...shades of the agony of public school sports, when I was always the one to duck the whizzing ball and earn the derisive groans of my team-mates.

I'm scared I'll be lonely, humiliated in my bulging track suit, thousands of miles from people who know I'm a person and love me despite my deficiencies. I know I'll miss my family desperately.

Most of all I'm afraid of failing. In the next month, I'll have to turn around the tendencies and tastes of a lifetime and set up new patterns of enjoyment for myself.

Embarrassing though it is, I'm ready to admit my fears because I think I share them with millions of others who are stuck in lifestyles they hate but feel powerless to change. I think it can be done. A month's sojourn won't solve all my problems, but I hope it can give me a running start on a new way of life.

November 27, Santa Monica Calif. — The question is not whether

I'll ever be used to linden tea, which tastes like a wet wash-cloth. The question isn't even whether the Pacific Ocean whooshing on the beach outside can soothe away the indignity of a spoonful of saltless vegetable sog for dinner. The question is: Can pampered North Americans find health, happiness, and longer life by eating like Third World peasants? Nathan Pritikin, a wiry 63-year-old California scientist, says they can.

Pritikin has invented a tough prescription to cure the woes of our ruinous lifestyle. For 26 days, clients here at his Santa Monica Longevity Center live on a 600-calorie-a-day diet of a handful of whole grains, 4 ounces of skim milk, half a fruit, and unlimited amounts of raw and cooked vegetables in a dizzying variety of concoctions. Between the eight small meals each day, everyone walks. By the end, overweight people have lost an average of 13 pounds, and even heart patients have worked their way up to an average of five miles' walking a day. And that's just the beginning. For the rest of your life, you're supposed to stick to the Pritikin regimen of no fats, no sugar, no salt, no caffeine, no tobacco, no alcohol (well, maybe a glass of wine now and then) and less than ¼ pound of lean meat every day.

At first glance the program seems severe, if not downright ghastly. Who can imagine a life without juicy steaks, mocha ice cream, morning coffee, or fettucine alfredo? Who, counters Pritikin cunningly, can look forward to a life of crippling disease, painful angina, or early death?

It's hard to argue that point. Though doctors debate, pro and con, whether Pritikin's program can really "cure" heart disease, no one seriously disagrees with his diagnosis. North Americans, he says, daily consume a diet of 40 per cent fat. Perched at the pinnacle of the food chain, we're happily gobbling two pounds a week of sugar and high-fat foods, polluted with 3,500 new chemicals which reach their ultimate concentration in our bodies. Combined with smoking, inactivity, and lack of fibre, that makes us sitting ducks for cancer, heart attacks, and a dozen other diet-related horrors that cut us off before our time.

Pritikin's drastic remedy —slashing the daily diet to 10 per cent fat, 10 per cent protein, and 80 per cent carbohydrate—

has polarized the medical profession. Some experts agree with the diet but say it's just too tough to maintain for a lifetime. Others argue that the results haven't been tested enough. But the Pritikin Program for Diet and Exercise has leaped to best-seller lists everywhere, Santa Monica has become a new Shangri-La, and celebrities from Yehudi Menuhin to Candice Bergen are munching their way through high-fibre menus.

The program's allure, the genius of it, I think, is its stark simplicity and irrefutable aura of wholesomeness. And, let's face it, its extremist character. None of that wishy-washy "moderation" that diet experts have always counselled. On Pritikin's regimen, the foodaholic, besieged by gourmet delicacies and deep-fry morsels on every street corner, can at least trade in an unhealthy food obsession for a healthy one. The program, after all, amounts to an obsession. There are hours of chopping vegetables, walking or jogging, and poring over food lists that hold endless surprises and shocks even for the health-conscious: no margarine, soya beans, honey, molasses, peanut-butter, cheese, egg yolks, granola, nuts, or seeds.

The rewards, however, can seem almost miraculous. I've always been a sceptic, as churlishly suspicious of the wonders of yogurt as I am of Uri Geller. Weight-loss gimmicks, from mare's urine to banana diets to water-gulping, have left me profoundly unimpressed: the long haul, not the quick loss, is what counts. But how can I not be dazzled by the scores of Pritikin case-histories, like the 90-year-old woman who came here seven years ago, crippled by arthritis and heart attacks, who is now winning medals for marathon running? And a 61-year-old man I have just met who was in intensive care awaiting triple-bypass heart surgery only three weeks ago. He came here instead and today walked nine miles without pain or fatigue.

For me, right now, it will be a miracle if I can make it through until the end of this first week. If not overcome by green pepper fumes or walker's wobbles, I'll let you know how it feels to eat like a Third World peasant in the midst of a world of temptation.

November 30, Santa Monica, Calif.—Sleepy, headachy, and irritable, my friend Beryl and I have staggered through our first few days of caffeine withdrawal at this no-nonsense shrine of pure living. I thought it would be good food I'd miss the most, but the vision that torments me right now is a steaming cup of fragrant black espresso. You never know how hooked you are until you quit.

Our first problem was to wrestle with a sense of unease at being surrounded by cardiac patients, diabetics, and other victims of the affluent life. The moment you arrive, a smiling desk clerk hands you a name tag with a dime and the Pritikin Longevity Center's phone number taped to the back—in case you become ill or exhausted on one of your daily walks.

If guilt over our unhealthy lifestyle brought us here in the first place, pangs of social conscience dogged us through this sprawling palace of physical culture, where everyone from the skinny staff (devotees one and all of the Pritikin program) to the track-suited clientele seems obsessed with medical histories, blood pressure, and triglyceride levels. Did we really want to become like those humourless golden joggers on the beach, panting and sweating in the act of self-worship?

We got over it. I reminded myself how typical it is for women to feel that everyone else's well-being comes first. We're so busy fretting about the needs of others that we hastily attend to our own needs with a quick chocolate bar or a stand-up meal at the kitchen counter. My doctor (everyone here is assigned a doctor) clinched it with a stern look and a declaration: "This place was made for a lady like you. You can prevent for yourself all these ailments you see around you."

Prevention. Within a day of our arrival, we were all wearing Pritikin T-shirts emblazoned with the eight-meal-a-day schedule, swarming to our nutritional lectures and medical tests, and dutifully spooning up our morning mush: a sticky mound of boiled cracked wheat, with no salt, served with a sprinkle of cinnamon.

Prevention. It isn't easy and not everybody makes it. Mario Puzo (*The Godfather*) didn't. He checked in, spent his weekends roistering in Las Vegas—wine, women, and song, a staffer said—and hastily checked out after nine days. Will *I* make it?

December 3, Santa Monica, Calif.—Here I come, walking fast and loving it, and that's just the little miracle I came here for. Beryl and I are heading down the Promenade, miles of public walkway just outside the Pritikin Longevity Center, bright blue sky above, the Pacific Ocean frothing onto the vast beaches to our left, and a balmy 80 degrees F. of California warmth caressing us as we go.

We reach Santa Monica Pier, a rinky-dink old seaside amusement park with the seedy charm immortalized in dozens of movies. Past the candy floss, the pizza, the only fresh-popped popcorn on the pier, past the corn on the cob (keep walking fast) and the tinny music of the ancient carousel, past the patient fishermen (No Overhead Casting, No Cutting Bait on Benches, No Jumping or Diving from Pier), and on to the end where sailboats will take you out to see the seals on the rocks. It's a mile and a half from the Longevity Center to the end of the pier and back, and that's just one of my prescribed daily walks here. Three miles a day is my average in the first week.

Well, you might think, so what? What's so special about walking a few miles? Aah. Remember that old 1950s parlor game classifying people as Mesomorphs, Ectomorphs, and Endomorphs? Mesomorphs were the muscled little activists who always seemed to be chasing a ball and actually enjoying it. Ectomorphs waver in my memory like Casper the Ghost... I think they were pale and thin. But Endomorphs, now there I can identify. Rounded, indolent, and sensuous. Yessirree. Now picture an Endomorph growing up in the days when La-Z-Boy rockers, not Adidas running shoes, were the symbol of leisure. Nobody ever told us that one day we'd be sorry for all the evenings we spent settling down with a new cookbook instead of sprinting out to play handball with the boys. Unfortunately, the more you don't exercise, the more you are loath to begin.

Sporty types simply can't understand this dreadful, leaden reluctance. "I gave a track suit to my plump Mama," complained a friend, "but she just won't put it on." No. Well, being thin and sprightly, you wouldn't understand how shame can paralyze a person into not beginning. The pudgier you are and the more you need it, the less you're likely to join those well-meant slim and trim classes where everyone is bound to be thinner than you. The more lithe and bright-eyed the missionary who nags you, the more discouraged you are about putting on that track suit. For the out-of-shape, exercise is a boring, embarrassing chore, which is why so many nearly-new large track suits are mouldering in the backs of cupboards. And which is why I came thousands of miles from home to make a start in a non-judgmental, non-competitive atmosphere where I could actually get to the point of enjoying activity.

The Longevity Center believes in aerobic conditioning— forcing your heart and lungs to work hard to develop greater capacity and endurance. Just like athletes, all of us physical wrecks at the Centre are now equipped with individually calculated training heart-rates that we are supposed to maintain for at least 30 minutes during each walk. To my absolute astonishment, I found that by my second walk, I was enjoying the training heart-rate. It's a comfort to know that your pounding heart and labouring lungs are operating at a safe limit and doing just what they're supposed to do to get stronger. And, for the first time in my life, an easy stride and the flush of exertion seemed their own reward.

December 4, Santa Monica, Calif. —It's 36 hours since I smoked my last cigarette.

That's longer than I've been without a cigarette since we first tried them in the schoolyard when I was 12 and I was the poor fool who actually liked them and got hooked. Quitting has been one of the most surprising and emotionally jolting experiences of my life. Why hasn't anyone written about the flood of feelings that can knock you flat when you quit a habit?

I was prepared for every kind of physical symptom. You are addicted to a chemical, said Jack, the leader of our quit-smoking group here at the Pritikin Longevity Center, and you can expect three to 10 days of withdrawal, including drowsiness, sharp cravings for the drug, headaches, and confusion. Nicotine, he told us, is a poison. Every time we light up, our body reacts as though it's being attacked. The adrenalin pumps, the blood sugar jumps, and our hearts speed up. Up and down, up and down, we jolt our bodies with nicotine all day until by late afternoon we're burned out and exhausted, our brain cells muffled by carbon monoxide. It's insidious how this drug makes you like it, he said. Your imagination is a partner in your addiction. You think you're getting pleasure when you light up, but what you're getting is relief from withdrawal symptoms.

I didn't give symptoms a chance to catch up with me. I leaped from bed that first morning, straight into my running shoes and out the door for a fast two-mile walk. There was a shaky, tender spot inside me quite separate from the cravings (I dealt with those the way Jack taught us — with five oxygen-jolt deep breaths). At breakfast, the tender spot resolved itself into an unexpected sadness. John, who gave up his five-pack-a-day habit a week ago, came over to hug me. Hang in theah, honey, he told me. Margaret came over to offer me her last five sugarless mints (a strict Pritikin no-no because they do have calories) and to make the astute suggestion that I write this column in the breezy lounge instead of in my previously smoky room. Ernie, who is old and finding it hard to quit, stopped beside me and tenderly patted my head without a word. Beryl, my companion in madness here, patiently dogged me all day like a lifeguard, ever ready with celery sticks. I felt like an invalid taking a first few, weak steps... how to read a book without smoking, how to exercise and then rest without smoking, how to finish a meal without smoking.

I raged like a child in our smoking group. I was devastatingly depressed. For 25 years, I realized, cigarettes had been my reward, my little treat after a task, my rest and refreshment, my company when I was alone, my badge of identity in company, my courage, my familiar. I lit them for their warm glow on cold nights at bus stops. I lit them for their blue curls of smoke. I still love the taste, the rituals of lighting up, the feel of a full pack. Sitting here on a Santa Monica beach, I suddenly, ridiculously, felt my eyes burn and spill over with tears as I tried to picture a future me without cigarettes.

But how could I spend this much love and sadness on a poison that's killing me? What about the bronchitis, the stink of old smoke, the terrible midnight visions of dying of cancer, visions complete in every detail down to the sinister whoosh of oxygen machines, the rubber sheets, the pain? All that meant nothing yesterday as I walked around with a swollen heart. I would never have believed a week ago that to quit smoking you have to spend some time in mourning. I walked, I chewed celery, I breathed like a grampus when the craving grabbed me. And then I took a shower, and standing in the shower I cried some more, remembering how my dad always smoked, and how I was now saying goodbye to one little thread of attachment to a man with whom I always fought and who has been dead now for 12 years.

It can be the ultimate act of mastering yourself, said Jack. Don't snivel. It'll be tough, but flex your muscles…it's the biggest challenge. I don't agree with his warlike imagery. It's horribly tough to quit smoking, but for me, at least, it's been essential to snivel. I've been bursting into tears for a day and a half, and every time I feel a little lighter, a little freer, a little less entangled with my addiction.

And, for the first time in my life, I've written something longer than the milkman's note without a cigarette jammed between my fingers, a full ashtray at my right elbow and at least two reserve packs at my left.

December 10, Santa Monica, Calif. — In this funny closed world of ours at the Pritikin Longevity Center, where men and women mingle unashamedly all day in droopy sweat suits, there is still one last great divide. One great injustice. One unalterable but absolutely unacceptable fact of nature. Men lose weight twice as fast as women. And they have to work only half as hard to do it.

That's why, before I came here, I slipped into my suitcase a consolation copy of *A Woman Doctor's Diet for Women*, by a smart and funny Yankee, Dr. Barbara Edelstein. I'd always noticed a tremendous disparity in the way men and women lose weight. Men, who do not usually have to think about, shop for, or cook the food, attribute this, of course, to their great self-discipline. But it was wonderful Dr. Edelstein who first put it all in perspective. Men burn calories twice as fast for the same amount of exertion, she writes. A woman's body is naturally composed of a higher proportion of fat to muscle tissue than a man's, and muscle mass burns five more calories per pound to maintain itself than fat or connective tissue. This means that while a woman's appetite is the same as a man's, she needs only half the amount of food to maintain her weight. How can overweight women fail to get discouraged when doctors ignore such fundamental truths of biology and instead blame her self-indulgence and lack of willpower?

Good old Dr. Edelstein. I needed her yesterday when Virgil, our Oklahoma stockbroker, said in a rich, rolling baritone somewhat muffled by a wholewheat bun: "Ah've lost 12 pounds this week." We're all fond of Virgil. "That's wonderful, Virgil," we women chorused, and we could smilingly have pelted him with our boiled brussels sprouts.

The overweight men here have racked up staggering losses—12, 16, or even 18 pounds in the first 10 days. And many of them are eating the so-called regular diet, which includes a daily 1,900 calories' worth of baked potatoes, wholegrain bread, and hearty bean soups. In other words, they have only to curb their wilder excesses to have the pounds roll off. Though Pritikin's 600-calorie maximum-weight-loss diet could work for anyone, I can't imagine a woman keeping weight off permanently with that baked potato regimen.

Beryl and I, knowing we have come here to master a new lifestyle rather than simply to shed pounds, try not to be obsessed with weight loss. But every morning before dawn, as we soft-shoe through the lobby toward our pre-breakfast four-mile hike, we are drawn irresistibly to the scales outside the dining room. I've lost 9 pounds in my first 11 days here. Beryl, who is eating less (she passes up the diet dinner in favour of a plate of steamed vegetables, and she's one of the very few here steely-willed enough to do that), has lost only 5.

Of course, Beryl has much less weight to lose than I, but that should be balanced out by her manic devotion to long work-outs in the gym while I'm busy writing this column.

I called Dr. Edelstein in Connecticut this morning to find out if she considered Pritikin's vegetable diet suitable for women. After all, she had written that any form of carbohydrates are poison to overweight women.

"Well, Pritikin's is a man-made diet primarily for treating male-oriented diseases," Dr. Edelstein told me cheerfully. "A woman on the 850-calorie diet which I recommend will also live longer and feel better, but I think she may lose weight more easily. I'm very afraid of carbohydrates. I think many overweight women have a faulty metabolism, which we just haven't pinned down yet, and they simply can't convert carbohydrates to energy."

Both Edelstein and Pritikin emphasize the link between high-fat diets and the risk of cancer, particularly breast cancer. Dr. Edelstein thinks that her own, more conventional form of balanced protein and carbohydrate diet is as good a defence against fats as Pritikin's. But, she says, if someone can stay full and satisfied by eating vegetables all day, and can lose weight efficiently that way, why not?

December 11, Santa Monica, Calif. — The first incredible thing about the Pritikin diet is that if you can put up with a little oral boredom, you never need to be hungry. The second thing is that you can actually get used to it and begin to like it. Sort of. And the third thing is that never, never in your life will you have eaten so healthfully. Guaranteed.

This is what it's like to crunch your way interminably through a Pritikin day:

7 a.m. No coffee or tea, but would you believe a mug of boiling water with a wedge of lemon? I know it sounds ridiculous, but try it. It's less ridiculous, I promise you, than the old-sock pong of linden tea.

7:25 to 9 a.m. Cereal. Most mornings, it's an ice-cream-scoop-sized (3-ounce) serving of saltless, boiled cracked wheat. We garnish it with a few sprinkles of bran, a trickle of skim

milk, half a sliced banana, and a hefty shake of cinnamon.
The first morning, it tasted like Elmer's glue. By the second
week it tasted like ambrosia.

9 a.m. to 10 a.m. Half a citrus fruit.

10 a.m. to 11:45 a.m. The salad bar is set up in the dining
room, a colorful collage of lettuce, tiny tomatoes, radishes,
celery sticks, cauliflower and broccoli, red onions, green
onions, cucumber slices, and bean and alfalfa sprouts. The
dressings are no-fat concoctions, the best of which is the
Italian style with cider vinegar, a dash of apple and lemon
juice, and herbs. Across the room is the steam table, now
ready for the day's onslaught with trays full of brown rice (for
the non-dieters), steamed vegetable combinations like green
beans and onions, and vegetable stews.

In case our vigorous exercise schedule leaves us no time to
sit down for a salad, there are little baggies at the ready so we
can tote our low-cal fodder wherever we go. All over Santa
Monica you can see determined hikers in Longevity Center
sweat-shirts, furtively munching on celery sticks as they stride
past the local pizzeria. I am told that airline pilots, who are
regularly sent here by aviation insurance companies when
they are too out-of-shape to qualify for flying, are now trans-
porting raw veggies in cockpits all over America. They are
obeying rule number one: never get hungry.

11:45 to 1:30 p.m. Soup. Have you ever had vegetable
soup without broth, salt, pepper, or meat? The non-dieters
fare better, with thick bean and lentil soups, but ours is a
watery solace. The best of the dieters' soups are tomato-based
(start with canned tomatoes, herbs, and water, and throw in
any combination of vegetables you like), and the best that can
be said for them is that you can take them to work in a
thermos.

1:30 to 3 p.m. Baked potatoes for non-dieters, served,
naturellement, without butter or salt. On special occasions,
even the dieters are given baked potatoes as emergency
rations. The other day a group of us were invited to spend a
day sailing on a magnificent 58-foot Norwegian ketch. While
the civilians aboard sprawled about the decks knocking back
their chicken stew, we blushing Pritikiners ate our baked

potatoes and found them piercingly delicious. Baked potato and green salad may have to become our staple restaurant order, since they are often the least processed and most fat-free foods available.

4 p.m. More soup. Or salad. Always salad.

5:30 p.m. Dinner. First the blessed salad. Then a hot entree: curried vegetables, or felafel in a pita, or a lasagna made with skim-milk cottage cheese. Though the portions are on the small side, there is so much bulk with all the vegetation that we sometimes collapse in exhaustion before we can chew our way through all of it.

And healthy? After two weeks on the leafy greens, most of us feel so ebulliently sparkly-eyed and energetic that we make Heidi look anemic. You can almost hear the mental tick-tocking as people begin to realize how good they feel, and, perhaps, to figure out how they'll keep up this rigorous program when they go home.

December 17, Santa Monica, Calif. —I'm celebrating a little anniversary here. Care to join me for a mid-morning wedge of grapefruit and a whiff of ocean air?

Yes, it's two weeks since I stubbed out my last cigarette. And one week since I impulsively grabbed my one emergency reserve cigarette from a drawer and crushed it to sawdust before I could change my mind. For the rest of my life, I'm going to celebrate Nov. 30 as Jubilation Day, the day I did what I thought was impossible. I'm even going to save all the cards, letters, and telegrams that readers have been sending me here at the Longevity Center, and put them up like banners.

Not that I've got it completely licked. "Don't ever take that one little puff," our instructors warn us, "or you'll be hooked again." From talking to other addicts here, some of whom have quit several times, I know I'll never really be free of the desire to smoke. Still, from my shaky perch as a fledgling non-smoker, I'd like to share some of what I've learned.

First, get away from the rat-race if you can, to a cottage or country retreat. Take a good friend with you, someone who can be trusted not to nag or preach, someone who will give you a little loving-kindness. I would never have had the courage to try to quit if I hadn't the good luck and the privilege of being here at the Pritikin Longevity Center with a friend who cared if I made it or not. We've been cushioned here as never before in our adult lives. We wake before dawn without alarm clocks, rested and fresh, with nothing to do but put on our sneakers like kids at camp. Someone else cooks, cleans, and worries while we trot through our paces. Everyone has time to be kind. In our cool and spacious public rooms, with the tall windows overlooking the sea, smoking is forbidden. You go the whole day without once smelling tobacco. Depressurized, physically active, and surrounded by a tight support system, I was able to quit as painless as possible.

My question is this: since nicotine addiction costs our society millions of dollars in damaged health, why do quit-smoking havens like this one have to be restricted to the rich? I'll wager that within a few years, medical establishments and governments will see it as economically rational to set up withdrawal hostels for working people, whose employers might well contribute the holiday time.

If you're thinking of quitting, even without a retreat, remember that physical activity is as imperative as an unending supply of celery sticks. Constant brisk walking reminds you with every deep breath how much better your body will be working from now on. And psychologically as well as physically, a constant munching of celery and carrots works better than gum and candy, because it keeps reminding you of your new direction toward health.

Be prepared for waves of strong emotion. Last week I wrote about my own depression and crying jags when I first quit. It turned out these wrenching emotions were common among the other quitters here. One rugged guy, a tough ex-footballer who has done well out of timber and trotting horses, told me he sat on the edge of his bed and wept half the night when he first quit. The depression turns into triumphant elation within a few days... particularly if you focus unflinchingly on the tumble of your inner feelings and absorb some lessons from them. I was astonished to realize, for example, that I needed cigarettes most, not when I was working, but when I was alone. I've been a heavily addicted smoker for 25 years without knowing I was afraid of being lonely. Our smokers' group leader tells us to be prepared for the pressures and temptations of the "real world" by listing the benefits of not smoking.

Okay. This is my two-week anniversary, so today I'm running up a flag to celebrate feeling great, energetic, and clear-headed. And for having clothes that don't smell of stale smoke. For being able to linger and browse in stores without panicky irritation at not being able to smoke. For being able to walk 5 miles before breakfast without getting out of breath. For planning to wear perfume again, now that it will no longer be drowned out by tobacco, as soon as I'm out of eau de sweat suit and back home. Just to reward myself, I've bought a wildly extravagant bag of a fragrant, spicy potpourri. I'm going to put it in every room of my house and breathe deeply. For this new non-smoker, it's going to be roses, roses all the way.

December 18, Santa Monica, Calif. —It was down time last week. Everyone had a weight-loss plateau (I stuck fast at a measly 11 pounds), the high had worn off, and even exercise was beginning to seem routine.

So Beryl and I took a weekend off and headed up the Golden Coast for Big Sur and Carmel, basking in the most sun-drenched December that California has had for years. Up there in the mountains with wood smoke drifting through the bright air and the whales sounding and blowing in the sea below, we felt as though California must be Paradise Now.

I admit that I actually screamed "thar she blows" the first time I saw the whales. I had cultivated a certain composure by the time we reached a state park where we tramped through spicy sage bush to watch sea otters floating comically on their backs in a glassy green cove, and to see the seals "arnking" (honestly, that's how they sound) and lolling on the rocks. But if nature can pull your strings at all, then the California coast is no place to stay laid back. To me, it was thrilling to see wild deer feed daintily on the hillside at dusk, owls flap past us, and jays eat boldly from our hands. At Carmel we stayed at an inn practically smothered in flowers—

cyclamen, poppies, petunias, and geraniums—and the blue of the sea was outshone only by the brilliant splash of stars at night.

Eating the Pritikin way was astonishingly easy as we journeyed up the counter-culture coast. Even in roadside diners, young waitresses were respectfully supportive when we explained that we were on a vegetarian, no-fat diet. "Oh sure," they'd say (everyone in California is on some crazy regimen), and mildly bring out the boxes for us to read the ingredients on the label. Nearly everywhere we went we were able to get a plate of plain brown rice with a mixture of steamed vegetables, plus a glass of soda water with lemon. But here's the surprise. Not only did the simple vegetables taste wonderful, but we began to feel a compelling self-confidence as we firmly explained our needs to waitresses. We began to feel that we were in control of what we ate. Far from being embarrassed by our eccentric ordering ("and bring lots of vegetables please without butter") I began to feel rather special. Comparing notes with Beryl later, I discovered that for both of us, respecting our bodies and making clear choices was a heady step from passivity and overweight.

And then back to the Center for our last few days.

"Ah'm gonna miss yo' all," said John, looking bewildered. Even the macho men here feel it: a certain sharing, a camaraderie that goes a little further than they are used to. We've puffed out the miles together, eaten gloomy breakfasts together before dawn, listened to cello concerts and each other's groans as we gritted our teeth through exercises. By the end of this week, our group of 60 will have presented a special "graduation show" of skits and songs, packed up our bags, and headed for home with a mimeographed list of each other's addresses. But we probably will never meet again. Our hothouse buddy system—the encouragement we nicotine addicts gave each other, which meant so terribly much at the time—would fade out there in the glare of everyday life, where our differences seem so much greater than our similarities.

December 21.—Goodbye, California. It's been grand.

I came here nearly four weeks ago with a bundle of anxieties, a 25-year smoking habit, and a tremulous hope that it wasn't too late to trade in some rotten health habits for better ones. I'm leaving in a burst of exuberant optimism laced with sheer terror. Now that I'm feeling so great, can I really keep on living the Spartan life without the safety net of the Longevity Center?

I came here to quit smoking, and I've done that. I wanted to learn about a new way of eating, and I've done that, though at the end of 26 days I'd lost only 12 pounds. I especially wanted to learn to love exercise, and I've done that in spades. Striding off for my dawn walks, I feel as though I've got a handle on the day and the world by the tail. I no longer care if I'm the slowest off the mark or if someone else can walk twice as far as I can. The exhilaration of action, of decisiveness, of taking control of my life, is enough, I hope, to keep me going through the Toronto slush.

Will I keep on eating Pritikin-style? "Unrealistic, unpalatable," sneered an investigative scientist with whom I happened to be chatting this morning. He admits that, according to his research, Pritikin heart patients have a "remarkable survival rate". But he thinks the ardent self-deprivation of us inmates, ironically housed in the lovely oceanside hotel where Synanon used to cure drug addicts, itself smacks of a cult.

Maybe. But though I came here a sceptic, I'm now convinced that the standard North American diet, dripping fats and oils from every doughnut and hot dog, is suicidal. Steak-lover though I be, I've now sat through enough lectures and waded through enough material to wonder where the heck we got the idea that gorging on red meat, heavy cream, and greasy fries was a version of "the good life".

The evidence is beginning to click together. In 1977, Senator George McGovern's special committee on diet urged Americans to reduce sharply their fat consumption—and that means cutting out red meat, saturated fats, and polyunsaturated oils. Only a return to the pioneer diets of grains, vegetables, and fruits, said the committee, can halt the epidemic of heart, liver, and gall bladder disease, high blood pressure, diabetes, and cancers of the breast and colon.

Scientists have discovered definite links between breast cancer and a high-fat diet. Rats and mice develop breast cancers when fed a high-fat diet. One experiment reduced the malignancies from 80 per cent to zero simply by putting the mice on a non-fat diet. Japanese women, with one of the lowest fat diets in the world, also have one of the lowest breast cancer rates. But when Japanese women move to the United States, their rate of breast cancer quadruples. Studies among vegetarian Seventh Day Adventists, who suffer only half the average number of cancer deaths, show those who do get breast or colon cancer have eaten more fried foods and refined goodies like cakes and white bread. Those who ate more leafy greens and plant protein had lower cancer rates. Every responsible authority, from McGovern to the National Cancer Institute to the American Heart Association is now telling us to cut way down on fats.

Okay, I'm listening. If I once dismissed vegetarians as protein-starved fringies, may the Great Turnip forgive me. Now I know that we can get all the protein we need, and more, from a Pritikin-style peasant diet of whole grains and vegetables, the same kind of plentiful roughage diet which protects Africans from bowel cancer.

I'm also equipped, now, with a nifty little paperback about aerobic exercise which I picked up down here. *Fit or Fat?* by Covert Bailey snappily explains the whole maximum-efficiency approach to exercise, and also unravels a few mysteries, like how fat people get fatter while eating less than thin people. It tells you how to find your training heart-rate and how to set up a program for yourself just like the one we've learned here at the Longevity Center. I highly recommend it for exercise neophytes.

Is this really me, talking about aerobic exercise? Can I really change my lifestyle and ingrained habits? The answer is, I think it's possible. Today, the day I leave the Longevity Center, is the first day of the long, hard haul. I'm making a resolve right now to forgive myself my backslidings. To keep my new self-esteem flying high when skinny people who have read these columns try to patronize me. To remember, those cosy mornings in bed when the alarm goes off, how real is the joy of getting out there and walking fast. And to remember the most important thing the Longevity Center has taught me: taking responsibility for one's own health and well-being is the ultimate high.

December 26. — You might say that my homecoming was cool and undemonstrative. You might, if you were myopic, stone deaf, and looking the other way when I arrived at Toronto Airport on the last night of Channukah after a 26-day absence. I cried with excitement, of course. Forgot to show off my new, two-sizes-smaller dress. Tried to hug three kids, husband, and mother all at once. Dropped my suitcase on my toes and wanted to give everybody their presents.

The bliss lasted all weekend and right up till the middle of Monday when my boss, Scrooge Cornell, told me that I had to write a column for Wednesday after all. "Tell the people how you're doing on this diet now that you've left the Longevity Center," she said, with a gleam in her eye.

Well, if you've digested your turkey and oyster stuffing and brandy and are just settling back, sigh, with a cup of coffee, let me tell you that it's beginning to seem just possible to survive here in the real world on a vegetarian diet. The plane ride home was my first test. I'd phoned ahead to order a vegetarian meal and was astounded to be served a perfect Pritikin dinner: salad with a wedge of lemon, Perrier, steamed vegetables, and a baked potato. I admit that my seatmate's dinner of roast duckling looked more tempting than mine. On the other hand, I had just registered a further three-pound weight loss on the morning I left the Center, and in the first weekend home I dropped another five, for a grand total of 20 pounds in 28 days.

My splashdown into civilian life had its hazards, though, bonus weight loss or no. For one thing, my friends took to flinching and hiding their cigarettes behind their backs when I appeared, for fear that I might have become a demon proselytizer. I even felt weirdly like a traitor to my class, an exile, when I ordered up a no-smoking seat in the plane. Shopping and cooking took up almost the entire weekend as I raided the fruit and vegetable stores and tried to make something appetizing from grey mounds of mashed eggplant. The family was terrific, bravely forking down a meal's worth of steamed vegetables as though broccoli were their heart's desire. Mind you, an astonishing amount of salami was quietly consumed during the evening. My most successful venture on the weekend was a spicy tomato-onion stew, which I would have brought to work with me if only the children hadn't forgotten the thermoses at school for the holidays. As it is, I had to make do with bags of greenery (you feel pretty silly, hunched over your typewriter with a green bean sticking out of your mouth at a jaunty angle) and an apple for emergencies.

Hungry? Yes, I've been 10 times hungrier at home than I was at the Longevity Center. There's only one answer to the constant temptation of a house full of goodies: more vegetables. The hunger is nothing, though, compared with the shock of early morning walks in a December downpour. Ice lurks at the bottom of innocent-looking puddles; crusty black mountains in the gutter crumble beneath the unwary foot. It's hard to tell which is more sodden: my parka, my sneakers, or my morale. Every mile in Toronto feels like 10 of the Californian variety. Not only that, but it's embarrassing: cars keep slowing down in astonishment at the sight of a large lady in her husband's soaking-wet Steelworker jacket, race-walking along St. Clair Ave. at 6:30 a.m.

Still, I've done it. I've made it through the first few days in the "real world" without backsliding. A dozen times since I came back to my old nicotine-soaked haunts, I've felt the sharp stab of longing for a cigarette. Smoking behaviour is so ingrained that I can well imagine that a year from now, taking up some occasional activity that I used to associate with smoking, I'll have to fight the craving all over again.

But that's all right. I haven't felt this exuberant, this alive, this much in control of my life, for years and years. I'm no athlete, no puritanical health nut, and no missionary. I've tried what seemed like a sensible approach and it's working so far. I'm going to try to keep it up. What's more, I buoyed and delighted by the number of people who have told me since my return that they intend to quit smoking or have already done so after reading my columns. I said when I started this whole venture that if a "walking compendium of urban vices like me can change in midstream, it should give heart to every overweight huffer and puffer in earshot." It looks as though both parts of that equation are, at least a little bit, coming true.

To everyone who is undertaking the struggle, I'd like to repeat that catch phrase that became a sort of battle cry of my whole Pritikin saga: "Hang in theah, honey."

Hang in there.

Well, I tried. I've never gone back to nicotine, but after exactly six months of vegetables and speed-walking in the singularly un-Californian atmosphere of Toronto, I slipped gradually off the wagon. My own pusillanimity doesn't mean Pritikin is passé. I still think it's one of the best diets I've ever been on, for sheer nutritional common sense and satisfaction. It's simply that I couldn't keep all those bright orange balls up in the air at the same time: just staying alive, getting to the bank on time, refraining from cigarettes, being a mother, and getting the column handed in by deadline was the utmost expenditure of self I could afford. The argument, I realize, is circular. The longer I ignore the chiding voices of those two stern angels, Diet and Exercise, the harder it is going to be for me to live up to other obligations.

Meanwhile, my fall from grace met with some fascinating reactions from readers who met me in person and detected without too much trouble that Pritikin had not reigned permanently supreme in my life. Women were impulsively sympathetic, for the most part. But there were those, men and women, whose faces went slack with inattention the moment they realized I was not the walking embodiment of a panacea. If I didn't have a magic cure for those extra pounds, I had nothing that could interest them. This extraordinary single-mindedness showed me again how deep and fierce is the vulture grip of popular media on all our brains. Thin, thin like the sinuous fashion models, the

TV nymphets, the gaunt tragedians of the soap operas, the bikinied blondes on the front pages of newspapers, thin is the only acceptable female shape.

Jiggle. Flab, waddle, chubby, bulge. Blubber.

All our words about fatness are comic-repulsive; naturally, since fat people åre society's last legitimate scapegoat. You can no longer openly despise people of different colour, people who lisp or limp or talk with an accent. But fat people are considered the guilty authors of their own misery. In a world spilling over with abundance, where gourmet cooking and fine dining are badges of chic affluence, to be overweight is, paradoxically, to look poor and be loathsome.

A revealing documentary on CBC-TV's program *The Nature of Things* quoted research that shows how very fat people may be helplessly trapped by their genetic inheritance. In Holland, babies born during the end-of-war famine grew up to be thinner than the average; babies who were born during the few months after food was airlifted into Holland grew up with an abnormal number of fat cells. "The problem seems to be inherent in the genes," said Dr. Dan Roncari of the University of Toronto, who headed the study.

"People think obesity is caused by gluttony," confirmed British researcher Michael Stock, "but there are just as many thin gluttons as fat ones. It looks to us as though obesity is a thermogenic defect." Stock and his colleague Nancy Rothwell, both thin, served as the maddening subjects of their own experiments: they didn't gain an ounce when they and other thin volunteers added 1,000 calories a day to their diets for eight weeks. "I eat a lot," Rothwell confessed happily, "at least six chocolate bars a day in addition to a lot of regular food. But I have trouble not losing weight." Now Stock and Rothwell are researching "brown fat", the kind that keeps thin rats thin no matter how much they eat.

All this was brisk, informative, and even distantly reassuring. But in retrospect, what I remember is the way the camera lingered in fascinated horror on the wobbling bellies of the obese, in ghastly jump-cut contrast to starving African babies. The camera is society's cruelly judging eye: fat is a wilful crime in the eyes of the majority. Few thin people realize how thoroughly the fat accept that judgment. A businesswoman I know, a shrewd, empathetic, and successful person who is overweight, casually told me one day that she had perfected a technique of brushing her teeth and combing her hair without once looking in the mirror. And, in my experience, few thin people are honest enough to admit how much smug satisfaction they get from skewering the hapless obese. I once went to a doctor to help me with a diet. She spent 15 minutes describing her intense horror of her own mother's body. Then she said, cool as a knife, "Of course, she wasn't as heavy as you."

The most spectacularly touching and revealing book ever written about the subject is surely *Such a Pretty Face: Being Fat in America* by Dr. Marcia Millman. The sad secret at the heart of many a fat woman, she reveals, is a demand for the totally unconditional love that, in all likelihood, she never received as a child. It's an unrealistic demand. Fat women are the objects of fear, contempt, and even rage in our society. And, of course, social stigma always leads to self-hatred. Millman is brilliant in discussing the before-and-after fantasy life of the obese, the Frog-into-Princess dream that one day the fat woman will emerge into perfect, thin beauty. It's a treacherous fantasy, Millman says, because until that magic transformation, the fat woman is waiting, always postponing her life. Fat women, Millman notes, don't have nice winter coats.

But why is overweight the special demon of women? Kim Chernin, in the challenging book *The Obsession*, describes a typical locker room scene—normal women grabbing at their thighs and stomachs with exclamations of disgust. Why is it women who starve themselves out of their female shape and into a boyish asexuality? Why are men with beer bellies acceptable but fat women repulsive? Chernin talks about the deep anxiety our society feels about ample female flesh. It is an exact parallel of the stern disgust with which Victorian doctors wrote about normal female sexual urges—at that time considered a foul aberration to be expunged with medical treatments, strict regimes, and even surgery. Will a future era see our universal obsession with fat as similarly skewed?

Let *The Nature of Things* have the last word. A young,

breathless, bone-thin dancer looks into the camera and says, "Aesthetically, female flesh, well, it isn't in. It's not acceptable." Sometimes, she says, her whole being rebels against the rigorous diet. "Your body is saying 'I want to be a woman.'"

Fatness and female flesh: the last taboo.

If the weight battle, was, at least temporarily, a lost one for me, there was one battle in the self-improvement wars that I won, and that stayed won. Though I am the last to preach at those who light up, I couldn't resist one foray into the topic of non-smoking, especially when I found out that women, along with the Third World, were the last and most lucrative markets for the beleaguered tobacco companies:

It's just about seven weeks since I quit smoking myself. And I want to tell you that reading the U.S. Surgeon-General's Report on women and smoking, in preparation for this column, was the roughest thing I've done since I quit. By the time I finished this gloomy 419-page document, my head was throbbing, my nerves scraped raw, and if there'd been a cigarette in the house I would have smoked it the way a drowning person gulps for air.

That's understandable, I guess. Women smoke because of "negative affect", according to the report. In English, that means stress and rotten feelings. And if anything *drips* with negative affect, it has to be a report which tells this recent quitter that only one in five women who quit actually makes it, and that it will be 15 years till my health risks are back to the same level as a non-smoker's.

Almost all the report's news is bad for women: more teenage girls than boys are starting to smoke; they're smoking younger and younger; more females are smoking more heavily; by 1983, lung cancer will be the number one cause of cancer deaths among women. You may already have read some of the other ugly findings in the report: that smoking is linked to still-births, placenta praevia, decreased fertility, messed-up menstrual cycles, earlier menopause, Sudden Infant Death Syndrome, ulcers, wrinkles, smaller and sicker babies, heart attacks, vascular diseases, and cancer of the larynx, mouth, esophagus, kidney, pancreas, and bladder.

If this is the kind of news that makes you feel frightened and guilty (and reach for another cigarette), stop for a minute. Here's some news from the report which should make you angry, and anger is a more constructive emotion than guilt. The report says that cigarette advertising has seriously warped the editorial content of women's magazines. In seven years, *not one* of the leading women's magazines in the U.S. has carried an article "that would have given readers any clear notion of the nature and extent of the medical and social havoc being wreaked by the cigarette-smoking habit." It's a shocker. Women's magazines stand indicted as corrupt. Research shows that their Technicolor cigarette ads are successful: young girls see the cigarette models as independent, attractive, sexy, young, sporty, and healthy. And on top of that, the magazines are guilty of suppressing vital information.

The Surgeon-General's report, though it nearly drove me back to demon tobacco with its despairing statistics, ended by cheering me up, faintly. After all, with so much fresh information about women and smoking, there are bound to be new and perhaps workable approaches to the problem. Consider this: the reason women are so much less successful than men at quitting, apparently, is that the statistics are skewed by the large number of homemakers, who are the heaviest female smokers of all and the least triumphant when it comes to kicking the habit. Cigarettes, says the report, are "their companion" in a lonely situation. This kind of insight — not the blaming and sneering of the anti-smoking lobby — is what will help people eventually to get free.

And consider this: rebelliousness is part of the addiction. Young girls who start smoking are twice as resentful of authority as non-smokers. Adult women smokers are more extroverted, assertive, power-oriented, opinionated, forthright, tense, and neurotic than non-smoking women. Also, on the average, thinner.

And this: "Women have more life stress than men," says the report, and "smoking is used as a major coping device" even by women who should know better: women doctors, nurses, psychologists, and managers, more of whom smoke than their male counterparts.

Because guilt is your worst enemy, take this thought away

with you. My generation (women born between 1931 and 1940) achieved the dubious distinction of having the highest-ever proportion of women smokers. By 1966, 45 per cent of us were smoking. We were part of a social swing, the first generation of women to grow up thumbing our noses at the prissy stereotypes of "ladylike" behaviour. If we were tough enough to fight those crippling images, maybe we have what it takes to liberate ourselves from nicotine.

BIRTH AND NEW LIFE

I REMEMBER LYING ON THE VAST WHITE-SHEETED BED AS
though I were on a raft, floating. The white curtains stirred at
the window in the summer air; ripples of sunlight and scents of
green leaves lapped at me. From other rooms, the sounds of the
older children playing came to me as though they were part of
the one sweet element of summer. Beside me, touching my side,
lay the new baby, wrapped and sleeping in her cotton blanket.
Her face was turned to my breast, her hair still misted damp
from the exertion of sucking, her lips just parted from the nipple,
her small fingers wrapped around my larger one. I felt that I held
her alive by the passionate tenderness that flowed out from me
and mixed with the soft air. Her steady breath, minutely rising
and falling, was like the expression and culmination of a love
that I could not separate from the wholeness of the summer
world; it held us both.

She did not know yet that I existed separately. To speak of her
sleep as "trusting" would be wrong. To her, the softness of the
blanket, the warm pulse of sweet milk going down her throat, the
blood heat of my finger, the yielding firmness of my skin, and the
different firmness of the bed were all part of a single blur of
sensation. I felt, lying beside her in the flush of new life, that not
only did I provide her with a universe but that I *was* her universe.
And I felt an eager acquiescence that it should be so.

Fifteen months later, I came home one evening in the midst of
an exhausting election campaign, knowing that the weaning was
almost complete. The baby romped with me on the bed; we
were delighted to come together, like lovers rushing back to the
meeting-place, bringing presents. She staggered about on the
tousled mountain of pillows and blankets, falling onto her bottom
with peals of laughter, giving me the present of her high-spirited
evening with her brother and sister. I laughed with her,

acknowledging her fine confidence and pleasure. Then she lay down beside me for her nightly nursing but, already on her side and one hand on my dress, she lifted her head with its soft wisps of hair and looked at me with a new expression of mischievous inquiry. Something made me feel that it was a question, and I found myself answering, a little sadly, "No more milk; it's all gone." She knelt up beside me with a serious smile, my daughter, our two lives no longer breathing with the same breath, and patted my dress closed with an almost maternal gesture. "All gone," she said, and jumped up again to dance.

Between these two moments, the early nurturing and the weaning, lay, as with my other two children, a time of enfolding intensity that I have never known in any other kind of love or work. I'm quite sure that this mother time was the making of me as a person, and the making of my three children. Yet I've never seen this fundamentally important interaction recognized or ever acknowledged in films, newspapers, magazines, television, popular music, or any of the aggressive, tawdry, or sentimental noise that passes for our culture, and even to speak of it is to put oneself in a defensive and somehow ludicrous minority. This worries me. If that first year or so is as important as I believe it to be, then society ought to make room for it:

I was amazed last week to read that Ontario provincial court Judge Paul Pickett threatened a woman spectator with a contempt-of-court action for breastfeeding her infant daughter in his courtroom. Amazed but not, as the kids say, totally amazed. Only two weeks earlier, a Beaches mom had called me indignantly after she was thrown out of a favourite local restaurant because, its boss claimed, it "turned the stomach" of another customer to see her nursing her baby in a quiet corner.

What a panoply of revulsion we have here! What a recoiling of dainty sensibilities! And how could both these women display so drastic a deficiency in modesty, good sense, and, as the flustered judge would insist, "courtesy"?

Simple. They are in the grip of what the late, great, English psychoanalyst, D. W. Winnicott, called "primary maternal preoccupation". If anyone but a new mother displayed such moon-struck single-mindedness, he claimed, she would instantly be labelled psychotic. But the same behaviour in a new mother is completely normal. For at least three months, as most mothers can tell you, the rise and fall of an Ayatollah or a Ronald Reagan is the merest silly trifle compared with the imperceptible rise and fall of baby's breath.

It's a state of tranced devotion and rapt concentration, and it's a darn lucky thing for babies that mothers give in to it. It's a state of mind in which it would seem almost... well... *discourteous* to ignore baby's cry of hunger. After all, in the unclocked eternity of an infant's every moment, "just a minute" might as well be "forever". A baby can't imagine a five-minute delay. She can't snap her fingers to hurry the waiter along, or nag at the cook, or sneak a little pre-dinner snack. When a creature is that dependent, with a ferocity of need which non-parents simply can't imagine, an immediate response from mother is the barest minimum of courtesy.

We can hardly expect all restaurant owners and provincial judges to be aware of these more refined and delicate shadings of courtesy. Theirs is not a world in which the union between mother and new baby is so close that the breast is no longer an object of lustful regard but simply the way you feed the baby. I learned this lesson years ago when my particularly hungry baby kept interrupting the visit of an old friend. Rather than having to sit in an isolated room, missing the conversation, I decided to nurse the baby where I was. As my hand went to my housecoat zipper, our friend (a calm family man and talented scientist) flung himself back in his chair as though he'd been nipped by a rattlesnake.

"You're not... not going to... well, do *that here*?" babbled the man of science.

It's hard for a new mother to understand that mentality which associates loving nurture with obscene sexual display. But there it is. Two warring views of the world. Which shall prevail? The babies, of course, must have right of way. It is to them that the ultimate courtesy is due. Picture Diane Phillips, caught by a sudden thunderstorm with her toddler and her newborn, taking refuge in a nearly empty restaurant where she and her husband often dine, where she felt she was disturbing no one. Can you imagine the insensitivity of the owner, who told her to nurse the baby in the washroom? What, take a newborn infant into that germ-infested ugly environment and *feed* her there, standing up? And this, if you please, in a society where businessmen love to have lunch with the waitress's bare breasts practically garnishing the salad, while feeding a baby is classed with the excretory functions!

I myself have never seen a nursing mother violate the bounds of polite society. A fold of clothing or baby's blanket usually hides all. Since display is the last thing on her mind (the seamy motives belong to the shocked observers), she is usually discreet to the point of invisibility. Obscenity has never been more clearly in the eye of the beholder.

Primary maternal occupation is universal. You will find the same passionate bond in the high Arctic or the lower Sahara— anywhere, in fact, that it isn't spoiled by external deprivations like famine or other distress. Recently I read in *New York* magazine about the growing group of older professional couples who are having their first babies later in life.

"I've never known anything to enter my life so fully as my child," marvelled a forty-seven-year-old father. "You experience a quantity and quality of love you never imagined before and that is absolutely unique."

A forty-one-year-old vice-president (a mother, this time) said, "It's all such a big surprise. I mean, the emotional attachment you feel toward a child."

An investment banker, who congratulated himself on his prudent fiscal planning before venturing on parenthood, said, "The expenses are working out just fine. But what you can never understand beforehand is the emotional expenditure you're going to be making."

Linda Wolfe, author of the article, was moved to comment on the surprising naïveté of these worldly older parents, who had, until their children came along, "somehow missed out on emotional truths known to the simplest of peasants from time immemorial." The wider truth seems to me to be that our culture has so dismissed the power and importance of parental love, so derided the vitality and beauty of motherhood, so denigrated the tender feelings of the father, that the miracle is that there is anyone left who stumbles on the knowledge that the nurturing of new life is so much more terrifying, painful, exhilarating, illuminating, enraging, exhausting, wonderful, and important than investment banking. Society does not and cannot need anything more than it needs infants who are soundly and lovingly reared.

It is just for these reasons, though, that it's impossible to write about parenthood without kindling the fury of someone upon whose sensibilities you've inadvertently trodden. Modern life, with its infinitely multiplying choices, has inflicted concomitantly more guilt on all of us. It isn't possible to be resigned to fate when there is no fate, only one's own free choice. Parents, with all that emotional intensity in reserve, can be tigerish when you dare to hint that they have made a wrong choice in the most important undertaking of their adult lives. And then, too, since we are dealing with issues as crucial as human life and its capacity for wholesome growth, every decision and every dissent seems fraught with terminal consequence. I recognized, for example, an envious sadness in me when I heard and wrote about a new approach to those crucial post-natal moments:

> Remember one of the most sacred tenets of childhood wisdom? Never touch baby birds you may find in the nest, or the mother bird will abandon them. In fact, it was almost instinctive whenever a child encountered a newborn animal of any kind: hands off, because you might interfere with something delicate and mysterious happening between mother and babies.
>
> We were right. Scientists have long known that all mammals experience a "sensitive period" immediately after giving birth, when a deep bond is formed between mother and offspring. Violate that, and something can go haywire: the mother may reject the infant, leave it to die, or even attack it herself. Why did it take so long to apply the same simple, obvious wisdom to human mothers and babies?
>
> Maybe we've all been so hocus-pocussed by medical wizardry that we didn't stop to think...or dare to question.

What brand-new mother dares to rear up on the delivery table and demand, "Hey, where are you going with my baby?" But scientists in England and the U.S. have been proving for a decade that the "nestling" principle applies just as firmly to human beings. If you don't separate a mother and her baby in that incredible hour after birth—that shaky, exhausted, triumphant, over-whelmingly emotional hour—something terrific happens. Months and even years later those babies are still benefiting from that crucial hour of "mother-infant bonding". They cry less, smile and vocalize more, are healthier, score higher on IQ tests, and are breast-fed longer and more successfully. Rarely are they battered or neglected. All through infancy, they get more cuddling and maternal attention than other babies.

In Toronto, a young psychologist, Dr. Donna Kontos, tried out the new theory on four groups of mothers at St. Michael's Hospital. All the women were matched for similar health, racial, economic, and marital backgrounds. The first group of 12 women had one hour alone with their babies immediately after birth. For half an hour, the naked newborn lay on the mother's stomach, skin-to-skin, under heated blankets. The second half-hour, mother and baby lay close together, face to face. Then the baby was taken to the nursery, and subsequently delivered to the mother every four hours for feeding. A second group had the strict hospital routine: baby whisked away immediately after birth. A third group followed the routine but then had rooming-in (an increasingly popular method of keeping mother and baby together in the same room) for the rest of the hospital stay. The fourth and last group had both "extended early contact" and rooming-in.

Mothers and babies in all groups were observed carefully at birth, and then again at one month and three months post-partum. Sure enough, the early-contact mothers had significantly greater attachment to their babies. They smiled more, cuddled more, looked at their babies face-to-face more, and sang to them more. The rooming-in mothers also showed more "bonding", and those who had both early contact and rooming-in ranked highest of all on Dr. Kontos' checklist.

"What's more interesting is that even those mothers who

had just one extra hour with their infants scored higher three months later," Dr. Kontos remarks. "That shows there is a critical, sensitive period in the hour after birth. In that hour, the newborn is typically quiet and alert, looking around and responding to voices. After that, the baby falls into a deep sleep of three to four hours."

Most of us mothers never had the chance to spend that priceless quiet hour with our newborns. Yet most of us went right on to do a fine and rewarding job of mothering just the same. But think of the few who are emotionally shallow, isolated, potential child abusers. It could be that our hospital routines tip the balance toward inadequate mothering for this minority. Certainly, there's already evidence to show that mothers of incubator babies suffer from a severe loss of self-confidence, at least until they get their babies back in their arms. And mothers who don't have early contact often seem to spend more time cleaning their babies than talking to them, said Dr. Kontos.

Worse still, that standard hospital routine of storing babies in a glass-walled nursery where their mothers can't get at them seems to lead to more breast-feeding failure. And, Dr. Kontos says, there's absolutely no medical reason why hospitals should insist on this potentially damaging separation of mother and baby. Smart hospital administrators are dispensing with those starchy rules. Soon, I hope, new mothers will no longer yearn helplessly outside the glass wall, while their newborns cry helplessly within.

We should have been listening all along to the "baby bird" message: something tender, deep, and essential is transacted between the mother and her new child. Mess around with that at their peril.

It's important to say, over and over again, that every one of us fails as a parent. No one is perfect; no child's childhood (especially from her point of view) is perfect. There is pain and shortcoming as well as love and happiness. Above all, society forces choices upon us for which we may be only partly responsible. A woman who has been conditioned to value her body as an object for the seduction and manipulation of men—a tenuous grasp of power, short-lived as it may be—might, for example, be loath to breast-feed her baby and may disguise her reluctance as an insistence on "being free" or "wanting to share the feedings with her husband". A woman who has no emotional support from her husband may resent the baby's demands, and respond with guilty petulance to talk about maternal responsiveness.

A lucky natural birth, with a healthy baby and a relaxed, intimate breast-feeding, may be the best of all possible worlds. But a fretful mother who feels "tied down" may be better off with the bottle. A happy and well-supported mother at home may be the best beginning for an infant, but if it's a choice between essential income and that roseate picture, then the choice is clear.

What is distressing is not that many mothers make "wrong" choices, but that they are often pushed into those choices and then, of course, told that they must take the blame for any unfortunate consequences. No wonder there's so much keyed-up argument about childbirth. Most women simply aren't aggressive or informed enough to defend themselves against the push and shove of special-interest groups. Medical specialists and drug or equipment manufacturers sometimes place the demands of their ego, status hunger, ambition, or greed above the well-being of infants.

It was a tense, exhilarating, and at moments oddly frightening meeting on "Childbirth in the '80s" In front of a packed and partisan audience, a small drama is acted out which seems to pit two "motherhood" issues against each other.

On one side of the podium, two men. Both are advocates of high-technology childbirth. They want the province to spend upward of $6 million on a glossy new computerized system of maternity care, focused almost exclusively on the 3 per cent of high-risk mothers whose newborns need crisis intervention.

On the other side of the podium, two women. They worry about 85 per cent of normal women giving birth to normal babies. They want warmer, more humane, medically safer environments than the high-tech jungles of the modern hospital.

I am wholeheartedly on their side. Of course, we must have the technology for the minority of babies who are at risk.

But I was nearly killed once by a badly bungled dose of anaesthesia which I neither wanted nor needed but which was forced on me in the course of a perfectly normal delivery. Later I experienced both the triumph and the healthfulness of a natural birth, and the relief of expert medical aid during a difficult birth. Now, after talking to hundreds of other mothers and studying mounds of documents proving the dangers of escalating medical technology, I am convinced that women should have far more choice and far more say in the design of maternity care.

That's why I felt subtly menaced by the two men on the panel with their bland assumption of "scientific" authority. They were Dr. Paul Swyer, chief of the famous neonatal unit at the Hospital for Sick Children and rightly a hero to those whose tiny babies he has saved; and John Aitchison, an engineer, president of Bell Northern Software Research, and chairman of a hospital council committee whose report is the subject of hot current debate.

The men monopolized the stage, using twice their allotted time to flood us with self-justifying statistics—all of which have been disputed by other authorities. With their glib technocratese, their relentless focus on machinery, management, control, salaries, and hierarchies, it was like listening to a discussion of the F-16 fighter plane.

The women, on the other hand, were fast, smart, down-to-earth, and convincing. And they got the only laughs of the evening. Family physician Dr. Cynthia Carver and York University anthropologist Dr. Shelly Romalis worry, as I do, that once all that gleaming medical machinery is in place it will be used indiscriminately. Indeed, with runaway technology in the labour room, that's already happening, despite the more humane "frills" of father participation and rooming-in. The audience laughed and groaned, with a kind of shudder of recognition, as Romalis described the routine now imposed on normal women giving birth: arrival at hospital, wheelchair, enema, prepping, sterile drapes, lying on a table while an electronic probe is inserted in the vagina and attached to the skull of the unborn baby, stirrups, anaesthesia, episiotomy, and often, forceps delivery....

It's the American way of birth, all right, and it's what these men want us to import. But, here's the blood-chilling fact: the American way of birth doesn't work. The U.S. ranks about 19th in the world in infant mortality, despite (or perhaps because of?) its high-technology birth procedures. Holland, for example, has a much lower rate of newborn deaths, yet 38 per cent of the babies are born at home, with trained midwives. We need both approaches to childbirth: the whiz-kid technology for the high-risk few, and the sensitive care, better nutrition, and non-smoking programs, plus more natural birthing, that have produced much lower mortality rates in countries like Sweden.

If the Ontario government buys Aitchison's Big Business model for maternity care, it's buying a costly dinosaur. The consumer health movement has come into its own. Now is the time to give equal power and equal say to the women and the public health experts who understand that giving birth is not a disease.

Looking back, I see that I shouldn't have been surprised by the vehemence of the response to this column. My own strong feelings about childbirth should have alerted me to the equally strong convictions that would be held for the other side of the argument. And I think I was wrong, too, in my follow-up column, to accuse some readers of worshipping doctors. Their fury sprang not from the insult to medicine, but from their own very natural outrage and profound pain that they had not been fortunate enough to have the easy, natural birth or the perfect child of their dreams:

We are a nation still enslaved to the priestly magic of medicine; we might as well dance around bonfires and carve ourselves with blue tattoos. If modern medicine is not a religion, can anyone tell me why the slightest questioning of the Doctor-hood brings down venom and abuse on the questioner's head?

To be fair, after I criticized the proposal to have the government of Ontario spend $6 million to surround childbirth with more and more technology, there were far more letters of delighted agreement than there were of snide insult.

But it's the vituperation that interests me. Especially the charge, from several mothers of the brain-damaged, that I am "smug", that I "laugh" at those with damaged children, and that I want to "deprive high-risk women of healthy babies so that a few fanatics can have a party while they deliver."

No, no, no, no. You are convinced, possibly because of your personal tragedies, that doctors hold the key to healthy babies. I am not convinced. Though perinatal technology may snatch some babies back from the jaws of death, the evidence is now slowly and horrifyingly building that high-technology childbirth may kill and maim as well. It's precisely the health and well-being of the baby, not the "joyful experience" of the mother, which is at issue here.

We know, for example, that routine hospital practice has grossly interfered with normal breast-feeding and mother-infant bonding, and some experts have already traced an epidemic of child abuse and learning-handicapped children back to this early medical intervention.

My second example: electronic fetal monitoring, one of the highly touted tools of the new childbirth technology. It's supposed to be magically better than the old system of an experienced nurse or doctor listening to the unborn baby's heartbeat with ear and stethoscope. EFM, as it's called, involves wiring the mother during labour, either externally or by inserting a probe into her vagina and attaching electrodes to the unborn baby's scalp.

Major studies, including Banta and Thacker's research for the U.S. department of health, show that EFM is of no proven benefit to the majority of mothers. Quite the contrary. It's dangerous: it can lacerate the mother internally, and cause infection and stress during labour, and it instantly depresses the baby's heart rate. Which is one reason why it has led to a huge increase (some say 30 per cent to 50 per cent) in the rate of Caesarians, with their higher risk of infant and maternal death and damage. But the sale of EFM equipment is a $30-million-a-year business in the U.S.

The angry mothers who wrote me insist that we need this kind of technology for the 3 per cent of mothers who are high risk. But the sinister truth is that procedures like EFM are being foisted on nearly everyone. Once a technology exists, it gets used, whether or not it is risky and unnecessary. What about labour which is induced for the physician's convenience, resulting all too often in premature or Caesarian births? What about the known and proven risks of anaesthesia? One U.S. study claims that drugging in childbirth leads to respiratory distress and to widespread minimal brain damage—an average loss of 4 IQ points per baby.

I received a sad and cogent letter from a woman who was a senior nurse in the Hospital for Sick Children's neonatal unit. She was sickened, finally, by the focus on machinery and by the procession of passive mothers who politely acquiesced to everything. She was one of dozens of women who wrote to me to argue for two themes: preventive medicine and humane options in childbirth.

Maybe, just maybe, the clear-eyed iconoclasts will soon outnumber the tranced worshippers at the medical shrine. When that day comes, we can at last work out some reasonable compromises in childbirth, so that intervention is kept in sane balance with prevention.

It is only a very small minority of Canadians, though, who engage themselves in such arcane disputes about the proper way to bring babies into the world. For most young Canadians, babies have become as quaintly rare as spinning wheels. When was the last time you saw a normal, contentedly pregnant woman in a film?

Of course, it is mostly men who make the movies and write the popular songs, and ever since the Industrial Revolution they have been pried loose from fatherhood and sent out into the work place away from home. No wonder so many are alienated from family bonds; anyone who has ever been responsible for the daily care of a baby knows that love and attachment grow with the quotidian rhythm of physical care, and since men have been deprived of that opportunity, their bonding is more tenuous and their relationship with their children can slip all too easily into a pattern of law enforcement rather than loving response. The occasional venture that glorifies the father (*Kramer* vs *Kramer*,

Ordinary People) is an exception that proves the rule; ordinary fatherhood is seen as an extraordinary achievement, so rare as to be ennobling. This is a tragedy of enormous proportions.

No wonder that ever since widespread contraception gave women the choice, for the first time in history, to procreate or to move into the more highly valued world of male achievement, more and more Canadian women duly took the latter path. If motherhood wins you nothing more than zero personal income, lost seniority at work, years of isolation, and no community support, and, on top of that, a Philip Rothian contempt from the popular culture... then why bother?

Choice is possible. And since choice has become second nature to us, we have failed to notice that we are living in what history will undoubtedly come to call the Era of Birth Control. Far more than nuclear weapons (though they may indeed have the final impact, in which case there will be no history), birth control has shaken our times, tilted all our familiar patterns askew, and sent us sliding helplessly in several new directions like coloured chips in a kaleidoscope.

Now that there is a choice, the rewards of motherhood are less obvious—especially to a generation raised on the instant gratifications and plastic thrills of television. If you have been conditioned to lust after perishable high-tech toys and treats, and to aspire to the subtle chic of predatory sex as a consumer item, the glamour of diaper-changing and floor-scrubbing may seem elusive. Feminism has little to do with it.

Of course, that also depends on the brand of feminism you buy. I've often observed that the minority of feminists who make a bitter and negative analysis of motherhood are those who are far too young to have contemplated having babies, or those who have never had babies, or those who have had theirs and are safely past the time of having to make a choice.

Women, however, have not traditionally had the choice to opt out of motherhood and its attendant lack of personal freedom. Without a doubt, the physical realities of maternity have kept women dependent on men through all of history. As a child, I was enraged by that inexorable fate—and, let's be honest, I was also the youngest in my family and consequently irritated by any babies who happened along to steal my limelight. I resolved then that childlessness was the only free and reasonable state for an adult woman bent on equality.

I began to change my mind, rather sheepishly, when reality moved in on me in the shape of my first pregnancy. I had never experienced such triumphant elation. My lifelong grudge against male privilege melted away into a gentle pity for creatures who could never know the ripeness of procreation. Feminism, I realized as I plunged into that honeyed babymoon, must take account of the life imperative. A philosophy that denies or ignores what so many women experience as central is not much of an analysis.

Indeed, many women I know manage to combine feminism and motherhood in a comfortably pragmatic blend. They are aware that the price of motherhood is very high, and feel that the cost should be shared more democratically than it is now. Feminists have been among those who fought for more humane childbirth, maternity pay, day care, neighbourhood support centres, and a heightened social empathy for the tasks of parenthood. Feminists mothers have been the fiercest exponents of a more generous view: more help for mamas, less blaming, less singling out of mother when things go wrong.

Despite everything, men and women continue to make loving homes together in which to raise up children. Of course, they can't help being affected by our collective contempt for the child-rearing process. Constant demands for "adult only" apartments and "child-free" restaurants remind us that parenthood, with all its mess, emotion, and long-term commitment, is unfashionable. The emotional numbness and fitful sensation-seeking that characterize our culture may well undercut parents' ties to one another and to their children. And yet — most marriages will not end in divorce, and most children will not be badly damaged, and most parents will make the usual number of mistakes and still manage to raise happy and capable youngsters. The naturalness of the process struck me again one day when my sister-in-law visited our home with her young son:

> Our little nephew Benjamin visited us the other day. All other serious column ideas immediately decamped. A 9-week-old redhead with a sense of humour and Delft blue eyes is more

enchanting, when you stop to think of it, than another dreary column on food prices or equality.

I was watching Benjamin play a game with his mother, Wendy. He lay cradled in Wendy's outstretched arms, looking up at her, with his very small pyjamaed feet planted on her stomach. She was babbling one of those mother-babbles (something like "abba-babba-BA" that makes you wince when you see it in print), and, on the "Ba" syllable, jumping him up in the air. What made it into a game was that now and then Wendy would break the rhythm and stop. Benjamin would lie there looking expectant. Then a toothless grin would dawn on his face, he'd kick his feet out straight as though Wendy's tummy were a trampoline, and start the jump himself with his own version of the babble: "A-a-ah!"

The game is fascinating, not because it's unique, but because it's part of a universal pattern. And not only are such impromptu games the stuff of which human beings are made, but they are so serious and important that the entire Board of Education could crumble and, so long as parents and babies kept playing, children would still grow up happy and intelligent.

Wonderful baby play depends on the presence of someone who is absolutely crazy bezonkers mad keen about the baby. A bored babysitter won't do. An exhausted, permanently distracted mother probably isn't up to it. It has to be someone who is so delightedly interested in the baby that she (or he) will good-naturedly go on repeating that silly game so long as it amuses him. She has to be alive and alert enough to the baby's feelings that she spots the exact moment when he grins and wiggles his toes and is ready to add his bit to the game. And in order to notice that, she has to be the same caring person who was there last week and yesterday and will be there tomorrow; continuity is all important. Given all these subtle preconditions, she will register the baby's toe wiggle, know what he means, and change the game to make room for the baby's new initiative.

From fragile and fleeting moments like this, a baby like Benjamin fuzzily begins to learn that someone is paying attention and cares about his impulses; that if you give a smile, you get a smile; that he is not passive and helpless but can set his body in motion by his own will; that this motion is pleasurable; that there is a pattern to events, something like cause and effect; that sounds other than crying can be repeated and mean something; that eating and sleeping aren't the only gratifications; that the world is a good and safe place...

Caring for a baby is made up of thousands of these moments every day. The ignorant may scoff; they may assume that baby care is all burps and diapers and mindless janitorial work. But the most sophisticated educational psychologist in the world couldn't duplicate what is going on here—unless, of course, it's with her own baby—because this is learning without teaching, learning enabled and enriched by the sheer loving responsiveness of the adult.

AFTER THE PAMPERS

I AM SITTING DOWN TO WRITE THIS ON A DAY WHEN I HAVE just learned that a friend's beloved youngest child was killed last night by a drunken driver. That news has filled up all the space in my mind, in my room, and in my typewriter; it turns into reality the unspoken fear that is present as the background of all the columns in this chapter.

Most of us undertake the enterprise of parenthood so lightly. We don't realize in the moment of our loving embrace, or even as the fruitful months of pregnancy ripen onward, that we are about to become lifelong hostages to the world's most unbearable threat: the loss of a child. I don't think I'm any more morbid than other parents. I wonder if they, like me, savour the preciousness of everyday life all the more intensely because, now and then, they also taste the bitter undertone of threat, the possibility of the ultimate agony striking at random.

All of us know that one day we must part with our parents. Most of us realize, however unwillingly, that partners must part. But none of us, I think, can face that violation of the human order which is death of one's child and therefore of one's future. Back in 1978, in the wake of a terrible news story, I tried to write about the dark pit of fear over which we skate so lightly every day of our lives:

> All over the country, parents flinched in empathetic horror from the tragedy of the St. John's School canoe trip and the sudden storm that stole 13 young lives on Lake Timiskaming.
>
> The news of any child's death is like salt on an open wound to someone who is a parent…the ultimate nightmare, the blow we feel we could not face. It's as though, when we first have children, we peel off a top layer of skin. For the rest of our lives, we're extra-vulnerable. When the parents of St.

181

John's are bereaved, we can't help but share some of the pain, a wrench of fellow-feeling that goes far beyond the conventional sympathy.

It's a strange fact of life that we first begin to believe in death in the months after we give birth. Up until then, we're immune; death is so unthinkable that it's a mere abstraction. But once we hold our own baby in our arms, we've got a stake in life so immense that the possibility of its loss becomes heart-shakingly real. Just last week, before we were all haunted by those upturned canoes on Lake Timiskaming, a colleague of mine was musing about this underlying thread of fear. "People keep telling you to let go of your kids, let them be independent. I allow my 10-year-old daughter to ride her bike to school, because everyone said I'd be overprotective if I didn't. Then I was driving to work and saw her riding down the middle of the road and through a stop sign."

All of child-rearing is a gradual letting go, inch by inch. You let the one-year-old win the fight to crawl to the farthest corner of the room; you let the two-year-old negotiate the stairs; you try not to tread on the back wheels of the trike as the three-year-old pedals down the sidewalk. There's tremendous pressure on parents, as my friend discovered, not to be "overprotective". One school of thought (the St. John's school of thought, as it turns out) says that boys especially have to take risks and overcome hardships in order to "become men", to have self-respect, to gain the toughness to compete and win in adult life. My personal school of thought is that any child's life is already filled with enough crises and hardships without imposing artificial (but really dangerous) ones.

A baby copes with danger when he experiences the fear of abandonment, or the tremendous rage that threatens to shake apart his fragile emotional safety. A kindergarten child copes with big-city danger every day, conquering the lump of ice in his stomach when he confronts speeding traffic, gangs of bullies, or dogs as tall as he is. And surely all of us can remember the more looming dangers in the mind against which we struggled nightly: the fears that our parents might die, that a fire might leap through the house. We can't really protect them from all that. Half the time, we don't even know what secret adversary they are wrestling in their minds. And when it comes to real, physical dangers, we always have to walk the tightrope between their impatience to be free and our unspoken knowledge of how easily things can go wrong.

I haven't yet reached the point when I'll have to worry about the fool who will take one drink too many before driving my daughter home from a party, or the impulsive moment of teenage bravado when my son will dare a stunt too daring on some yet unimagined motorcycle. Yet I know that tonight, when I read in the papers again about those 13 lost lives, I'll have to choke back the urge to babble admonitions about the future: "Don't ever ride a motorcycle in city traffic... don't walk alone in parks at night..."

The young, rightly, would laugh off these parental fears. We have to rely on the hope that we've brought them up so that they're not self-destructive, not so insecure that they'll have to prove themselves dangerously. Meanwhile, we have our fears to conquer. Chief among them, I think, is the fear of being labelled "overprotective". Few mothers I know can cope with this put-down from a school principal or male sports director. Instinctively, we feel that our primitive mother urge must be wrong, exaggerated, a drag on our children's independence. Then we hear about a tragedy like St. John's, and we know what those parents must feel today. I hope that their grief is not shadowed by agonizing self-reproach. We all struggle to know what is right for our children; our hearts are sore for those from whom luck looked away.

A multiple tragedy is the dramatic extreme of a parent's dilemma. Its opposite is small-scale daily survival; he or she who has never been a full-time parent of a preschooler cannot know how that daily task challenges the soul. Even a teacher who spends every day with six-year-olds can have no idea of how much harder it is to be the loving, angry, frustrated, exhausted, adoring, and disorganized person who is responsible, when you come right down to it, for every inhalation and exhalation of that small child, every hiccup and undone shoelace, every wrinkle of the id and ego. What makes it all so much more difficult is that none of the minute-by-minute challenges are clearly identified as critical moments up to which one must live. If you could only remember, as you lean down to pick up the hurled teething biscuit for the tenth time in one day, that this is an important act of parenthood and not just another ache in the small of your back.

Nothing arouses my furious scorn more quickly than the auntie or dad who babysits a five-year-old for a day or two and pronounces it all a breeze. Or the childless teacher who offers up a complete psychiatric diagnosis, complete with brilliant smile and nod of dismissal, to the parent in the open-house line-up. Nothing goads me to a more baffled state of perplexity than the vast, yawning indifference of society to the lives and problems of parents.

The problem is an urgent one: How can we enable parents to do a better job of child-rearing?

Everyone is bitterly aware of the failures. So many blank-eyed vandals, mindlessly destroying what the rest of us must pay for. More and more damaged kids, stacked in a holding pattern like faltering airplanes around our jammed treatment centres. More and more semi-literates zonked out on rock and grass and 15 years of immersion-TV. See them jerking and twitching, wired to their pinball nirvana.

Hardly anyone agrees about the causes. Hardly anyone, aside from an overworked core of professionals, plugs away at prevention and cure. For most people, it's enough to have a nice, satisfying rant now and then when something dreadful happens. Let there be a murder and the land is filled, briefly, with the buzz of axes being ground. (Welfare! Godlessness! Feminism! Permissiveness!) Meanwhile, quietly, some people go on working away at the real roots of the problem. Character, trust, optimism, imagination, decency, all are nourished in infancy. We know the first six months are crucial, and that the warmly responsive mother—babbling back to her baby, playing peek-a-boo, stimulating speech and play—is a more solid foundation for school achievement than all the punitive "3Rs" programs you can invent later on.

But such richly alive parenting is a learned skill, and there aren't many experienced grannies and aunties living next door any more. A typical young mother in suburbia is isolated, with no one to talk to for seven hours a day. It's hard for her to be a joyfully creative mother. Besides, she doesn't know the moves. She may never have held a baby before she held her own.

This isn't a big flaming cause. You can't spout fire and brimstone about young mothers who are too unsure or emotionally malnourished themselves to do the best job with their infants. It's hard to raise money for the cure to this malady because the remedies don't sound hot-shot and dramatic enough. The government will cough up millions for high-technology gizmos for premature babies (ah, the prestige, the big bucks, the medical hoo-hah, the lovely quantifiable machinery of it all), but a few thousand dollars for a simple, down-to-earth project to help women become better mothers? Forget it.

And yet. And yet such projects do spring up and struggle along, because the real need is there. Some mothers approached Sacred Heart Children's Village, a treatment centre in Scarborough, and said they wanted a self-help group. Sacred Heart was enthusiastic. Now, thanks to a handsome grant from the Sisters of St. Joseph, and rooms lent by an Ontario Housing Corporation building on Kennedy Ave., the Mums and Tots Drop-In is a five-morning-a-week, rip-snorting success. More than 30 mothers (part-time workers, married, single, a few on welfare, more who are not) come, free of charge, for mothers' discussion groups and an expert play program for babies and toddlers. An alert mother can learn a lot just watching the early childhood specialist draw the youngsters into song, games, crafts, and imaginative play.

I sat in, one cheerful morning, as Bonnie, a newcomer to the new mothers' group, cracked everyone up with her wry wit. "The pediatrician's appointment is my big excitement," she said. "Getting up! Choosing something to wear! Going out on the street and then talking to someone!"

In both mothers' groups that morning, the mood was warm and excitable with the pleasure of shop talk: temper tantrums, bargain stores, toilet training, nutrition. My baby days are long gone, but the memory is still vivid of that intensity and preoccupation. And the fatigue. And the need to talk with other women who were equally immersed in the most important job of all.

The mothers talked about how low their self-esteem had fallen ("We're doing the dirtiest jobs, eh?") and how they went home singing, charged up, from the group. These mothers weren't in trouble with their babies to start with. But they could easily have become overwhelmed and confused, swatting their kids into silence instead of loving them into growth. The Mums and Tots Drop-In is just one good answer. There are others. Such small-scale and unpretentious efforts are our best hope because they strengthen what is good and prevent pain before it happens.

It's fashionable nowadays to sneer at all the experts who have blighted our fine, feckless spontaneity as parents. This view may be shared by all those who spontaneously know how to *be* parents — after my first two, I felt pretty fine and feckless myself. Earlier, however, I found myself in the position of the youngest child of a family, one who had never watched a diaper being changed or even experienced holding a baby in my arms...and there I was, getting into our car while a smiling nurse plunked a little pink-wrapped bundle in my arms, said "Enjoy your baby!" and whisked back into the hospital. I promptly burst into tears. "Oh, please," I silently whispered to some hoped-for deity, "just let me keep her alive till she's at least sixteen." I didn't dare hope for any more than that, given the abysmal absence of any child-rearing skills. Luckily, it turned out that children themselves are the best teachers.

When my two oldest children were very small, in the late 1960s, there was virtually nothing available to help the parent with sex education. Vague admonitions to "tell them just what they ask and no more" didn't really prepare me for that day when they asked for the "more" that I was leaving out.

In my day, we learned about sex in giggling groups under the streetlights after supper. The shrieks of laughter were wrenched from us in shock and disbelief as big kids of 8 or 9 told us, in brutal four-letter words, how we had been conceived. The mystery was all the more obscene and frightening because the clues were so fragmentary: dogs seen copulating, jokes overheard.

Would you believe that, for the vast majority of kids, it's still like that? Recent studies in England and the United States show that more than half the parents of 11-year-olds have never mentioned intercourse; even fewer talk about birth control; 40 per cent of the prepubescent girls had never heard about menstruation from their parents; fewer than 2 per cent of parents told their boys about wet dreams.

If anything could point up the tragi-comic silliness of human nature, it must be this paralyzing shyness between parents and children. We spend thousands of dollars and hours of concern on their orange juice and nursery schools, and then send them out to learn about sex from the porno books at the corner store and the smutty half-truths of Grade 5 sophisticates.

Some kids, of course, raise their parents more astutely than others. My own, for example, neatly ambushed me when I was still smugly thinking how enlightened I would be three or four years down the road. Unsuspectingly, I strolled into the middle of a debate between my 2-year-old son and 3-year-old daughter.

"I say that mummies make the babies," my daughter explained, "but he says daddies do, too."

"Yes, mummies and daddies both," I beamed. I congratulated myself on not telling them more than they wanted to know, and figured our first little step in sex ed. was all wrapped up.

"What do the daddies do?" my daughter pounced. I fought down my surprised laughter and ploughed on with a vivid account of the happy adventures of egg and sperm. All this, I was shakily feeling, was a bit much and a bit soon.

It wasn't over yet. A light dawned on my son's face, a light which I later came to recognize as the spirit of enraptured scientific inquiry. "How does daddy get the sperm to the egg?" he asked sweetly.

And that's how two kids not yet old enough for tricycles taught me to speak straight and true when serious questions were being asked.

All children wrestle with the profound questions of life and death, whether we want to recognize it or not. At 5, my daughter wanted to know whether people made babies every time they made love. Enter the subject of birth control. The conversation resumed a year later, when she asked what happened if people made babies by accident. (There were adopted kids in the neighbourhood, and an unwed teenage mother.) I said what I could about how love and acceptance sometimes grow along with the baby. And about adoption. And, when pressed, about abortion. There was a long silence. "Are you telling me," she said, in a tensely contained voice, "that some mothers kill their babies before they're born?"

So then our talking rippled out to encompass the agony of choices, morality, and the care men and women owe each other. It's been like that with all three of them. Over the years, as they check out with me the whispered rumours of perversions, dangers, the mechanisms of sex, and the discoveries of their own bodies, their fierce urge has been not only to know, but to sort out their own ideas of right and wrong.

Maybe the listening is a hard discipline because we're as caught up in the big questions as the children are. The other night, my 8-year-old whispered to me, from the midst of a bedtime hug, that I should dye the new gray hairs I'm beginning to sprout. I knew what she was saying; I've reassured her so many times that most people die when they're very old. So I whispered back that I could be counted on for a good many years yet.

The thoughts of childhood are very long and deep. Birth, death, love, and safety are all intertwined, and if we brush aside one of those questions because we aren't ready, we may never get to hear the others.

The first time I was surprised into openness remains very vivid in my memory. It's a kind of benchmark to which I return again and again in my dealings with children, to test how well I'm measuring up. When my first child, Ilana, was one and a half years old, she had a particularly tender relationship with my gruff father. It was a relationship that proceeded in spite of my rather grudging watchful eye: I was far too old to remember first-hand my father's adoration of babies, and my relationship with him was far too prickly to allow either of us to recognize or admit that we loved each other. Nevertheless, my small and blue-eyed charmer doted on her "pa-pa". I remember a winter day when, reluctantly, I had to press my father into emergency babysitting. I delivered Ilana to my parents' house, gave my father a long list of fussy instructions, and told him not to bother taking her out, since he would never be able to manage the complexities of her snowsuit and boots. When I returned, a couple of hours later, it was just in time to catch a glimpse of them from the back, heading down the snowy street for a walk... the big old man in his seventies, with his shambling walk, and the tiny girl in an elfin-hooded snowsuit — mittens dangling cockeyed, boots on the wrong feet and desperately unbuckled, but her hand reached up to fit snugly into his and both of them expressing total contentment in every line of their bodies.

A month later, he died very suddenly. I moved into my mother's house with the baby to keep my mother company in the next trying weeks. For the first few days, I didn't recognize the baby's restlessness. Then one day I stood at the bottom of the stairs and watched her climb doggedly, one step at a time, bent on some private search of the upstairs bedrooms. A few minutes later she was back and climbing down, backwards. Half way down she stopped, turned around, and fixed me with a worried blue stare. "Pa-pa all gone?" she asked.

It had not occurred to me to explain to a one-and-half-year-old infant that she would never see her pa-pa again, and indeed, faced with the sudden illumination that I had neglected something important, I could do no better than to nod and say sadly, "Yes, pa-pa all gone."

I learned, in that moment, that adults underrate children's comprehension so severely that it's as though we inhabit two different worlds... and our adult one is the more ignorant.

Of course, parents have to keep re-learning this simple lesson about telling the truth to children. It's as though we get so caught up in the country of adult complications that we forget that children are fellow citizens. And while it's true that none of us can control the emotional weather to create a perfect climate for them, we shouldn't forget, either, that when things go wrong, the same rain falls on their heads as falls on ours.

Divorce is like escaping from a burning house," Warner Troyer says to me. "If a whole family jumps out of the second-story window, everyone's bound to be hurt a little. Would anyone say, 'It's only a broken arm; don't bother calling the ambulance'?"

If anyone has a right to grin rather fiercely while bandying around these metaphors of pain, it's Troyer, a twice-divorced father of eight, who has spent the past two years listening to 400 kids talking about their emotional bruises, cuts and broken bones. Funnily enough, the resultant book, *Divorced Kids*, isn't bleak or pessimistic. Yet eight New York publishers rejected the manuscript, some with angry comments like this one: "I'm divorced myself, and my son has not been the slightest bit affected."

Troyer laughs at the recollection. "I'm like a walking Rorschach test. I could almost tell you people's marital history depending on how they react to the book." Unbelievably, almost all the divorced adults interviewed for the book were adamant in their refusal to call the ambulance. "Children are so adaptable," they kept telling him.

Troyer knows all about these glib disclaimers. He used them himself—until he started listening to children in his role of "travelling bartender", the impersonal outsider with the tape recorder. Their voices (and most of the book consists of their conversation) are blunt and uncomfortably shrewd about clumsy adult lies and deceptions. The little ones are, by turns, wistful and pragmatic. ("We don't need no Daddy," says a 4-year-old. "Mummy cuts my meat. I can do it too.") The practised cynicism of the older children, coupled with their wide-open vulnerability, makes you wince. But it's fascinating, useful stuff.

"At first it was very painful," Troyer admits. "Then it was humiliating to realize I'd made all the blunders these kids were talking about. And finally it was amusing. My own kids laughed at me. They said 'Dad, we could have told you all that if you'd ever thought to ask us.'"

Walk into any big city classroom and one-third of the children will be "divorced". They, too, could tell you what Troyer found out:

That kids need warning of the cataclysm to come. Almost all the kids in the book were stunned by the suddenness of the separation. "My Daddy went away and said he'd be back at 7:30 and then my Mummy came instead...and I didn't see my Daddy any more and now I can't see him." The sense of betrayal and loss is ferocious.

That they need to be told they are not guilty of causing the separation. "The biggest surprise to me was their guilt," Troyer says.

That they need, desperately, someone who will listen to them seriously. "Parents get to talk to their lawyers, but who do we talk to?"

That the complete loss of one parent is an agony. Surprisingly, Troyer avoids special pleading; he doesn't rage against the manipulative mothers or the callous fathers. "My focus is on what the kids said they needed." And what they said was that, beyond all reason or family feuding, they were doggedly, breathtakingly loyal and loving to both parents.

That grandparents, relatives, and friends idiotically but consistently shun the newly divorced child—just at the point when the separating parents are steeped in self-absorption and rancour, and when the child most urgently needs loving attention and affectionate role models.

That, contrary to prevailing myths, kids often welcome a parent's new lover or mate if it brings real happiness to the parent. New relationships enrage and alienate the kids only when the mother is promiscuous, when the adults lie about what's going on, when the new partner tries to buy love with gifts, when the new boyfriend butts in as an authority figure, or when the new girlfriend asks to be called "Mom".

That, most of all, they need to know what's going on. It's their lives, too. Thanks to adult stupidity, too many of them are in a kind of permanent mourning. Typically, one small girl whose father lived only 30 blocks away was kept in the dark: "I don't even know where he is. Maybe he's dead. Maybe he's trying to find me and doesn't know where I am."

Hostages in an adult game. Anyone who thinks their child, or their nephew, neighbour, or grandchild, came through a divorce untouched should grab Troyer's book. It's worth the pain of self-knowledge, because, as Troyer bravely shows us, there are ways to make it better.

It's a measure of our increasingly conservative times that we have less and less patience with the foibles of the young, less tolerance for the "pain of self-knowledge" it would take to change our behaviour as well as theirs. A rash of parent-education courses has spread across the country. Some are helpfully supportive; some try to teach the parents to manipulate children into the desired responses; others lean on catch-phrases like "consequences" or "tough love". Flailing about for help with children who have turned out so differently from what was expected, many of us resort to the quick painkiller of blaming someone else—preferably the school, other kids, or our own kids. Anyone but ourselves.

For a few years there, having children seemed almost trendy. Grown-up flower children were settling down to raise families with a new fervour of commitment. Backpacks were every-where, co-op nurseries sprang up like daisies, and innovative playgrounds were the rage. Now, suddenly, the talk is all of discipline versus permissiveness. Time to slap on some con-trols, say disgruntled adults. Suddenly, it seems, Canadians have gone sour on their kids.

The backlash has gone further than we may imagine. Parents in their thousands are snapping up *Dare to Discipline*, a paperback by James Dobson, which proposes that we use pain to control our children.

"The shoulder muscle is a surprisingly useful source of minor pain; actually, it was created expressly for school teachers," chuckles Dobson, explaining how to squeeze the muscle hard enough to force a child into obedience. Approv-ingly, Dobson tells how his own mother "cracked him with a shoe, or a handy belt", and once thrashed him with a buckled corset. His pièce de résistance, though, is a description of a "desirable" incident when the mother of a 15-month-old girl ordered the child not to step outside the door while the mother went out to get firewood.

"Suzie decided she didn't want to mind her mother," says

Dobson, so mother "stung her little legs a few times with a switch."

Dobson sees children as a "Now Generation" out of control, spoiled rotten by "too much love". His imagery is revealing. Kids, even babies, are described as "brazen, defiant, stiff-necked, rebellious". A parent will draw a line, says Dobson, and the child will "flop his big hairy toe over that line." Any show of defiance by a child under 10, he says, should be met instantly with the application of pain, a "marvellous purifier".

One night, Dobson's book was being promoted (though he underplayed the "pain principle") by a Thunder Bay high school teacher on a TV talk and phone-in show in which I participated. The viewers voted, by a narrow edge, that Ontario should keep the strap in the schools. Caller after caller wanted to bring back corporal punishment. A policeman vowed that my approach of loving attention "scared him to death." He had been strapped in school, he said, and he wanted his 6-year-old son to have the same experience.

What's going on here? I have the glimmering of a theory. Dobson and his followers are frightened and angered by youngsters whom they see as sullen, rebellious, ungrateful, and immoral little vandals. Well, nobody's urging with their revulsion. Who can warm to a pot-smoking schoolyard bully of 12? Where Dobson gets muddled is in his definitions. These spoiled kids, he says, are the products of "permissive" parents who give too much love and not enough discipline. These "too-loving" parents, he says, let their kids run wild, indulging them one minute, screaming at them the next.

Since when is this the hallmark of a loving parent? These are lazy, unloving parents who have emotionally abandoned their kids. They're not "permissive", they're plain inadequate. Love is hard work—a lot harder than letting your children nod out in front of the TV four hours a day, smiling sweetly when you first order them to bed and resorting to screams and blows half an hour later. That's not love; that's laziness.

It's tough work responding to every cry of a newborn infant. It's hard to hear the fright or anger in your 2-year-old's tantrum and not to respond with a tantrum of your own. It's

hard to tune out your own concerns and listen to a pestering
3-year-old with such concentrated attention that you suddenly understand his behaviour isn't defiance...it's despair
about being left at a strange babysitter's house. When you're
overworked and worried about the mortgage, it's hellishly
hard not to respond to a 4-year-old's plea for a new trike with
an impatient dismissal, a rude put-down, or a bribe of candy.
Taking the time to listen, taking it seriously, working out
alternatives with the child...that's what I call loving work.

The best children I know—the most self-disciplined, creative, alive, and affectionate—have had this kind of "permissive" attention. The most successful children in school are
those whose teachers respect them, listen to them, involve
them in planning and rule-making, and treat them as worthy
human beings. The whiners, the obnoxious kids, the sullen
little despoilers...maybe they're the ones with self-absorbed
parents who didn't try hard enough, who veered sloppily
between emotional neglect and angry attempts at control.

Maybe the parents who lust after simple answers (the
strap, discipline, control) are counsellors of despair. Perhaps
they failed to love early enough and intelligently enough.
Parental devotion isn't measured out in absent-minded
indulgence or in blows. It's measured out in concentrated
hours of serious attention being paid. And, as heaven is my
witness, the rewards are more joyful and more glorious than
the child-swatters will ever know.

The loving work of parenthood is so much more difficult than for
previous generations. Time was when parents might reasonably
assume that their children, in the familiar biosphere of the home,
would grow leaf and branch like their parents. No one in my
childhood had to worry about my values or beliefs. The boundaries of my parents' world were close and inviolate, and within
their parentdom our imprinting, for better or for worse, took
place undisturbed.

Then came television, the Great Leveller, mowing down all
the bright young minds to the same stunted level, the same
limping, maimed language of Los Angeles parking-lot attendants
or Brooklyn cops. Television's children have escaped their par-

ent's realm through the magic box. Today, middle-class parents listen aghast as their children demand junk food, threaten aggression with the language of cheap criminals, and address each other in the telegraphic gruntings of the cartoons. If parents want their children to grow up with some of the familial values, they can no longer rely on osmosis. They will have to fight to protect the child's time for wholesome play, and to prevent tawdry commercial desires and attitudes from reigning supreme in their child's mind.

It's not an easy battle. Most of us are outnumbered, out-smarted, and outgunned by the fellas who run the TV empires. I sometimes wonder, when people worry about the stranger who might tamper with their child, whether they are at all concerned about the molester who has possession of their child four hours a day. He is the Phantom Babysitter, and he's a menace.

Take an honest look at it. Your child, if she's an average Canadian kid, will spend about four hours a day, every day, hypnotized by the Phantom's strobe-lit fantasyland. By the time she's 11 she'll have thrown away more of her childhood hours in television-viewing than in any other activity except sleep. Typically, she'll have started mainlining TV at the age of 2.

I've been watching, studying, and writing about children's television for some years. I believe it's no coincidence that we now have a high incidence of impulsive, hyper kids who insist on instant gratification, who show massive rates of learning disabilities, who often seem to gloss over a yawning emotional vacuity with a brassy sophistication beyond their years.

The Phantom is the most powerful teacher in history. Both Canadian and U.S. researches show that violent television encourages children to hurt other children, to use brute force as a quick and moral solution to problems, and to be casually callous to the sufferings of others. Programming clichés have spawned a whole adult society with twisted perceptions of reality: in the U.S., adult viewers who drink in more than three hours of TV a day seriously believe that the majority of schoolteachers are young white males; that people have a 1-in-10 chance of being attacked in the streets; that we need more law-and-order cops like Kojak; that the U.S. population is the world's largest. The same study revealed that normal kids are now haunted by fears of violent attack. No wonder. All Saturday morning cartoons are now in the high-violence category of more than 10 violent acts per hour. Popular hits like *Space Stars* (61 violent acts per hour) and *The Roadrunner* (56) outdo even the most quick-fisted prime-time punch-ups like *Police Squad* (34). According to the National Coalition on Television Violence, there's been a 300-percent increase in TV violence since 1957. I didn't need the studies, though, to tell me that something was amiss. Some years ago, when Kung Fu was the TV rage, Toronto nursery school teachers were reporting a startling rise in injury-causing attacks by 4-year-olds.

Whenever I've criticized children's television in print, I've been shocked by the quality of response from children themselves. The most devoted viewers wrote appallingly incoherent, abusive, naïve letters clearly showing that they couldn't separate or distance themselves from the programs in question. When I attacked *The Brady Bunch* as a simperingly artificial sitcom, dozens of Canadian kids wrote to tell me that "this wonderful show teaches us how a good American family should live." Kids wrote to tell me that the *Bionic Woman* was "true", and besides, "she only hurts people when she has to." "*Scooby-Doo* doesn't make us violent," they wrote violently. My worst fears were confirmed.

The sad part is that the Phantom doesn't have to be a lobotomized gangster. Good television, rare as it is, can stimulate children to imaginative play. Kids watch TV with a real yearning for identity; good programs can reflect back to them a supportive and humane sense of themselves and others. It can reinforce the decent values that parents are trying to teach. The non-profit Children's Broadcast Institute, which promotes responsible and creative programming, believes, as I do, that the parent can blunt the damaging effects of bad TV and enhance the good. Watching TV with your kids, commenting on the programs (if only on the poor acting or animation), discussing the values, and helping your child get some critical distance, may be the best defence—short of turning off the set.

It's an enlightening experience to live through the mind-numbing TV immersion that is the daily lot of millions of children. I suggest you duplicate it for just a few days, watching whenever your kids watch. Observe how it gobbles up your leisure time, numbs you into a kind of drugged acquiescence, and lures you into slack-jawed hours of more and more viewing.

One of the most devastating charges that future generations will be able to hurl against the TV merchandisers is that they stole away the child's birthright of play. Teachers report that children have lost not only the knowledge of the old games — the rhymes, chants, and rules — but even the imaginative power to invent new ones. Parents say that when they limit their children's TV-watching to a well-chosen half-hour each day, the youngsters' resilience, energy, good humour, and playfulness come surging back. But there's something a little sad in the spectre of adults having to teach a listless generation how to play:

They say that marbles are the rage in Winnipeg now. All spring, the kids turned up at 7 a.m. at school to play Foot Snaps, Placers, and Choo-choo train; the teachers used the names of marbles in English class; and the trading was so hot and fierce that parents phoned the school to complain when their kids were on the losing end of a deal. Here in town, I heard some public school teachers on the radio describing how they're teaching the kids to skip Double Dutch. It seems a shame, in a way, that adults have to get involved.

Six hundred years ago when I was young, the games were part of a private world of childhood, a world with its own adamantine rules, wild exploits, mysterious chants, and medieval codes of honour as sternly immutable as Hammurabi's Law. You learned to skip Double Dutch ("Stop clashing") when you were about 6 and the big girls needed someone to turn rope. Your arms ached, and they never gave you a turn to skip, but finally you got the ropes going in an even slap-slap rhythm on the pavement, and then one day it would suddenly be you teaching some dumb little kid how to turn.

It's funny how each game had its private emotional pattern, the moment you half-consciously waited for. In kindergarten, it was the satisfying rhythm of "Rise, Sally, Rise, and close up your eyes, and point to the east and point to the west, and point to the very one that you love best," or the hot blush when you were tapped in A-tisket A-tasket. In skipping, it was the sound of "Bluebells, cockle-shells, eevy-ivy over", while the rope was swung gently back and forth without turning.

In Hide and Seek, it was that uncanny moment when you were "It", leaning against the side of a house, hiding your eyes against your arm and counting fast to 50. Suddenly, the scuffling and wild scampering died away, the evening was quiet around you except for the clatter of little kids' trikes and the swish of sprinklers, and for one heart-lurching split second you felt as though everyone had really run off forever. Even the breathless glee of the last dash for safety — "Home free!" we screamed, reckless of skinned elbows as we raced down alleys and plunged through hedges of poisonberry bushes — even that gasping exhilaration wasn't quite as keen as the blind spookiness of that abandoned moment and the choke of relief when you could yell into the silence, "Ready or not, here I come!"

I loved the endless hot summer hours when I played alone. Once, after an Errol Flynn matinee at the Avenue, I made a pirate sword out of two sticks with the handle closely bound in red wool, and fought the Chinese elms in the backyard until Mrs. Pollock next door came out and scolded me for knocking off leaves and twigs. In the narrow driveway between the duplexes, I thunked my India-rubber ball (did anything every bounce so gloriously high, or land so sweetly and roundly in one's hand?) against the wall and chanted, with ritual solemnity, "Ordinary, moving, laughing, talking, one hand, the other hand, one foot, the other foot, clap front, clap back, front and back, back and front, tweedle, twydle, curtsey, roundabout." Or, bouncing the ball under one leg and then the other and then back again: "One, two, three a-lairy, Lost my ball in the City Dairy. If you find it, give it to Mary, one, two, three a-lairy." ("These games improve their eye-hand co-ordination," said the teacher on the radio. Thank God we didn't know it then.)

At Allenby School, we had a special pastime. The moment the first deep frost set in, we made a recess beeline for the high iron fence around the girls' schoolyard to make "slides". You claimed a foot-square patch of ground, tamped down a layer of snow, carried cheekfuls of water from the drinking fountain (careful not to let your tongue touch the metal), and dribbled it around to make ice, and then, facing the fence and holding two railings, you quickly slid your feet backward, one at a time, until the slide was like glass. Terrible feuds flared up about claim-jumping: I broke forever with Lois Feldstein when she laid claim to the slide I thought was mine. It was a deathly serious break, too, because we were co-authoring a novel we were sure was going to make us the most famous 9-year-olds in Canada.

Oh, the passion we brought to childhood games, the iron justice we demanded, the quickness we had in lining up allies, the strangling rage when something wasn't fair ("What's wrong, dear?" "Oh, nothing."), the thrill of the outlaw, the fear of the hunted as we skulked down back lanes and dashed across the forbidden shortcut of St. James-Bond United's tempting backyard.

But O-U-T spells OUT and out you must go, out from the secret kingdom of childhood games where adults had no place, no place at all.

ADOLESCENTS — THE
RIGHTS OF PASSAGE

WALK PAST THE VIDEO PARLOUR AND HAVE A PEEK INTO hades: It's dark in there, and in the wreathing smoke of a hundred cigarettes and joints, the darkly clad figures of young men move in a trance. A year ago, these same young men were in thrall to the pinball machines; a glimpse into the same door would have shown you a room full of electric writhings and sexual thrusts as they danced before their pinball gods. Now only their fingers move; they inhabit the noise — the siren shrieks, the chitter and bleep and sputtering explosions, the thin whine of rockets and mechanical shrilling of intergalactic ships — as nervelessly as motes of dust inhabit the air.

This is part of the new world of adolescence, and with fresh commercial excitements developing as swiftly as coastal weather systems, even video parlours may be out of date by the time these words are in print. Still, they provide a fit image of the helpless astonishment we feel as our own teenagers move into worlds we can neither penetrate nor approve.

Drugs are part of the adolescent atmosphere now, and few adults of my acquaintance know what attitude to take to them, let alone what actions are wisest. Marijuana is used so widely by the adult population that I became something of a laughing-stock to some of my newspaper peers when I questioned its use among the young, and the young themselves will tell you that there isn't a school or gathering-spot that isn't saturated in the casual use of the weed. I am sure that we can't afford to be so sanguine.

A picture in the newspaper showed him as a boneless sort of teenager, tardily pubescent, with a characterless face under carefully waved blond hair. He is David Hinsperger, 18, and he must have spoiled the day just a little bit for anyone who read the interview with him. Hinsperger is the jaunty little murderer who, stoned out of his mind, murdered a Toronto jeweller in the course of a bungled robbery.

"Well, like we got back to the apartment and I felt nothing," Hinsperger said. "Don't forget, we were high." Being high was (and is) the essence, the goal, the style, and the content of Hinsperger's life. He smoked marijuana in high school, "liked it", and went on to speed, acid, and other junk.

Because everything about Hinsperger—his appearance, his middle-class background—seems so normal, some readers will be tempted to think that all he needed was some discipline, some tough seat-of-the-pants lessons in right and wrong. But Hinsperger is part of a pattern of mounting violence among teens, and that "discipline" response is knee-jerk nonsense. If preaching and punishment could change warped characters, no Sunday school graduate would ever commit a crime, and our prisoners would emerge from jail as model citizens.

No, character and conscience are formed long before a child ever gets to kindergarten, and they are formed by the responsible, sensitive, loving care which most parents bestow on most children. My hunch is that parents are doing no better and no worse a job of this than they ever did. What's happened in the past 20 years is that an entire subculture— the world of drugs—has clamped itself onto society's underbelly and swollen like a leech. It's incredibly easy for kids like Hinsperger, the marginal kids with shallow consciences and limited inner resources, the kids who were always there but usually didn't become killers, it's easy for them now to find a criminal home away from home.

That just didn't exist when I was growing up. There was an unimaginable gap between the decent lower-middle classes and what we called "the underworld". The kids who got into scrapes were on their own; they never made contact with adult criminals, and they usually straightened out eventually. The drug market, created and manipulated by adults for a huge market of youthful suckers, has filled that gap. Hinsperger blurred his boring high school life with marijuana; he blurred his boring work life with drugs; he blurred the night of the killing with drugs; now he is blurring his life sentence ("The month I've been here seems like a week because I'm mostly high") with prison-bought drugs. All the way along, he found it breathtakingly easy to sidestep normal society and slide into a drug world where criminal adults were eager to condone and abet his life of theft and drug abuse.

"Everything happened so fast," said Hinsperger, wondering how his little fun habit escalated to murder almost before he'd thought about it.

He's guilty, but society seems to conspire in his guilt. Do prisons tolerate the constant saturation of drugs because it keeps the prisoners docile? Do schools and parents shrug at the marijuana problem because so many middle-class parents, educators, and media people are tokers? Just this year, a report called "The Marijuana Issue" by Toronto high school principals stressed that thousands of kids are dozing away their adolescence because society seems to wink at the offence. Drug escapism is too new in our society, on this scale, for us to have many answers, but I think the principals made some good points. Simple possession must remain an offence, they said; otherwise kids think "it's no big deal." Punishment should be strict — not jail terms (think of Hinsperger nodding out in jail, a hero to fellow murderers) but community-service penalties. Education is crucial. Most teens just don't know or believe that cannabis is a suspected carcinogen, that it lowers the production of male hormones, that it damages brain cells, that it's being proven worse than tobacco and alcohol.

I hate to sound like the screaming right-wingers but I think there isn't much question that the leap in teen violence is closely linked to drugs. Like it or not, there is a straight line between the joints that made Hinsperger feel good and the bullets which ripped the life out of Israel Erlich. I don't know the answers to the drug problem but I know we have to make a start. And I think we should start where most of the kids start — with marijuana, their contact point with crime.

Among all the forces that pummel our teenagers (and most of them, after all, are the same old forces that pummelled us in our day), there is one that has a permanent and debilitating effect—sexual stereotyping in a difficult job market. Joblessness is a spectre that particularly causes panic in Metro Toronto, with the largest concentration (50,000) of unemployed young people in the country, and a steady, menacing rise in youthful crime. And closely linked to unemployment is the massive dislocation that experts predict for our young women in the next decade, when technological innovation will bump thousands of under-educated file clerks and secretaries from their office jobs.

It's astonishing, at a time when every provincial education ministry across the country has begun to harumph about the need for more technical and trade training, that the way our young people really learn and prepare for the job market is dictated more by primitive prejudice than by any rational analysis of employment trends. According to a survey of one thousand Ontario schoolgirls completed in 1980 by researchers at the Ontario Institute for Studies in Education, "sex-role ideology was important in career planning." Sex-role ideology. That's a hybrid of voodoo ("Girls can't do math") and cynical realism (I'll never get to be manager").

But at least these girls erred on the side of realism. Though 60 per cent of them aspired to upper-class occupations, like that of doctor, only 40 per cent actually expected to attain them. Disturbingly, only the girls with markedly liberated views about woman's role aspired to non-traditional occupations; those with traditional ideas about the feminine destiny chose, of course, more limited and conventional aspirations. Worse, and more surprising, was than more that three-quarters of the girls had what the researchers called "blatant misconceptions" about working women. They thought that 40 per cent of female college graduates never marry, that career women get divorced more often than housewives, that married women only work for a few years until the babies are born...in other words, these girls, brought up to believe that their heart's delight would be to marry and bear children, have a negatively warped idea of the impact of serious careers on the rose-covered-cottage dream. They really seem to think that by training to be supermarket check-out girls or office file clerks, they are guaranteeing themselves a rapturous lifelong marriage and cherubic children.

Ignorant and prejudiced, they are heading into an adult world
that will crush their hopes and break their hearts. To call this
education is a travesty, and yet my guess is that many parents in
Canada today still oppose or are wary of women's studies courses
that give girls at least a glimmer of factual grasp on their own
situation.

Equal opportunity? Canadian research reveals that half of all
male teachers are prejudiced against women and a quarter
believe in some form of sexist indoctrination for girls. Now comes
one study after another to tell us how deeply ingrained is the bias
in our educational system. The Association of American Colleges
called its 1982 report "The Classroom Climate: A Chilling One
for Women?" and disclosed that both male and female teachers
use dozens of kinds of behaviours that create "an inhospitable
climate" for girls. Canadian studies have long since shown that
girls' ambitions begin to decline in high school; now the ACA
assures us that the dampening-down process is reinforced in
college, where male-bonding jokes serve to unite male teachers
and students in derision against the women. Female students are
interrupted more frequently, spoken to less often by teachers
from elementary school right up through university, and even
denied credit for good ideas which are only rewarded when they
are taken up and repeated by male students. Male ambitions,
naturally enough, begin to rise in college, as their egos are
flattered at the expense of women.

Even if sexism didn't cripple our children and stunt their
future choices, it would be wrong just because it is an unexamined
set of prejudices. Nearly all the ills that beset our children are less
fearsome when the youngsters are equipped with critical skills. A
kid who can think, analyse, and reject prevalent ideas is well
armed against the meretricious nonsense enshrined in the popular culture. And yet this critical stance is just what our schools
most ferociously resent.

A personal experience illustrates this vividly. When my oldest
daughter was thirteen, in 1978, she insisted on attending a large,
solidly middle-class, and well respected high school smack in the
centre of Toronto, mostly because her friends were going there.
The school prides itself on a long history of conservative and
traditional educational values—values that began to look like

rigid and narrow-minded dogmatism once we got closer to
them. But that's jumping ahead. My daughter was happily and
unrebelliously ensconced in grade nine, and even working as a
junior reporter for the boringly rah-rah student newspaper,
when grade nine initiation rites came along. The instructions for
the initiation were drawn up by the school's female gym teachers
and sent home on mimeographed paper. It seemed that only
grade nine girls, not boys, had to take part. The girls were to
dress up as babies, carry rattles, wear diapers over their clothes,
and crawl around the cafeteria floor saying "goo-goo" as they
went. As the event transpired, it was an ideal opportunity for the
watching boys to snicker, loll about, and pinch girls' rumps as
they crawled by. Girls who refused to participate were, according
to one youngster I spoke to, made to go out on the sports field,
wear a sign on their chest saying "SUCK," and practise that old
chestnut of an exercise known as "I must, I must, develop my
bust."

In view of the known infantilization of girls in our schools, and
the systematic denigration of their hopes and dreams and self-
esteem, this childish bit of nonsense seemed a bit much. My
daughter stayed home that day, and I wrote what I fondly
thought of as a reasoned and calm note of explanation to the
principal. He did not reply. Nor did he reply to the four or five
other mothers of whose protests I had heard. When my daughter
wanted to write an earnest account of the initiation for the school
newspaper, the editor (an athletic chauvinist of almost stupefying
conventionality) insisted that nothing critical of school events
might ever be written in the newspaper.

All this would be a tempest in a tiny teapot if it weren't for the
stifling implications of the way the gym teachers and the principal behaved. A women's-studies consultant for the Board of
Education heard about the girls-only initiation and arranged to
talk with those responsible at the school. When she arrived, she
found a phalanx of bitterly hostile girls from the athletic association, grim-faced gym teachers, and an utterly uncooperative
principal waiting to attack her. She was astounded by their
implacable refusal to listen. "They insisted that it was all good
fun, only 'outsiders' would complain or 'make trouble', and that
there was nothing to discuss," the consultant told me later.

The throttling of criticism, the defensive lashing out against anyone who questions established values, is exactly the behaviour that makes our adolescents vulnerable to trash. When teenagers are taught never to question, they are unlikely to turn a sceptical ear to the blasting rock bands urging them to get stoned. If compliance is the habit we insist on, we had better be ready to see our youngsters comply with those who have more persuasive powers than we have: the seducers, exploiters, and hustlers who sell everything from religion to drugs to kids who don't know how to be critical.

A man and his son driving on the Trans-Canada Highway were involved in a crash. The man was killed instantly. The son, critically injured, was rushed to the nearest hospital, where the chief surgeon was hastily summoned from the golf course. The surgeon ran into the operating room, prepared to examine the boy, and suddenly exclaimed, "Oh my God, it's my son!" Who was the chief surgeon?

If this riddle baffles you, that makes you sadly typical, according to Dr. Peter Cole. He's presented this time-honoured feminist litmus test to thousands of high school students over the last few years, and not one has ever guessed right.

"They'll come up with the most convoluted answers — twins, mistaken identity, adoption, clones... anything rather than realize that the chief surgeon is the boy's mother," grins Cole.

The grin is not an entirely happy one. To Cole, the response to the riddle is a measure of how tightly Toronto's kids are shrink-wrapped in stereotyped thinking. Recently Cole met with me to share some of the insights gathered during his three years as director of Toronto's Family Planning Services.

"I've been the token liberated male at dozens of high-school conferences," Cole told me. "The first thing I tell them is that I'm no expert: a man can't really be a feminist. And I see no purpose in judging and blaming other people for their degree of liberation. The idea of criticizing housewives, for example, is obnoxious to me."

Cole's whole pitch to his young audiences is as unthreatening as his disarming introduction. Diplomatically, he focuses on how male stereotypes frustrated him in his own adolescence. How, for example, in his early teens he stopped kissing his father "even though my dad was very affectionate and emotional and I *liked* kissing him. "How strangled he felt in his relationships with other young men: "We were only supposed to talk about boats, cars, sports, and stereos. It was absolutely taboo to display vulnerability, so if you broke up with your girlfriend you lost the only person with whom you could talk about your feelings." How work was supposed to be the number-one priority: from adolescence on, young men feel under pressure to choose careers, to be upwardly mobile. "You can't change jobs creatively or afford the luxury of peripheral interests, because it would look shiftless on your curriculum vitae."

But only when Cole talks about "making the first move" does he rouse a sympathetic ripple of laughter from his teenage audiences. "They resent the pressure for the boy to be the pusher and the girl to be the pushee. Men have set themselves up as the experts in sex and pillars of strength in everything, and the boys feel trapped.

He can't rouse a flicker of empathy, though ("just nods and yawns"), when he describes how leers, raunchiness, and locker-room talk make girls feel humiliated, "like pieces of meat". And when he talks about men suffering emotional pain and desperately needing the support of close male friendships, the boys are frantic to deny both the need and its solution.

"Things haven't changed—and they won't change—because kids aren't changed by rhetoric. They're changed by role models, and these boys have very conservative role models in their teachers and parents. Unless a boy has multidimensional male teachers, men who read poetry *and* run the marathon...chances are he will grow up one-dimensional himself." Trendy adult male hypocrites aren't much help. "It's easy to call women Ms. and make your own coffee, but how many such men still pressure their secretaries to have sex?"

High-school girls, says Cole, are angrier and more perceptive about stultifying stereotypes, but they still play the games dictated by males. "And they'll grow up conflicted and disillusioned because they won't find men mature enough to partner them."

Cole, recently married for the second time, left me on a note of gloom, contemplating his future children's struggle against the suffocating sexism of their peer group. My experience with high school students is not nearly so wide as Cole's, but I have a hunch that the outlook is not quite so dismal. Kids may pretend to be as conventional and blank-minded as sheep when they flock together, but I think a new sensibility may lurk underneath, only to emerge when they have made it safely to adulthood and dare risk the pains of individuality.

Until then, young adolescents are strongly susceptible to peer pressure. Sexuality is the overpowering subject in their lives and it is presented to them by those powerful communicators of pop culture — television and radio — in the most stereotyped and violent way possible.

"Don't you think 12 is too young to go to dances?" asked the plaintive mother's voice on the phone. "Why should the junior high school push all these youngsters into sexual awareness so early?"

Ask the tides to roll back, madam; ask the leaves to jump back onto the maple trees. That would be easier than to shield your child from the glutinous swamp of the sexploitation culture in which we live. School dances are the least of it. We live and breathe the stuff, inescapably. You can't have Farrah Fawcett or her clones wobbling their assets across the ninny-box every night without the message being printed in your child's brain.

Have you listened lately? Late last Saturday night, I watched TV as rock singer Rick James leaped about in his skinny-tights, screaming: "If you don't want it, I'm gonna f---you right outa the door" (he didn't use dashes). His back-up singers, two tartly dressed little skimps, joyously squealed, "Pull my trigger!" as James declared his intention to shoot them with his love gun.

I was startled enough to launch a little investigation of my own into the music our youngest adolescents are buying these days. With the help of some knowledgeable young clerks at Sam the Record Man, I selected and listened to a bundle of the most popular rock and disco music, and learned that it relies almost exclusively on themes of drug use (it's lucky for the simple-minded lyricists that "smoke" and "toke" rhyme) and grossly explicit macho sex. Mind you, I didn't include the extremist punk-rockers in my survey. And I'm not even going to be able to quote from Frank Zappa, the one-man Gong Show of rock, who made his millions by musically pulling down his rompers (favourite themes, spewed with indescribable venom: woman-hatred, oral sex, anal rape, and gonorrhea).

No, I stuck to the middle-of-the-road music. And what's top of the pops? The multiple female orgasm. Female climaxes are featured on at least six of the 30 records I listened to, always with rhythmic panting, drum-beats, moaning paroxysms and screams. Amidst the cacophony, an astute listener will hear subliminal tidbits. A typical version, played at school dances, is this one by a female group: "Push, push/In the bush. Push, push/In the bush. I like to do it, I like to do what you like to do. So baby let's go to it. (Girls chanting rhythmically:) Are you ready? Do you like it? Do you like it like this? Are you ready? Do you like it? Do you like it like this?"

The album jackets sum it all up: women holding champagne bottles between their legs; half-naked women in chains; wet-lipped women; parts of women; a woman with a wad of bubblegum being pulled off her naked breast; a naked, headless woman holding a TV set in front of her torso (the record is called *The Tube*); a woman's crotch menaced by a huge hairy spider. Acres of the stuff.

"Exploitation of women does make money," shrugged a store clerk. "And since rock music is an expression of teenage lust, aggression, and frustration, and is heavily dominated by males, of course it's anti-woman."

The big issue to him, and to others knowledgeable about the music industry, is the mass manipulation of the teenage market. "The record companies and the radio stations exercise total mind control over the kids," he said. "It's only one step away from 1984."

Censorship isn't the answer. You might as well try to censor the polluted air the kids breathe. Record-banning, like any other witch-hunt, would only reinforce the music's rebellious glamour. In fact, parental disgust is an essential and much-desired element in the music; rock "artists" long to be banned so they will become instant millionaires like the Rolling Stones.

I don't think teenagers will rush out to perform unnatural acts after listening to their daily dose of mind-numbing decibels. No, the danger lies much more in the sick, distorted sex-role images the kids are soaking in through their pores. Never in history has there been such a massive propaganda campaign, avidly lapped up by very young and impressionable girls, promoting the image of woman as a moaning, slavish, manipulative, adoring, masochistic lump of quivering flesh.

Sound exaggerated? Listen to the songs your youngsters hear on radio. I can't quote the lyrics in a self-respecting newspaper. But I can tell you that the commonplace vocabulary of teenage music is the four-letter word (all of them) and that the common theme is either sneering abuse of women ("If you won't----me, baby, Well----off. You ain't nothing' but a----tease") or the hysterical, grovelling please from women begging for sexual attack. How do 13- and 14-year old girls feel, in the company of boys at school dances, hearing amplified female orgasms blasted over the PA? And how do they feel when the lyrics tell them, in brutal language, that resistance to sexual coarseness is just "uptight" repressed prissiness?

Despite its power and pervasiveness, I don't think this music, drenched in sado-masochistic imagery, needs to win the day. The best line of defence against it is the alert parent, not the angry one who reacts when it's too late. In homes where sex is discussed, early and openly, and all stereotypes are debunked, kids don't need sick images or the naughty thrill of dirty lyrics. In homes where critical skills are encouraged from the start (argument, debate, good conversation, probing at the status quo), the adolescents are likely to be clear-eyed and aware.

Maybe there's a sucker born every minute, but your child doesn't have to be one of them.

I wonder, though, if I was being a little cavalier there. Perhaps not every teenager has to be a sucker for commercial interests. But the pressures of the peer group, the ache to belong, and the avalanche of images from advertisers are all beyond what we experienced one generation ago. Perhaps more than any other cohort of parents in recent history, we need to make extraordinary efforts of the imagination to realize the difference between our time and theirs.

Puberty is painful enough. It was painful enough back in the Sen-Sen era, when the gleaming teeth of Barbara Ann Scott loomed over my childhood: but can you imagine what it's like to grow up in the shadow of Brooke Shields?

I walked past a magazine rack the other day and four glossy versions of Brooke's face beamed forth at me; I went home and saw her rear end on TV; my kids went out and saw the rest of her in *Endless Love*. She's so flawlessly perfect and so pervasive that my eyes don't even register her any more. My brain simply notes one more Brooke Shields manifestation and moves on, as though she were a stop sign. (How long since you actually read "STOP"?)

That's the problem. The Lolita syndrome is subliminal by now. Brooke may have shocked us when she first posed à la prostitute at age 10, but most of us no longer even twitch when she markets her honeybuns. Or when a dozen little tartlets follow in her wake, peddling furs and jewels and cosmetics with their best 12-year-old come-hither looks.

Don't think the message has been lost on our own babes in TV-land. Visit a department store these days and you'll hear the weeping and gnashing of teeth behind the fitting-room curtains, as 10-year-olds fight with their moms for tighter and tighter jeans to show of their bony little tushies. They may not know what they're flaunting or why, and boys are still strictly "YUCK", but they know they gotta flaunt or die.

They know it because of sales hype like that found in a Canadian magazine called *JAM* ("Just About Me/A Magazine for Pre-teen Girls"), which fell onto my desk from the numbed fingers of my editor. Not all of *JAM* is irretrievably nauseating. Just most of it: like the hard sell of clothes, cosmetics, and consumerism. The glinty-eyed obsession with money is unnerving. There's a feature on the comic book character Richie Rich, twinkling with diamonds and dollar signs; a story about an obnoxious Teen-Age Tycoon; a column on Earning Your Own Bread (more dollar signs), not to mention Banking With Your Piggie, Be A Super Spender, Making Your Cash Count, and a handy glossary of banking terms.

All this for 10 and 11-year-olds? C'mon. And since when did pre-teens drool over "hunky guys" or complain to a "Fashion Fairy Godmother" that their wardrobes urgently need a brand-name up-date? Too much, too soon, and too darn silly, especially the list of possible kiddie jobs, headed by "model", and the column of showbiz burble from a teeny-bopper who celebrated her 13th birthday with a wing-ding in a New York nightclub.

Watch out for your little girl, mama. This decade will see the most concentrated assault on the pre-teen mind since Which Twin Has the Toni, and her brain cells may be permanently frizzled. Did you know that a major publishing house is about to bring out a line of teenage romances like Harlequins? They'll be called "Sweet Dreams" (what would these hustlers do if they couldn't coat the sex with sugar?), and the themes will be "dating, shyness, popularity..."

There's only one thing that gives me comfort in all this. And that's a young person of my acquaintance who fits the pre-teen category. Recently, she made a grand sweep through Eaton's on an 11th-birthday buying spree. In a positively terrifying outburst of sophistication, she snapped up Jelly Bean shoes, mauve hair combs, stud earrings, bangles, and snazzy purple cotton knickers. I eyed her tenderly, this changeling who can trade sly quips with me about New Wave music as she drifts off to play with her doll house, and whose fashion sense is subtly undercut by the aroma of apple cores and bubblegum emanating from her chic little shoulder purse.

I showed her, straightfaced, a copy of *JAM* and waited with some trepidation for the verdict. She dropped it on my desk with a scornful gesture.

"If you'll notice," she said, "the whole thing is filled with jeans company ads. That's the total giveaway." So saying, she marched off with her teddy bear securely tucked under one arm.

Avaunt, you greedy manufacturers with your prepubescent lip gloss and your whole stock-in-trade of popsicle prurience! Someone I know has got your number. Don't call her; she'll call you…maybe.

"You were dead right about the Brooke Shields syndrome," said a discouraged father. "The only problem is, you didn't tell us what to do about it."

If I only knew. Here's a thoroughly decent citizen, the kind of parent who bicycles with his kids and Bundles Up for Wednesday, and he's helpless to protect his 10-year-old, 70-pound daughter from a frenzy of self-loathing because she can't get her jeans tight enough or her bottom small enough.

Amazing, isn't it? An entire generation of granola-fed little girls is socially tormented because it can't live up the boyish beauty standards of some anally obsessed male fashion designer. It must be the most twisted success story in the annals of advertising.

The brainwashing is, of course, relentless. Enormous close-ups of denim rear ends are everywhere: billboards, TV commercials, magazine features, and even, Timothy preserve us, Eaton's and Simpsons flyers. But why are children so vulnerable to it? I'm nagged by a recurring observation: even some of the most devoted parents are surprisingly indolent, or perhaps over-confident, about sharing their values with their children. Oh, there are the book banners and censorship types, and heaven knows, they're energetic enough, popping dos and don'ts and moral precepts down their kids' throats like codliver oil pills. They'd like to scrub the world clean enough to keep their children in perpetual snowy innocence, or, failing that, to prevent their children from contact with "wrong" knowledge. Not only is the task hopeless, but real moral education has almost nothing to do with muzzling and blindfolding children and keeping them on a tight leash.

The kind of education I'm thinking of is more elusive and perplexing, and requires you first of all to take your child seriously. Oddly enough, people don't always respond to or reward their child's first moral awakenings, perhaps because they dismiss the possibility that even a baby's cute gurglings can be a perfectly serious communication. I remember watching a baby in a supermarket cart, blissfully drooling over a lollipop. Baby's mother smiled at her distractedly. Baby responded with a chortle and shoved the lollipop right under mama's nose. "Ugh, get that sticky thing away from me," recoiled mama, slapping it away. Would she have slapped away a bouquet of roses from her husband? Would she later give toddler lectures on sharing? A first lesson in generosity should be to receive a gift courteously.

To take children's thoughts seriously, you have to start with the premise that they are fully human, however inexperienced. I was once enjoying a picnic with my family when my 5-year-old daughter, obviously brooding on something she'd heard from older playmates about homosexuality, suddenly blurted: "But if a man and a man make love, they wouldn't fit together properly!" I was still absorbing this bombshell when I noticed a couple at the next table glaring at us furiously. To them, no doubt, a child's earnest struggle to comprehend should have been slapped down. To them, children should be cute itsy-bitsy sweetums, repressed little dissemblers who go on year after year dutifully shielding mommy and daddy from the terrible knowledge that they know All.

Friends used to sneer when I would doggedly explain to my children, at the mild ages of 3 and 4, why I disapproved of TV programs riddled with racist stereotypes or police violence. Well, I did feel a little foolishly earnest. But at least the kids knew that I took their minds as seriously as their clean fingernails and vitamin-stuffed bodies. Values and—more important—the habit of critical analysis don't trickle down automatically. They don't get absorbed by silent osmosis. Kids have to see that their own thoughts have weight and value in the flow of family life, and they have to see and hear their parents speaking about principles, acting on them, and struggling with moral perplexities. If the inner life of the conscience is not seen to be important in the parent's lives, how can we expect the children to sprout it suddenly in adolescence? If we preach at them, how much of a favour are we doing them? On the whole, I think we protect them better in these strange times by giving them the sword of reason than the armour of rigid dogma.

Our children are going to have to sort out a lifetime's worth of advertising lies, con artistry, and political manipulation, and we won't always be there to explain.

I noticed the other day that a large number of the boys hanging around the local high school after classes were sporting moustaches or beards. This gave me pause. Try as I might, I can't recall a single youth who had either the hormones or the chutzpah to cultivate such a badge of adult manhood in our own departed days of adolescence.

Physically, they do grow up bigger and faster now. Culturally, they are far more sophisticated than the teenagers of the 1950s. Inevitably, we parents are being pushed to stop projecting our own youth as the perfect model of suitable behaviour and to start considering that our children are facing more complicated lives than we could have imagined. Luckily for them and for us, all the evidence shows that they are capable of more informed judgements than we would have been. The problem is that we haven't caught up with them yet. We're still reacting with the old reflexes, still leaping to protect and, yes, control them when they've long since journeyed beyond our ken.

Among the middle-class youngsters I've come across in my research are these: a 16-year-old whose parents have split, moved out of town, and remarried—the girl now lives alone, her rent in a sophisticated downtown high-rise paid by her absentee daddy; a 12-year-old whose mother coaxed her to hide some illicit drugs in a school locker—her reward being a share of the LSD; and a

16-year-old boy who hates to visit his divorced dad, ever since dad came out of the closet and began living with...a 16-year-old boy.

These extreme cases are not the norm, thank heavens. But they do represent some of the burdens of choice and moral confusion that our children bear. The more I've learned about the lives of the urban young, the more I've realized that we can't shirk for much longer the task of remodelling our laws to bring youngsters' freedoms and rights into line with their burdens.

Change isn't easy, and change in something as elemental as family life can be as frightening as though you'd gone out to buy some milk and come back to find your house painted a different colour and a stranger looking out your window.

That's almost how jolting it was to read a brief called "The Medical Consent of Minors" and realize that the authors, members of Justice for Children, a non-profit foundation for child advocacy, are calmly discussing their belief that kids under 16 should be able to seek or refuse all kind of medical or psychological treatment—without their parents' knowledge or consent. In fact, they say in their brief to the Ontario government, young people already have that right under existing common law, though few doctors themselves realize it. So long as a child is capable of understanding the nature and consequences of the treatment, he or she is capable of "informed consent" no matter what the chronological age, argues Justice for Children.

Now wait a minute, I yelped to myself. Should children really be able to get confidential treatment for drug abuse, venereal desease, pregnancy, or abortion? Aren't parents then abandoning their responsibility to nurture and protect? Aren't youngsters being asked to shoulder an intolerable heavy burden of decision-making?

My mind flew back to a depressing half-day I spent, a year ago, in the waiting room of the Teen Clinic at a downtown hospital, where I had taken my then 13-year-old daughter for a routine physical check-up while the regular doctor was on holiday. While I waited, I was riveted by the loud conversation of two young teenagers.

"Hey, is this your first or second?" one girl asked the other. "My second. Nothin' to it. Just like pullin' teeth," replied the second. They went on to compare, with grisly callousness, the details of their abortions, their boyfriends' sexual habits, their intentions to "keep doin' it" and the opinion of one girl that "My mom respects me more now, y'know?"

An hour later, while I was still queasily digesting this slice of teenage life, I was finally called in by two young doctors who had been examining my daughter. To my amazement, it turned out they they had been prying and probing psychologically as well as physically, coaxing my 13-year-old to confess whether she fought with her parents, whether being the daughter of two achievers "put her under pressure", and whether she "needed anyone to talk to without her parents knowing." She was as mortified as I by this invasion of privacy, and we both went away convinced that teens and their families need protection from presumptuous clinicians.

So I brought this uneasiness with me, this irritated conviction that the parent and no one else is the child's best advocate, to the Justice for Children brief.

"That's fine when parents and children have a good relationship," argued Marion Lane, general counsel for the foundation. "If there's decent communication, your kids are not going to run off to get medical help without asking for your guidance. But what about those whose family life has broken down? What about the 16-year-old girl I know who is now in a mental institution because, two years ago, her parents and doctor forced her to have an abortion? Didn't she have a right to make her own decision?

The "what abouts" got more and more convincing. What about the immigrant girl whose father was deeply depressed after the death of his wife? The girl showed up at a suburban family agency begging for counselling, but was refused because the grief-stricken father wouldn't give permission. What about the fact that hundreds of messed-up teenagers can't get help from the Toronto Board of Education's own social workers because the parents won't agree? What about the epidemic of teenage venereal disease and pregnancy (50,000 teenage pregnancies a year in Canada), out of control largely because teens won't go to family doctors for advice because they have no guarantee of confidentiality? Clearer laws could mean the difference between despair and a fruitful life for thousands of youngsters whose road to help is now barred by an absent, uncaring, or hostile parent.

The debate about children's rights is barely beginning, and already it is awesomely complex. What is clear is this: the family has been shaken up and sometimes jounced apart by the earthquake of social change. Those of us who have strong and enduring bonds with our children shouldn't be too viscerally indignant when these changes are brought into the open.

SUFFER THE LITTLE CHILDREN

TURN OVER THE BOULDER OF ACCEPTED FACT AND THE little grubby truths begin to crawl out. Underneath the language of knightly chivalry was the reality of rape; behind the official pieties of countries where abortion is banned there are millions of coat-hanger butcheries. Under the bland assumption that our own children are the most blessed and schooled and vitamin-plumped children in history, there is the truth that they are, in reality, the landless peasants of urban Canada.

They have no votes; they have no money; they have no legal rights; they have no power; and when hard times set in, gallant governments wield the knife on women and children first. In 1979, the International Year of the Child, I began to dig around behind the façade of rainbow-coloured track shoes, bilingual kindergartens, and Ronald McDonald signs on every corner, to find out what was really happening to children. And I learned that for those who do not have a sure foothold in the middle class—those who have been nudged aside by accident of poverty or handicap—it's a long, long way down from the privileged world of childhood to another world, an explosive Third World within Canada of children who are forlorn, needy, and officially ignored.

Raymond, age four, was a citizen of that world of poverty and hard knocks. I met him in the course of investigating children's services in precisely the year that I bitterly renamed the Year of the Cutbacks when I saw first-hand the children who were suffering as the government slashed programs and budgets. Raymond was a bright-eyed, dimpled kid, a pupil at TREAT, a suburban Children's Aid Society nursery school for high-risk children. Raymond was as high-risk as they come: six months before I met him, he'd been a withdrawn and depressed child who screamed and cried himself to sleep at night. His father had vanished. His baby brother had died in a gruesome household accident in which Raymond himself was involved. His one-year-old sister, suffering from a respiratory ailment, kept the family awake at night. Raymond's mother, twenty-two-year-old Dianna Joudrey, was trying to make ends meet on Family Benefits of $409 a month, while paying $300 rent for her inadequate apartment. Dianna Joudrey knew that something was going terribly wrong for Raymond; her nerves were strained to the breaking-point by her own troubles and Raymond's wild, demanding behaviour. Then a Children's Aid Society worker suggested TREAT.

"The difference in him is fantastic," Dianna told me. "Honestly, he comes home singing his little songs and telling me all about school. He's so much more grown-up now."

The psychologist's report told the same story, more clinically. When Raymond was first tested, he blushed and hid his eyes in embarrassment because he didn't know the words for airplane, ball, or horse. In half a year, his IQ jumped by ten points. He became a relaxed, outgoing youngster with a best friend in class. He chattered easily with me about his favourite toys in the playroom, and greeted his mum with a rapturous hug. Even more important, Dianna admitted that she had learned to enjoy him more. Grinning from ear to ear with pride over her blossoming boy, Dianna showed his "report card" from TREAT to all her relatives. The dangerous sense of anger and struggle had gone.

TREAT had no special magic. All the ingredients were well-known formulae for rescuing distressed children: one dedicated child-care worker for every four children; careful assessment and special goals for each child; an open door for mothers who wanted to phone or visit for supportive advice; a parents' discussion group; close contact with other agencies, especially those to help mothers build self-esteem.

It worked for tiny two-year-old Stacey, a frail blonde moppet who had suffered bruises and broken bones at her mother's hands. When Stacey first came to TREAT, a caseworker told me, "she was frightened to cry out loud. If she fell, she would just lie there, with tears running down her face, looking up with big, pleading eyes, but not making a sound." Not only had Stacey learned to laugh, play, and make noise, but her young mother had learned to stop hurting her. TREAT's particular brand of seemingly nonchalant supportiveness to desperate young mothers was a key ingredient in this kind of success. Arriving in the morning to pick up the children for school, the young caseworkers would linger in the doorway to offer a cigarette and chat, or deliberately express delight over the child's curiosity or energy so that a hostile mother could see that her child was not a monster.

In its two years of existence, TREAT reached ninety-five children, helping many of them to raise their IQs by twelve to fifteen points. Some of the children learned to talk, to use the toilet, to trust adults, and to experience pleasure and hope, for the first time. Not all of them had lives as dramatic as those of Stacey and Raymond. The thrust of TREAT's work was prevention. Out there, in the world of bleak high-rises, there are thousands of young mothers who are simply too immature, unloved, or harassed by poverty to know how to mother a child. Sometimes they don't know any better than to leave their babies for hours, or days, alone in a crib or locked in a bedroom.

"Closet children, I call them," child-care worker Pat Williamson told me. "We get kids who have never been out of their apartments before. They'd be lost if they were sent to an ordinary day care or kindergarten. But if we get them first, they have a chance of making it."

How many are there? Pat gave me a look. "Zillions."

"In 1979, the Year of the Child, TREAT's $83,000 grant from the federal government ran out. The Ontario government, despite TREAT's proven record of preventing abuse and crisis, said it had no money to give. TREAT closed down. Stacey and Raymond and all the others went back to the crowded apartments, the shouts and bruises, and the empty future.

As the Ontario government systematically closed the training schools, treatment centres, and group homes, and sent the kids back into the community, it was also cutting back on services in public schools. According to the late Dr. Robert Jackson, the province's own commissioner on declining school enrolment, the Ontario government had "pocketed the savings" on dwindling school populations, rather than channelling the money back into the schools. Hundreds of teachers were fired by panicky school boards; art, music, counselling, speech therapy, English as a second language, even books and pencils, were slashed from school budgets. Meanwhile, the provincial per-child grant shrank year by year, and inflation shrivelled the amount even more. "What case histories do you want?" raged an elementary school principal when I called him for an interview. "Do you want my seven-year-old who brings crusts for lunch? My immigrant kids who are lost without English classes? My ten-year-old with two charges of indecent assault against him?"

Or Alberto. Alberto was a plump and appealing nine-year-old, expelled from his special-education class for "using language which was corrosive to the moral fibre of the school." Alberto, lovingly sheltered by his loyal family, was not dangerous or violent and not even very retarded. His parents were desperate to get some education for him. "There are at least two hundred kids like him in Toronto who have been thrown out of the school system. The minute a school gets hit by cutbacks, it dumps its most difficult children," the agency director told me. In the Year of the Child, Alberto sat at home. "Alberto is normal," he chanted with anxious eyes. "Alberto is normal; Alberto watches TV."

In the Year of the Child, Ontario trimmed thirty-five dollars off it per-capita grant to schools in the name of economic restraint.

The parents of pre-school children are also facing a desperate problem: a chronic shortage of day-care centres where the toddlers can be left safely while their parents work to support them.

Anastasia, as thin as a 12-year-old urchin, shyly tells me that she is 21. She is all bones and eyes, like Cicely Tyson, and as wary of me as a fugitive. It is only when she turns to 10-month-old Belinda that her face lights up with radiant, unguarded love.

I've intruded into Anastasia's life because I picked her at random as one of more than 900 mothers on the waiting list for infant day care at 19 Metro centres. She agreed to see me, and then asked me not to use her real name. (In fact, the only laugh I wrung from her was when I asked her to make up these pseudonyms, and she giggled happily at the moment of fantasy.)

There isn't much fantasy in Anastasia's life. She's a single mother who lives, works, and breathes to make a life for her baby. By 6:45 each morning, Anastasia has delivered a clean and fed Belinda to a babysitter in her own Ontario Housing apartment building and arrived at the bus stop for her 45-minute ride to work. She sews the side seams on baby clothes at a textile factory, bringing home $109 a week. After paying $112.50 monthly rent, $9 for the phone, $19 for OHIP, $30 a week for food, $6 for carfare, and $30 a week to Belinda's babysitter, there's nothing left.

At 5 p.m., Anastasia returns to her bare little apartment (no rugs, no curtains, no TV) to spend a quiet evening with the baby. It's about three months since she spent an evening out, she admits. But she doesn't complain. You can tell at a glance that beautiful Belinda is a passionately loved baby: her huge eyes sparkle with curiosity and playfulness, she makes vigorous baby-talk speeches, and scoots her infant seat around the kitchen table with chortling abandon.

"She needs a high chair," says Anastasia, sprinting to the rescue. "That's what I'll buy if I can get her into day care." Metro-subsidized day care would cost $1 a day. "And some Fisher Price toys," she says, suddenly burying her face in Belinda's tummy and eliciting a new cascade of chuckles.

Even more important is the kind of intelligent, stimulating care Belinda might receive in a properly supervised home daycare setting. In a quick, anxious outburst, Anastasia reveals: "The last babysitter I had was minding four other babies and some bigger kids. Belinda screamed when I took her there, and when I picked her up at night she was soaking wet. I don't think she was fed on time."

Belinda is one of 40,000 Metro children who spend most of their waking hours with unsupervised, underpaid, and often overworked babysitters. According to the Metro Social Planning Council, 25 per cent of these sitters are in chronic poor health; 13 per cent of them plunk the children in front of the

TV for more than four hours a day; one-third never read stories, do crafts or sing with their small charges; half never work on the children's language. There are hair-raising stories about women minding 17 preschoolers at a time, or locking the kids in an apartment while they run to the store or to visit neighbours.

Home care supervised by experts would be a good alternative for Anastasia and Belinda, and might just give Belinda a head start on the education her mother is lacking. But this is the Year of Child Cutbacks, and Metro Social Services may be forced to cut half a million dollars from its $20 million budget for day care. There will be no new infant day-care spaces this year.

Irene Kyle is the director of Cradleship Crèche, a Toronto day-care centre with 64 children, ages 3 to 6, and 150 more in supervised private homes. Wearily, she filled me in on the random methods of day-care funding. "We're lucky; we have a ratio of one teacher to every six children, because we accept a lot of children with special needs. Metro Social Services sets a per diem budget for us but it's never based on real costs, always on their estimates of what our costs should be. This year there's a $37,000 gap between our costs and the Metro budget." The difference will be made up by the United Way, and by scrimping. Field workers who counsel parents will double up on phones, the little playground that's gradually sinking into the adjoining road will have to crumble, and the waiting lists will grow longer and longer.

"Oh, the waiting lists," groans Irene Kyle. "At least 6,200 parents are looking for day-care spaces, half again as many as are already in centres."

Her own waiting list turns up Anastasia, and a sick mother, and a father who had to quit his job and go on welfare to care for his three preschoolers when his wife had a schizophrenic breakdown...and 60 others, at this one small centre alone.

Day-care centres, Kyle says, are turning into "ghettoes of the poor." Eighty per cent of her clients are single mothers because even the lowest-income couples don't qualify for a Metro subsidy and yet can't afford the $75 weekly unsubsidized fee. The need seems overwhelming. Even if we could win the battle of the waiting lists—and as fast as spaces open, the waiting lists fill up again like holes dug in the sand at the ocean's edge—there would still be enormous improvements to the system to be made.

Even the oldest and best day-care centres, like Cradleship Crèche, are starved and stinted. Last year, angry Metro politicians turned down the Crèche's request for a 3 per cent increase, calling it a "Cadillac service". It doesn't look like Cadillac to me. For all the dedication of the teachers, for all the bright nature projects on the walls, the play corners and crafts and birthday cakes, the 24-year-old concrete building on Regent St. seems woefully inadequate. The toys are battered, the rooms crowded, and for some toddlers who spend an exhausting nine-hour day here in the company of 60 other children, there is no corner where one can be quiet or private.

I watched while one curly-haired charmer, her eyes brimming, had a cut lip doctored with an ice cube. She had been hurt by a playground shove. There was something horribly resigned about the way her chubby, blood-smeared hands lay passively in her lap. Another little one, having given up on the wild melee of the playground at recess, lay on the ground just outside the door, sucking her thumb until it was time to go in.

The children are exceptionally well-tended at the Crèche. These stray observations are not meant to cast any reflections on the care but simply to say that this is equal to the best day care we have, but it is too hectic, too strapped for funds, staff, and space.

In response to my series of articles about children's-services cutbacks, about thirteen thousand citizens sent coupons to Ontario's Conservative premier, William Davis, asking him to stop cutbacks that were hurting children. All of them got a pleasant form letter assuring them that Ontario's services to children were second to none. And that may have been true, but it was irrelevant, because the services just weren't good enough.

In Canada in the 1980s, not only the government but even the public will to struggle to help our children was in danger of atrophy. Child-welfare agencies, sourly trapped between public distrust and government stinginess, seemed paralysed, sinking further and further into bureaucratic bickering and self-serving excuses. But when community projects sprang into existence, filled with fresh vigour for the fight, these agencies sat back with a resentful leer.

The woman sits on the bench, apparently idle. You would never guess she is a front-line warrior in the battle against child abuse. She looks bright-eyed, maternal, brisk, and cosy at the same time, and her name is Marilyn McHugh. Come the end of November, she will be out of a job, but I'll get to that later.

Soon, the mothers will come out of the Ontario Housing high-rise slum to let their children play in the driveway—that's where the bench is; that's the only place to play—and McHugh will be there. Maybe she'll offer to hold a squalling infant while the mother ties a toddler's shoelace, or lend a couple of dimes for the phone.

McHugh is an outreach worker for a three-year-old project called Parent Resources, set up with a federal grant and subsequently funded by the province, to reach mothers who are isolated, under stress, and "at risk" of abusing their children. Besides its four street workers, the project has two bright toy-cluttered drop-in centres where mothers can put their feet up, have a coffee, and indulge in shop talk with other mums while watching their children play.

"We have lots of mums, poor and middle-class, whose children aren't at risk at all," McHugh explained. "It's just a great neighbourhood resource for everyone." Apparently, one of the joys of the centre I visited, in a schoolyard portable near Pape and Danforth, has been to watch the middle-class mothers grow more sensitive to and supportive of the poverty mothers.

Meanwhile, McHugh turns up in the darnedest places. "I've seen her walking these streets for three years now," said a bemused local shopkeeper. What she's doing in those laundromats, parks, and greasy spoons is striking up conversations with mothers who may be too lonely and desperate to ask for help.

Sometimes, her approach takes weeks of excruciatingly delicate manoeuvring. "Around the OHC, I kept hearing oblique comments about a young mother who hadn't got out of bed in months," McHugh recalled. "I squeezed in her door with a neighbour one morning. Just hung around, washed the dishes. Sure enough, there were three kids, ages 2, 4, and 6, fending for themselves." McHugh visited three or four times a week for a month before the severely depressed mother suddenly told her: "You can sit on the bed if you like." Finally, one bone-chilling morning in the bleak little apartment, it was: "You can get under the blanket if you want."

McHugh was thrilled. "That woman's okay now, an active member at the centre, and her kids are just fine. She's gone from a high-risk mom, you see, to low risk."

"Mom" is the word you hear; not "client". Part of Parent Resources' great strength in the community is that it has no authority. McHugh and the others will report abuse if they have to, but more frequently they'll talk the mother into calling for temporary Children's Aid Society relief herself. The aim is not to police but to offer the off-the-cuff practical help that an extended family might.

A Parent Resources success story: a woman with four children was evicted from Ontario Housing because her alcoholic husband ran off without paying the rent. So the woman went to stay in a hostel. Then she couldn't get back into OHC because she didn't have a permanent address. Because she didn't have an address, her mothers' allowance was cut back. Then, because she was indignant, her children were taken into care by the Children's Aid. On her reduced allowance, she could find only a room with a hotplate, so the CAS wouldn't let her have the children back. It was a three-year fight to help the woman straighten out her life.

An independent evaluation team was impressed by the amount of real change seen in the high risk mothers. How do you measure, though, the number of kids who *aren't* being screamed at, hit, or locked up? Not easily. But when you learn that Parent Resources runs two centres with seven skilled staff, serving a minimum of 300 families a year, on the ridiculously tiny annual budget of $150,000—and when you've trailed around for a day, as I have, behind McHugh, with her magical motherlode of oranges, crayons, and caring—you have to marvel at the tangible amount of healing and helping that is being done here.

I followed McHugh into one seedy OHC apartment where Dorothy, a confused and battered soul, was slumped on a grubby couch. Though it was mid-afternoon, Dorothy's 3-year-old twins were still in pajamas. "Why haven't you brought the boys to the centre?" McHugh asked, pulling out crayons for the twins. "We've missed you."

"Aaaw. I dunno, Marilyn. You know, I got troubles." But as the vivacious twins scrambled around their mother, demanding a picture, Dorothy picked up a crayon and drew for them. "House? Okay, see the house."

Afterward, McHugh beamed triumphantly. "You know, before she came to the centre, Dorothy would never have dreamed of drawing with the boys. In fact, she didn't even know enough to talk to them."

Prevention does work. It works especially when a project is so deeply rooted in the community. Because of its warmth and closeness to the neighbourhood (mothers who use the play centre also sit on the volunteer board of directors), Parent Resources has won the trust of deeply alienated people in a way I've rarely seen. Now all that is about to go down the drain. The problem is that Parent Resources is a demonstration project. It was set up to demonstrate methods of preventing child abuse; now that its worth is established, the funding is at an end. For $150,000 a year, Community and Social Services Minister Frank Drea could and emphatically should keep this invaluable service alive. But his assistant deputy minister, Peter Barnes, told me on the phone that "we will have to choose whether to spend money on more research or to use up all our funds on projects like this."

"If only people could vote on this," a Parent Resources worker said wistfully, looking around the lovely bright clutter of the play centre, "I just know they would vote for it."

In a way, the public did vote for the project. Five thousand readers clipped out coupons from the *Star* and sent them on to the provincial government, asking Frank Drea to save Parent Resources. The behind-the-scenes negotiations that ensued were revealing. Provincial government officials insisted to me that the province should not get into "direct service". It might create a dangerous precedent, they argued. After all, the province had a deal with Children's Aid Societies to provide all direct services to children. It would be unthinkable for the government to offend the CAS and set up a possible future obligation by helping children directly. Finally, an embarrassed ministry agreed to cough up the funds for Parent Resources if a Children's Aid Society would agree to administer the money and supervise the project.

Thus was Parent Resources offered a potentially lethal form of famine relief. If they gave up their autonomy (part of their trustworthy appeal to their community), they would be given enough money to keep them skeletally alive. The only hitch, then, was to coax the Children's Aid Society to act "in loco parentis" to Parent Resources. Once CAS senior official told me frankly, but off the record, that the CAS wouldn't lift a finger to help the little project because Parent Resources had been openly critical of CAS failures. A spokesman for the Catholic CAS told me, also off the record, that it didn't want to get involved because when the heat was off, a year or two down the road, when the press was looking the other way and the public had forgotten, the provincial government would quietly drop the funding. Then, with the Catholic CAS nominally in charge of Parent Resources, it would look like the villain if it suddenly cancelled the project.

Not one of these bureaucrats, from the provincial government down through all the ranks of the Children's Aid, ever mentioned to me the fate of the children whose lives were being improved, and possibly saved, by Parent Resources. I believe there is a withering blight that shrivels the imagination of bureaucrats and reduces them to tunnel vision. The blight is called Cover-My-Ass. It leads decent men and women to harden themselves to the suffering of the innocents, in exchange for the security of their salaries and the status quo.

In the end, the Catholic Children's Aid worked out an agreement with Parent Resources, and enough provincial money was found to keep the little project open for at least another year. Not exactly a shining chapter in the annals of child protection.

But not an uncommon chapter, unfortunately. Time and time again in the last half-dozen years, our institutionalized indifference to children has ended in suffering—or even death—for the most defenceless. Every time such neglect hits the newspapers, public outcry pushes the government to defend itself, back off, revise, or make partial amends. What cannot be mended, though, is the trail of damaged young lives. In early 1980, the story that gripped Canadians from coast to coast was Wendy Koenig's journalistic revelation in the *Edmonton Journal* of the treatment meted out by child-care "professionals".

Miss Arthur frightens me.

Miss Catherine Arthur, executive assistant to Alberta Social Services Minister Ralph Bogie, Miss Arthur whom I will never meet, is as scary to me as a bat in the living room, not meaning any personal harm but all the more alarming for that, blundering blindly into your life and leaving behind a trail of shattering moments. Miss Arthur came into my kitchen, via the newspaper, in the news item about five disturbed children in a government-funded treatment centre in Peace River, Alta. The story told how the five children in the home, most of them native children, all of them emotionally disturbed, had been punished according to the precepts of behaviour modification.

A 13-year-old girl was forced to smear her menstrual blood on the bathroom walls. A 12-year-old boy, a bedwetter, was forced to urinate on his sheets, sleep on them, and then wash and dry them in the morning, missing his breakfast and walking the 3½ miles to school if he wasn't finished in time. At night, the child-care workers could hear him sobbing for hours in his wet bed.

A 9-year-old boy, a child who rarely speaks and is thought to be retarded, was punished for mixing up the sign language for food and drink. He was not fed. He then ate from the dog's dish on the porch and was punished by being forced to eat dog food covered with Tabasco sauce. When he could not or would not wash the dishes, he was forced to stand at the sink, hands in water, for 12 to 16 hours without food, drink, or rest. The child-care workers, seeing him there at 3 a.m., with hands bloated from the water and a crust around his mouth from not eating or drinking, were told to walk by and ignore him.

My mind went skittering out of its comfortable paths when I read the story. I had to force myself not to think of my own trusting 9-year-old standing at that sink. For 16 hours. How does a 9-year-old stand there for 16 hours? Did he get sick from hunger and exhaustion? Did his legs tremble? Did he cry? Or did his eyes throb and his throat ache from not crying? How does it feel to be 9 years old, with no one in the world on your side?

We know whose side Miss Arthur is on. "Listen, I'm 100 per cent sensitive to how this looks to the public when they first come across it," confided Miss Arthur. Still, she said, forcing a child to sleep in his own urine or to eat pepper-spiked dog food are "common ways of behaviour management, prescribed in thousands of papers written by professional psychologists and psychiatrists who say it's the present-day way of curing people of bizarre acts."

Ah. It's common then. Nothing to worry about. Miss Arthur's language makes it all so clear. Note the nonchalance of "come across it", as though the torture of children were a daily commonplace among the insider-professionals, though a bit of a jolt to us sentimental proletarians when we first notice it. We'll get used to it. And how reassuring, that appeal to quantity and to the blank-eyed deity of science. "Thousands" of articles. The present-day way. And notice Miss Arthur's final, spiteful verbal flounce: "I guess the alternative is to say we can't help disturbed children at all."

Uh-uh, Miss Arthur, not so fast. Disturbed children may act bizarre, all right, just as a wounded animal may snarl at its rescuer. But the "cure" is not to goad them in their open wounds. There are many humane and decent alternatives to the mental torture you defend. We are well past the time when we genuflected as the naked Emperor of Science rode preening down the street.

There will always be a Miss Arthur, to defend the use of

> painful techniques on the powerless. But there will also be the ordinary, decent people, like those in Edmonton who are opening their homes to the five children, who trust their instincts enough to be outraged. They know, even if Miss Arthur may not, that a sadist may wear a white coat, and cite thousands of articles, and smile and smile, and be a charlatan.

Miss Catherine Arthur was subsequently promoted within her ministry.

The peculiar horror of child suffering and the common instinct to identify with the victim (the unjustly punished child in each of us rises in righteous fury at such stories), make it easy for reporters to stir up public outrage about child abuse. But what is the quality that makes governments and bureaucrats so strangely immune to the same sense of outrage? For one thing, there have been enough Children's Aid blunders, sometimes ending in the death of a child, and enough subsequent inquests, to make it clear that those in authority often identify with the abusive parent. In one case, a social worker was so sorry for the parent, and so determined to save her, and so self-hypnotized into thinking that the mother had made great strides under her guidance, that she gave back into the parent's care a child who was promptly and gruesomely murdered.

There is another pattern, too. The bureaucrat wrestles to bring an unruly problem under control. Of all problems, child abuse may be the most unruly, because the interventionist bureaucrat must tread an almost imperceptible line between child protection and the sanctity of the family. There is never enough money, and never enough co-operation from self-protective social workers, teachers, and doctors. If you remove a child from a dangerous home, the back-to-earthers may scream about the rupture of the parent-child bond or the genocide of original peoples. If you leave the child in a dangerous situation, you may eventually come up against a messy death and a lot of indignant questions from the public. Perhaps the bureaucrat, trapped between many equally repellent choices, settles his irritation on the pesky little brats who cause the trouble in the first place—the abused children themselves, and the bleeding-heart reporters who want to save them.

This hypothesis may explain the course of events set in motion when a federal civic servant named Corinne Robertshaw, a lawyer in the Department of Consumer and Corporate Affairs, decided to investigate the problem of child abuse for herself. In April of 1981, shortly after a brown-paper envelope containing the rough draft of Robertshaw's report arrived on my desk, my story appeared in the *Toronto Star*:

> Canada's first major study of child-abuse deaths—a hair-raising record of confusion, neglect, and preventable baby murder—has been stopped short by the federal government, just a few months before the report was to be published. About 30 top child-welfare experts, alarmed that the study's searing revelations may never see the light of day, have apparently protested to Health and Welfare Minister Monique Bégin. But Bégin has not explained why federal government lawyer Corinne Robertshaw won't be allowed to finish her exhaustive report. I spent last night slogging through the report, with its painstaking analysis of how 54 children died in 1977. And I'm staggered that the government would stifle information so horrifying and so important.
>
> Homicide, says Robertshaw, is the fourth major cause of death among Canadian children, ages 1 to 5. Based on this first nationwide survey, Robertshaw estimates that 100 to 200 children are killed by their parents or caretakers every year in Canada, through battering or severe neglect. But the deaths are hidden. Child-abuse registries and homicide statistics would reveal only about 30 of these beaten, burned, starved, smothered, and broken little souls. How can we be placidly ignorant of the children who are being tormented down the block or in the next town? It's a chain of squeamishness and ineptitude. Doctors don't report strange bruises. Coroners don't recognize child-abuse syndrome. Police are muddled about whose duty it is to investigate. Inquest juries look murder straight in the eye and call it "death by unknown causes".
>
> Robertshaw pieced together the details of 54 deaths from police, court, Children's Aid, government, and newspaper records. Take Death No. 2, for example. That's how the

report grimly lists them. Death No. 2 was the 3-month-old son of a young professional couple. They were completely ordinary people, on the surface. They were opposed to "spoiling" and in favour of "discipline". The mother had been strapped as a child.

When the baby died, he was found to have a fractured skull, greatly swollen buttocks and thigh, previously fractured ribs and forearm, and injured thigh bones. Three months of beating and pain. Half a year later, a one-day inquest listened to the parent's flat denials ("He fell") and decided that death was due to "causes unknown", though psychiatric help was recommended for the parents. No charges were laid. The death did not show up as a homicide in Statistics Canada. You couldn't murder a dog and get away so lightly.

Death No. 15 was an 18-month-old girl whose scrawny corpse bore the marks of early fractures, neglect, and ruptured intestines. Neighbours had heard the screams. But six months earlier, when child-protection workers were called to investigate, they contented themselves with quizzing the apartment superintendent. Police also investigated and decided all was well.

Death No. 19 was a girl 4 months old. Her father was awaiting trial on charges of assaulting her, causing bodily harm, when she was only 2 months old. It seems nobody thought to get her out of harm's way. Two months later, he killed her brutally. He got two years less a day, increased to seven years on the crown's appeal.

Death No. 32 was a 10-month-old boy who had already survived burns and bruises by the time his mother kicked him to death. The post-mortem found massive damage to liver, pancreas, and lungs. The death certificate said "accident" and so did Statistics Canada. The mother got a suspended sentence for manslaughter.

Horror-stricken by the number of battered and murdered babies, even the professionally impassive report-writer concludes: "We should think of these deaths not as statistics but as defenceless children who died, and in many cases lived, under conditions of truly appalling fear, suffering, and despair."

How does it happen? How could it be that more than half these 54 children already were known to the authorities, yet still unprotected, when they died? Because, for one thing, our laws are an archaic muddle, and for another, we taxpayers begrudge the money to do the job. Coast to coast, even the definitions of abuse are a welter of confusion. The rules are dizzyingly different: is it abuse when a child has been strapped and bruised? Do you report abuse when you suspect it, or only when you believe it, or when you have proof? Even the child-abuse registries vary. Some provinces don't bother to list the already-slain. Others place parents' rights to privacy before the child's rights to be protected. Central reporting systems are so ragged that a homicidal family can trek from Newfoundland to British Columbia, easily slipping through the provincial nets of identification.

Many infanticides are never investigated because doctors are sloppy in filling out death certificates. Ignorant coroners can totally miss the symptoms of a child-abuse death. In Saskatchewan, unbelievably, only 66 of 170 coroners are doctors, and in 1977 they listed no child-abuse deaths at all. Robertshaw's scrutiny of 37 "sudden infant-death syndrome" babies in that province in that year, though, turns up at least eight who breathed their last under bizarre circumstances of violence, neglect, and terror.

Ontario has no reason to be smug despite recent efforts to improve. In one major Ontario city, the police, schools, Children's Aid, and public health nurses all admitted to Robertshaw their state of total confusion. Who should investigate, report, intervene? Nobody seems to have a clear answer.

Robertshaw's answer is a federal initiative to encourage clear, uniform reporting systems. We'll never be galvanized into action, she writes, until the public can get solid information about the extent of child-killing. One recommendation that leaps to my attention is the multi-disciplinary "flying squad" on the model of the team in Winnipeg. A group of doctors, nurses, police, social workers, and psychologists work independently, based in the community rather than reporting to one hospital or agency. They should have the power, Robertshaw says, to commandeer any kind of preventive help for any endangered child.

Revenge, blame, or punishment are not the point. To save

children from agony, to break the cycle of abuse, we need to hear what Robertshaw has to tell us. But when her report was submitted to the federal Department of Health and Welfare, Ottawa civil servants writhed in embarrassment. They had been fudging, twiddling thumbs, filing statistics, making excuses, sending out pamphlets, and collecting pay cheques for years. When Robertshaw won government approval for her study, she started a slow trickle of icy resentment down the hardened arteries of the federal bureaucrats. Eventually, that resentment was to snow her under and nearly bury her report.

As government insiders tell it, social workers in the Department of Health and Welfare last winter manipulated the minister, Monique Bégin, into killing Robertshaw's report before it could be completed and published. Just one hitch. A leaked copy of the report reached the *Star* and we blazoned it across the front page. When I reached assistant deputy minister Brian Iverson of Health and Welfare, he said, "We never intended the study to be so complete, so sweeping. No further work need be done. We will publish some parts of it but I'm not prepared to say which parts." A few months later, a truncated version of the report was grudgingly released to the public, and Robertshaw was sent back to her desk in the Department of Consumer and Corporate Affairs.

There it rests. In fact, Bégin hopes the report will rest in peace, permanently. Just to make sure there will be no restless public demand for action, she has set up a piddling little smokescreen of a unit called Clearing House on Family Violence. More pamphlet-mailing. Judging by my phone interviews there, the unit shows no sign whatever of following up any of Robertshaw's 100 superb recommendations.

I'll leave you with what she calls Death number 21, a 17-month-old girl. Father was a wife-beater. Mother illiterate. Both believed in "hitting gently" as a means of discipline.

Cause of death: perforated bowel and peritonitis caused by severe blunt force to stomach. Baby had been known to authorities as an abused child; courts had refused to make her a ward.

My verdict: Society guilty of neglect.

Prognosis: No foreseeable change, until we all undergo a revolution of the heart.

THE HEART OF THE FAMILY

I HAD JUST BEGUN WORK ON THIS BOOK, IN THE EARLY
weeks of 1982, when I was stopped short by the sudden death of
my mother, whom I loved aboundingly. "Elderly Widow Dies
In House Fire" read the headline of the news story that first
unbelievable day of my mother's non-existence, and in the midst
of the roaring waterfall of emotion in which I felt myself to be
tumbling, I was caught by that compulsion known only to the
victims of publicized events. I wanted to set the record straight.
"No, no, an elderly widow," I protested, though she was—but
the words took her far away from her own self and from me.

Then the hundreds of letters and cards began to come, many
from strangers. They kept me steady, those voices of friends and
strangers, as though they had joined hands to reach a lifeline to
me in deep water, Still, one or two of them well-meaningly
jarred. "You must feel so guilty," said one. "We understand; the
old become incompetent but stubbornly insist on living alone,"
said another. "She must have been the archetypal Jewish
grandmother," someone wrote. No, no, no. It was not like that.
The need to explain what she was, and what she meant to me,
stood like a shadow between me and this book for two months,
until I grappled with the shadow to write this.

On Friday evening, as was our custom, my mother came over to
our house for dinner, tootling up gaily in the trim little car she
had bought herself last year, a good year for real estate, and for
busy agents like herself. Upstairs, at my typewriter, I heard her
quick, light step as she came in the front door. She always walked
in that quick, proud way, holding her small body consciously
erect, defying time and gravity—and especially defying the
painful bunions on her feet that prevented her from wearing the

elegant shoes that my Aunt Milly sent from Europe. But she never talked about pain.

The summer before, her eighty-second summer, she had travelled with my fifteen-year-old daughter to Paris. They walked eight to ten miles a day, my mother indefatigably alert and interested. Adversity met its match in my mother; years of grinding work and disappointments were greeted with the same good-humoured resolve she brought with her to the better years.

Three summers before, my husband, three children, mother and I had travelled to the south of France. Late one evening, we alighted at the château Castel Novel in Périgord, once the home of Colette. We dined late on cold meats and pickles and a rosé wine of the region; the tablecloths were pink linen and we ate in a glassed-in porch that leaned out into the dark, rustling forest. My mother grew pink-cheeked after a few sips of wine, as always; at family festivities, her combination of diminutive regality and impish merriment was delicious.

That night in Périgord, the children were caught up in the mood of sensuous delight in our surroundings, the candlelight and the giddy, teasing laughter of which their grandma was the centre. As we all went up the ancient, curving staircase to bed, the children's giggles echoed off the stone walls.

"Don't your feet hurt, Grandma?" asked our son, weak from laughter and with twenty stone stairs still to climb.

"No," answered my mother, tossing her head as majestically as the wine would allow, "because I do not choose to let them."

My daughters remember their grandmother as someone fastidiously delicate. When you hugged her, you felt the softness of cashmere and silk, faintly scented with French perfume, all costly gifts from Europe, cared for and used for twenty to thirty years. Beneath the daintiness, though, there was the quiet strength of a woman who chose not to let things hurt her. When my father didn't earn enough to keep a roof over our heads (he was a travelling salesman who often spent more on expenses than he earned), my mother kept us afloat with a complicated series of delays and kindnesses she coaxed from bank managers. She house-hunted on streetcars and busses between long mornings and afternoons spent with her mother, then dying of leukemia. She braved the sneers of wealthier friends to go to work to support us in the tradition-strangled nineteen-fifties. In her seventies, after my father died, she jauntily travelled Scandinavia, Portugal, and Spain on her own.

Rattling across borders in a farmer's cart, how did my grandma Zlateh keep the two baby girls quiet under the hay? Did tiny Naomi Leah, Nachama Laiah, my mother, hold her hand over the mouth of her baby sister, jolting there on the wooden boards underneath the tickling straw? From Kiev to London, where my grandfather Zelig waited for them, it took at least a year. No one is now left alive to remember that journey, the silences or fear, the secrets kept, across how many forbidden boundaries.

But they learned to be good at secrets. In London, Zelig and Zlateh won the ultimate treasure for their first child — a British passport — by falsely swearing that Naomi Leah had been born in London in 1901. All her life, my mother hid the secret of her birth in Kiev. Those extra two or three years that might have given her away to some stern immigration official were kept secret, even from me. Officially, she died two months before her eighty-second birthday.

Golders Green, London. A seething Jewish slum. What did my mother gain there? Paradoxically and wonderfully, a precise English accent. A memory of the rich smell of Saturday-night dinner, the heavy, steaming pot carried home in her trembling small arms from the communal oven at the bakery. And a love of wild violets and primroses, and their fragile cold scent, in a spring woods outside London, on a school outing.

A picture, now lost forever in the flames, showed my mother at the age of nine, new to Canada. She had green-hazel eyes and a straight, fine nose in an oval face, under a haze of dark curls. She was so slender that Zlateh coaxed her to drink cream. She looked solemnly out at the photographer, holding a baby brother who was going to die.

I don't know where the sense of style came from. All the Glassmans had it. All six of the brothers and sisters were attractive, vital, with a taste for things like chaste blue Wedgwood plates and Royal Sarouk carpets, without ever having passed through that first, more usually caricatured stage of acculturation, those heavy ghettoized accents, florid susceptibilities, gross extroversion, and pinched money-hungers so dear to novelists. Mordecai Richler's relatives may have been flinty-eyed acquisitives, belching and scratching in their undershirts on St. Urbain Street. Mine never were.

Grandpa was a skilled cabinetmaker in Russia before he ran away from the Czar's army. Even though Grandma pushed him into construction work in Canada, he spent so much time and money on fine veneers and exquisite woodwork in the houses he made that he never got rich. My mother's physical elegance came from him, her father Zelig, and they shared an extraordinary pacific dignity. In 1958, at the Venice Film Festival, on a grand tour of Europe laid on by Aunt Milly and her husband Massimo, my mother and my grandfather walked arm-in-arm down the promenade from the Excelsior Lido Hotel to the festival cinema. Maria Schell walked ahead of them, ignored by the crowds lining the street. But when Grandpa appeared, regal in his white dinner jacket and silver hair, with my mother looking darkly glamorous in a black-and-white dress, the crowd roared forward for his autograph. They thought he was a distinguished foreign director. My Yiddish-speaking grandpa didn't understand a word of the Italianate furor; my mother, excited and embarrassed, blushed, sparkled, and held her head up.

Late at night, my grandma sat by the lamp, stitching copies of the French imports she had impudently studied in store windows downtown. My mother, eldest of the admired Glassman sisters, went to dances in ruched silk and swirling chiffon. She danced like a feather. A boyfriend had a job demonstrating ballroom dancing at the fancy hotels; the dancers would drift back from the floor to watch and applaud as he swept my mother around in his arms, my mother from Kiev and Golders Green in her watered silk and porcelain beauty.

In family stories, Leah is quicksilver, flashing through frosty nights on Grenadier Pond in her wickedly long-bladed speed

skates, or making all of Markham Street gasp as she drove her
father's new car (he beside her, proud and indulgent) all the way
home from High Park, and she only fifteen.

She even played on a women's basketball team; my father,
who everybody said looked like Clark Gable, was the coach. He
came into the office where she worked and said that he would
shoot himself if she didn't marry him. After the wedding, he took
her up north on a fishing trip. The photographs showed her in
jodhpurs, bravely brandishing an iron frying pan while the
French-Canadian guides showed off strings of enormous pickerel.

I never heard many reminiscences of the earliest years in Toronto.
Grandma had brought them up with a determined eye to a
better future, and there was little nostalgia among the Glassmans
for those old days when Grandma had run up and down University Avenue with a dying two-year-old girl in her arms, distractedly begging passers-by for help because none of the hospitals
would take in an infant with scarlet fever.

My mother remembered the boot-maker coming to the house
on Markham Street to measure them all for their new leather
button-up boots, but she also remembered the groans of her
mother giving birth upstairs, and the screams of despair when a
baby boy died of the diphtheria he had caught on the boat
coming over.

It's not surprising that my mother, coming from a home where
babies had died, was a strict follower of medical advice in the
wholesome upbringing of infants. She listened to the cruel
tyrannies of Alan Brown, famous paediatrician of the day, and
agonizingly refrained from cuddling us when we cried and from
feeding us between the rigid four-hour intervals he decreed. We
also had our fresh air, our oatmeal, our two colours of vegetables
every night (with their vitamins intact, thanks to her new-fangled
pressure cooker), our home-preserved fruits in winter, our brown
lisle stockings, our nothing-but-white-cotton-underwear-against-
the-skin, our regular bedtimes and regular risings, and our
biblical injunctions to scrupulous cleanliness, and in this calm
order, we grew.

Only in later years, hearing the resentful stories of other

daughters, did I realize what particular light-handed genius and grace my mother brought to the task of housekeeping. She was a gifted cook. Strawberries shone like whole rubies in her miraculously fresh-tasting jam. She could eat Danish pastries or French sauces in a restaurant and recreate them effortlessly at home; she scorned any sauce thickened with flour or cornstarch, and invented secrets, like a squeeze of lemon in the chicken soup or a touch of caramelized sugar to help brown a roast, that amazed her guests when the indefinable subtleties of flavour were explained.

Our small rented duplex gleamed with furniture polish and the silver tea service; linens fragrant from the clothesline were ironed to silken order before they were filed flat in the cupboard. All this quiet plenitude was achieved on the skimpiest budget, and with no nagging or fuss.

Our souls were tended to more diffidently than our bodies. Perfect grammar and clear enunciation were almost more important than religion; I was scolded sharply for unconsciously imitating a friend's sing-song inflection, but my mother was silent when we clamoured for a Christmas tree and didn't explain why we couldn't have one. She was shy and reticent in talking about abstract ideas, and believed in shielding children from difficult knowledge.

We were taught the strictest honesty. When, at age five or six, I was delighted to find a tawdry lapel ornament on the street outside Eaton's, my mother made me stop and think about "the poor soul" who had bought and lost such a pathetically cheap trinket. But when she wanted to articulate her most passionately felt convictions, my mother often had to fall back on platitudes.

She, who so valued her own feminine beauty, was baffled when I became a rebellious teenager, sullenly insisting on jeans, pigtails, and a calculated defiance of ladylike convention. "But even nature adorns herself!" exclaimed my mother, appealing to my poetic intensity. She was mystified when I laughed. She was not much given to introspection, but kept on scrubbing pots, patiently and efficiently, as I paced up and down the kitchen, spouting my half-comprehended gobbets of existentialism and Simone de Beauvoir.

We couldn't agree on anything, but she had the grace to interfere with me as little as possible. When I came back from a year in Israel at eighteen, we were able to be friends, and never quarrelled seriously again.

Being Jewish was problematic in some ways. Though her own Jewishness was never in question, my mother was so determined to put narrow sectarianism behind us that she nearly whisked us straight out of Judaism altogether.

When she was five or six, in London, she was deathly ill with scarlet fever. Waking in the whiteness of a convalescent hospital, she thought she had died and gone to heaven. "Say just one word, *tateleh*," wept my grandfather beside the bed, "say just one word in *mamaloshen* [mother tongue] and I'll give you a shilling." But she had forgotten all her Yiddish, and never spoke it well again.

She grew up in a time when being Jewish could get you shunted around Europe, sent back to point of embarkation, harried from one country to another, even murdered. I felt the first tremors of this when she registered me for kindergarten in 1944. "Religion?" snapped the school secretary. Pause. My mother's hand tightening on mine. "Hebrew," she answered. Hebrew? That was when I learned that it could be dangerous to say "Jewish".

So we were brought up in the watery pieties of Holy Blossom Temple, a ludicrously named Reform congregation, then in the flush of assimilationism, with its all-English service, Christianly throbbing organ, and gentile choir. The rabbi, Abraham Feinberg, once stopped a service to rebuke a man who was wearing a yarmelkeh. He wouldn't go on until the offensively ethnic skull-cap was removed.

After my grandma died, there was little to anchor us to the rhythm of the Jewish year.

I knew, as soon as I knew anything, that my mother was particularly beautiful, and I thought that her perfection was like a doom-laden judgement on me, who could never grow to equal her. She was astonished, later, to hear this from me.

If I envied anything, it should have been her easy competence in practical things, skill that grew from her calm sense of order, the way her violets and tomatoes and lilac cuttings leaped riotously into bloom for her while she benignly ignored them.

At the log cottages my parents would rent in Muskoka when we children were small, my mother would rise before dawn, flick my father's hand-tied flies into a nearby brook, and come back laden. We would wake to the sizzle of brook trout in the pan, and blueberry pies from yesterday's picking, their purple juices welling up through the crust.

Part of my mother's rare charm was her low, musical voice and her tact. She had the mild touch, the feel of just what to say when young colleagues appealed to her for advice or when she was drawn into other people's family storms. She never blurted. She could bite back a retort or hold a secret for twenty years, if she had to; there was plenty of reserve there, whalebone behind the silk.

When I gave my first child her first bath, it was the first baby I had ever held in my arms. I was so slow that her little fingers turned blue and she howled piteously. My mother stood by, arms folded, smiling encouragement. Years later, she confessed that she had yearned to snatch the poor wee thing and wrap her up warmly. But she didn't breathe a word at the time lest I feel inadequate.

Her age was one secret she kept, fiercely, so that her colleagues wouldn't dismiss her as an old lady. She was older than fifty when she nervously dyed away the few gray strands in her hair and went out to apply for her first job, as a receptionist in a new real estate office. Ladies didn't work, but we were broke and trying to pay for our new house in the suburbs. The real estate office coaxed her to become an agent. All through my teens, I realize now, when people asked me if that beautiful woman was my older sister, she was in her fifties and sixties.

She was a hard-working and shrewd real estate agent, but too scrupulous to get rich. But she made enough to support us all. And she would come home late at night from her work to scrub floors, cook—even the stews she made for the dog, flavoured with herbs and garlic, smelled so delicious that she had to label them sternly to prevent our eating them—and even to dig and haul rocks for a garden she had planned. She planted portulaca between the flagstones and transplanted crab apples. She weighed one hundred pounds. I would emerge from an evening's reading to find her out in the summer night, hauling boulders or wrestling a stone bird-bath into place.

We grew, my mother and I, to cherishing each other's real qualities instead of yearning for the ones that weren't there. She gave up on my ever becoming a lady—all those years of taking me to ballet lessons, posing me for photographers with satin bows in my hair, all those years of gentle reproofs when I smoked and swore—and took delight in, of all things, my Jewish home. Many of the old customs I had to learn out of books, and then, "But this is just what Papa used to do!" she would exclaim, coming in before Passover to find me and the children hunting through the darkened house, candles in our hands, for the hidden bits of leavened bread that had to be ritually burnt.

The last Passover we spent together, she and I cooked for three day in my kitchen. We laughed helplessly at our yearly-expanding extravagance. We had chickens to roast, ducklings, brisket, chicken soup with matzah balls light as small clouds, freshly made horseradish she wept over, gefilte fish as puffy and tender as quenelles, prickled with pepper, served elegantly, of course. My mother hurried after me as I rushed the plates to the table, stopping me to decorate each piece of fish just so with a coin of carrot and a sprig of parsley.

An ardent but collapsing acolyte, I marvelled at her style in the kitchen: inexhaustible, whisking away the dirty pots so that in the midst of many concoctions, the kitchen stood in trim order; her tiny form wreathed in fragrant steams and alight with energy and good humour. "My *Yiddishe tochter*," she said to me that year, beaming. It was a deep pride to her that I would consciously carry on the Jewish traditions she had nearly lost by taking them for granted. And I adored her.

On Friday evening, the last Friday evening in January, the last time I saw her, we prepared together for the Sabbath. The children were all home. She blessed the candles; after dinner, she taught my youngest daughter "*Oifen pripichek*", an old Yiddish song about a rabbi teaching the children their alphabet by the warmth of a pot-bellied stove.

She was not afraid of fire but of water. When my brother and I were no more than four and five, she forced herself to learn to swim at the YWCA before taking us to a cottage that summer. Our first day there, she waded in and swam a measured breast-stroke back and forth between two docks, holding her head up high. "See, children?" she called to us flutingly. "Nothing to be afraid of."

My brother and I, who both loved the water, were puzzled. "Why is Mummy scared?" I asked my brother.

She was frightened of ill health, hospitals, decline, and dependency, so she treated them as she did any fears, by sturdily ignoring them. She didn't want to depend on me (when she broke her wrist once, she went to the hospital with a friend and called me later as though nothing had happened), but she treasured the warmth and love we shared, particularly in the years of my children.

She was nervous, sometimes, of my educated angers. That last Friday, we talked together about the feminist books I'd been reading and how many feminists of my generation seemed to hate their mothers for the repressed and restricted ways in which they'd been brought up.

"I hope," said my mother, with a slight quaver, as though this had long been in her mind, "you don't feel that I favoured the boys when I was bringing you up."

"No, no, no!" That was all so long ago, and she had done what seemed right.

"And I certainly hope you don't hate *your* mother; that would be awful."

"Oh *mamitchka*," and I covered her hands with kisses, "you know how lovable you are to me."

That last Friday was tinged with an extra emotion. "Mmph!" exclaimed my mother, giving my youngest, Jenny Leah Zlateh, a huge, playful hug. "You give me so much pleasure!" And she and I hugged at the door. I tucked up the soft collar of the mink coat around her small, bright, still beautiful face as we stood at the door saying good-night, good-bye.

On Sunday, it was the fifteenth anniversary of my father's

death, and the heaviest snowstorm of the year in Toronto. My
mother spent all afternoon by the cosy warmth of her fireplace.
My nephew, Stephen, who had a special closeness with my
mother because he had lived at her house while he attended
university, dropped in to see her about dinner-time, and sat with
her—she was in fine humour—to chat beside the fire. When he
left, she sat there still and called family and friends. Late in the
evening, she called us: "Just wanted to make sure everyone in
your family is safe home in the awful storm."

"Yes, all safe."

And quietly she went to bed, first letting the embers die down,
as always, and safely tucking the screen tight against the fireplace.
Went to bed and slept, my sweet mother, and didn't know that
heat was building in the vinyl chair by the fireplace, and soon
the orange flames would burst out, and black smoke roll through
her spotless house with the green plants on the windowsill, the
grandfather clock ticking in the living room.

At 4:30 in the morning, we woke abruptly to a banging at the
door. The window showed us the white light of snow, and a
police car blinking at the curb. "What a hell of time to come
banging," I said, crossly and irrationally. My husband climbed
into pants and stumbled downstairs. I followed, curiously. Half-
way down, at the landing, I stopped. "There's bad news," the
policeman was saying. "Your mother-in-law, Lee...there's been
a fire..."

The children woke terrified in the dark to hear my screams.
"Is she alive? Is she alive?" My eleven-year-old covered her head
with the pillow so she wouldn't hear the answer.

The policeman was young. He couldn't bear to answer our
question. "Phone the hospital," he said. My husband's face was
pulled back into lines of agony as he dialled, shaking. "What can
I tell you," the doctor kept saying. "You'd better come
identify..."

We drove up through the dark city, in the uncleared snow.
Groans were being dragged from my gut, as though on a fish-
hook. My whole body ached with unbelief and horror. Is my
mother dead? Then a hole has been torn in this safe dome of the
universe where I've been living so calmly. Nothing is safe. A hole

has been torn; anybody I love might be ripped away from me by that dark, howling vortex outside.

"No, no, not Leah," wept one of my uncles later. "But Leah is indestructible." So she seemed, my invincibly beautiful little mother, proudly looking twenty years younger than her age, her quick empathy always so alive to others.

At the hospital, they opened a door and showed me her small body under a sheet. My mother's body that gave me life; I knew all its little softnesses and gentle decline, its worn loveliness. The sharp and terrible smell of smoke clung to her, who was always so pristine. They told me later that they found her near the bed. She could only have taken a step or two. Probably, they said, she never knew the flames were eating her house alive, and that black, oily smoke had stolen away her oxygen while she slept. The room with the fireplace was gone, with all its treasures, its family photographs we had laughed and sighed over. Curtains melted, walls cracked, blackness and chaos fell on her orderly dishes in the cupboard, silver candlesticks fell crumbling in the heat, the grandfather clock bent double. But the flames spared her bedroom; they did not touch her where she lay on the rug, her breath gone.

That endless Monday, they began to bring back to me the blackened and smoke-reeking belongings snatched from her smouldering house. Her mink coat, the last thing I saw and held her in, was an oily ruin. She had had it for twenty years, a treasured gift from my aunt. She left it to me in her will. A friend took it away to a cleaner to get the smell out of my house. The cleaner called weeks later to say nothing could be done with it. The insurance adjuster went and got it and threw it away.

I hadn't known that I had so many tears; my face was scalded raw from them. I hadn't known I was so unready to give her up. The days passed. Those wretched, groaning sobs were no longer dragged out of me by shock and the violent suddenness of loss. My brothers came, and the house was filled with friends and relatives for a week. Gradually, my mother stopped being only mine. It was as though she had stepped back a few astonishing paces, so that I could suddenly see the lines of connection running between her and all the others she had touched. Friends astounded me with their letters, friends of hers who told me how they had cherished her sweetness, friends of mine who had known my mother through me and who now said, "I loved her." Chastened, I realized how little I had ever noticed. A postal clerk recognized her picture in the paper and wrote to me: "I always thought she had goodness shining in her face."

At night, a thousand times, my heart would thump me awake and I'd be calling inside my head" "Mum, Mum, wake up, danger!" A thousand times in half-sleep, I played and replayed the moments, tested the fog inside her mind (terror? did she know terror?), dashed through smoke and crackling flames to snatch her unconscious body from the bedroom floor and carry her through to safety.

Then these lurid insistent imaginings faded. I spent a month scrubbing thick black filth from little china flowers and crystal glasses, small fragile treasures, weeping as the soot and chemicals and water streaked down my arms: "Did this really come through the flames, and not my mother?" I started realizing things: how central a place she had in my life; certain delicate resemblances between my mother and my oldest daughter; how grateful I was for my extravagant habits of self-expression, coaxing and tickling and kissing my mother out of a lifetime of reserve and into the more open and loving years at the end.

"Elderly widow?" Never. She was as vivacious and self-sufficient as a sparrow on a branch. Guilty? No. No guilts, no regrets, beyond the one huge one of losing her. I hadn't imagined the size of the empty space she would leave behind. Women wrote to me to say that they knew about that void, and that when their mothers died, it was an ache that no one else could ever quite soothe.

I see that after all these words, I still have not the novelist's art of bringing her convincingly alive on the page. I had wanted to record something of the meaning and shape of her life: her intelligence and spirit; the way she threw back her head delightedly to laugh at family stories; her rare civility that seemed to hold the family in balance and still connected, so that even feuding cousins or alienated brothers could somehow keep their membership in the unit alive through her.

Two months later, I miss her with a physical grief that embarrasses me but is implacable. Sometimes I lean my forehead against a wall and feel I could call her back from nothingness; I wonder how I could have gone so many years not realizing how much I relied on her steady love, her sane good humour, her optimism, her example of indomitability and level good judgement.

The Jewish funeral service is stark. We stood in the heavy, wet snow, snow that matted on our heads, and were told: God gives life and God takes it away. You cannot have one without the other. Be grateful. I am grateful, and I know now, much better than before, how much we are all a part of a wheeling, turning circle of growth and death, but there is still a tight ache in my throat when I am alone and thinking of her, and a steady rainfall of tears.

There were things we shared and never talked about: the extraordinary satisfied peacefulness we each felt in our turn when we had served the Friday-night dinner and cleared everything away, the family fed, the candles still glowing in the clean kitchen. The intense sensual joy in cuddling and breast-feeding our babies. A private mischievous greed that took its piquancy from daily restraints, a naughty indulgence we shared together when we would impulsively make crêpes just to sprinkle icing sugar on them from a specially elegant shaker, or tea biscuits to drench with butter and freshly made berry jam. The way raspberries looked on the branch after rain. A sudden sharp ache of loss for Zlateh (her mother, my grandmother) when one of the children did something particularly reminiscent.

I couldn't write a chapter called "The Heart of the Family" without first trying, out of my love and debt to her, to write about my mother, who was the heart of my family, and is still its rhythm that goes on as long as I and mine will live.

Oh here is the story of our families;
We've looked for the roots of our family trees.
Escaping from hunger, oppression, and strife,
Our people have come here to start a new life.
Singing too-ra-lee too-ra-lee too-ra-lee-ay.

The children's voices rose up, scrambled for the high notes, and cheerfully belted home on the too-ra-lee-ays. Above our heads dangled a galaxy of dodecahedrons: twelve-sided paper ornaments, each side emblazoned with a symbol of that child's family. The "Cross of Jesus" bumped up against a menorah in the swaying air, and a Union Jack swung beside a peddler's cart.

The 30 children, ages 4 to 11, of Walker Avenue School were treating us parents to a festival that crowned two months of intense work. It all began last year when one of the black children at the school, with the help of his adoptive white family, searched for and found his natural mother. A study of black history followed. All the children watched some *Roots* television episodes and the older ones read a stirring biography of Paul Robeson. Then everyone got in on the act: kids were scurrying home with lists of questions for grannie or uncle. How did we come to Canada? Why? What did we bring? What did we leave behind?

So there we were last Friday night, beaming parents and grandparents sandwiched into the narrow city house that serves as a school. Everything gleamed and danced in the glow of candles: the children's paintings; the huge paper "family" tree that climbed the wall, its papier mâché roots sprouting out across the floor; and, of course, the children's eyes as they lined up to sing.

They sang about Jo-Jo, a daring and skillful little cook, delighted to learn that her grandma pulled toffee in a candy factory. They sang about Alison, who complained that her Loyalist background was dull, until she learned how her ancestors fled here in the teeth of the American revolution. The two most senior Canadians, it turned out, were Jason, whose Chinese ancestors worked on the railway, and Keith.

What kind of train did Keith's ancestors ride?
The Underground Railway whose passengers hide.
In Canada, blacks could be legally free...
Cross over the border to flee slavery.

Listening to the children sing, and strolling around afterward with a plateful of turkey and a glass of wine to peer at their paintings, I marvelled at the sheer variety of pain and suffering from which all these people arrived. Pogroms in Russia, the stony poverty of a Greek island, wars flaming across Europe. One moppet sang about his ancestor who plotted to kill the Swedish king. Zachary's dad brought his draft card to hang on the family tree; the Viet Nam war had turned him into a Canadian. Briar's mum brought her identity card from a World War II DP (displaced persons) camp in Germany. And more than one parent's eyes glistened as old pain and new liberty were celebrated.

My own Jenny startled me with the passionate lines she wrote: "Where am I going? I am going into the future carrying the tradition of fighting for equal rights. My branches reach out to shelter the people I will love some day."

Afterward, as we gossiped, laughed, and ate together, some of the parents said they were angry that there hadn't been more Canadian content. I didn't know what to say to them. It was the first time, in a lifetime of attending and then being a parent at Canadian schools, that the Christmas concert didn't make me feel like an outsider. It was the first time I had seen Canadian realities vigorously spoken: little Matthew, for example, telling about one ancestor who was born on a ship fleeing the Irish potato famine, and another grandparent, Japanese, who was interned in Canada during the last war.

I was proud and touched beyond words to see a whole school of children whose research into their pasts kindled in them a sense of racial tolerance and social justice. Every single one of them discovered forebears who were, somewhere, persecuted by someone else. And every single one of them washed up on these shores because in Canada you could be free. Could any Canadian content be more profound than that?

My life is full of little incongruities. "Do you really sell, er, pre-fab sukkahs?" I found myself asking on the phone to Lansing Lumber one day recently.

"Yep, gotcha," reassured someone laconically cheerful. "Fifty-three dollars, fifty cents, delivered to your door, with nails."

I felt as silly as the first intrepid soul who ever bought a plastic Christmas tree or a Styrofoam jack o'lantern. A sukkah, you see, is a harvest booth or hut. I build one every year, according to tradition, for the Jewish harvest festival of Sukkot. For eight days, we're supposed to eat our meals in a rickety backyard hut festooned with grapes and wheat sheaves, in chilly thanksgiving, and in memory of our ancestors who wandered 40 years in the desert.

I'm sure it all made perfect sense to my forefathers and foremothers about 3000 years ago. They would finish up the fall harvest and knock off work for about three weeks. Everyone would head for Jerusalem, where all the holy days were sensibly crammed into a few festive weeks.

It still made perfect sense to me when I was a student one year in Jerusalem. Everyone was still getting lots of time off for the big holy days, and we ate in holiday idleness in a huge straw-thatched sukkah in the balmy 80-degree warmth of a Mediterranean September. Some of the wild Jerusalem cats decided to be fruitful and multiply on the flimsy roof, and one morning a surprised little kitten fell smack into the middle of breakfast. We spent the whole holiday morning finding a way to reunite the kitten with its family.

That was all very well. But can you imagine how hectic it is in the brisk new world for a Jewish mama who also works fulltime? There's barely a minute to make the chicken soup and the apples with honey, let alone build harvest huts in the backyard. Which brings me around again to Lansing Lumber and its pre-fab. For years I've been making ramshackle monstrosities with anything handy: left-over tent poles, Scotch tape, bamboo blinds, twine, and branches snatched from the neighbours' autumn pruning. This year, I was clean out of tent poles and inspiration. When I heard about the pre-fab, I phoned at once, hardly blushing at all.

And let me tell you, a pre-fab sukkah is a lovesome thing. The kids and I scrambled about for a couple of sunny hours, drilling holes in two-by-fours, squinting at diagrams, dropping sheets of particle board on each other's toes. At last, we fitted the three half-walls together (a sukkah has to be mostly open, with a roof of branches), and there it stood, the grandest, finest sukkah in our family history.

But the work wasn't done yet. Next came the harvest, which we did, not with scythes and bill-hooks, but with cold cash: bunches of wine grapes on the Danforth, and clever little striped orange and green gourds at the florist. Then it was down to the ravine with the pruning shears and a bundle buggy. Indiana Jones Junior shinnied up a tree with a knife in his belt to reap some glossy red berries hanging in thick clusters. Meanwhile, I discovered some appropriately Mosaic bulrushes (cattails, really) along the creek. We found scarlet branches of sumac, clumps of purple aster, dried Queen Anne's lace looking sere and dramatic, tall stalks of evening primrose with golden seed pods, wild flowers shaped like bright yellow buttons, and enough burrs to pin our pant legs to our socks as firmly as bicycle clips. A true city harvest.

Later, I went outside to finish making ready the sukkah. The rules say you have to know it is temporary, so you must see the sky through the roof. And it has to be flimsy: a reminder that we're all just passing through. We thatched it roughly with boughs, breathing in the cold air, the evergreens, the swampiness of bulrushes, and the dried grasses smelling dusty sweet like autumn. We tied up the dangling bunches of grapes, Indian corn, and even some carrots and beautiful purple cauliflower.

Then it was done and I sat inside it for a few minutes. I thought it was not a bad metaphor for our blessings and our vulnerability: this fragile little house, filled with the temporary sweetness of fruit and flowering things, open to the sky and wind. It was good to sit there and catch the brief sunshine, to be aware of the coming cold, and to be thankful.

"I think I'll take the children to church this Easter," said my non-practising Christian friend. "I'm not really a believer, but still... it's important for the children."

I know. For 12 years now I've gathered up my own doubts, agnosticism, and laziness, bundled them off to one side, and celebrated the Passover Seder in our home. It began as "something for the children", an impulse to share with them what I remembered as the happiest festival of the year.

Like many another parent with no church or synagogue

affiliation, I wasn't sure what balance to strike between traditional forms and my free-thinking heart. Circumstances nudged us in the right direction. First, you have to take a religious observance seriously. Simply out of historical loyalty and loving memory, we did.

The Passover Seder at my grandparents' home was the exciting centre of the year: a two-hour service woven around a family feast. Silver and china gleamed, all the favourite relatives were there, and we children sat with our chins propped on the table, lapped in family warmth and the rich aromas from grandma's kitchen, as the men sing-songed their way through a rapid-fire Hebrew ceremony.

Well, I have no aged male relatives who can do the sing-song now. But in recreating the Seder I found that all my compromises made it blossom into something even more wonderful than it had been for me as a child. Certainly there's less solemnity. Since I have to conduct the service (my husband doesn't read Hebrew), there's an atmosphere of relaxed jollity as I dash to the kitchen to stir the chicken soup between prayers.

Digging into the meaning of the Seder, I realized that it's really a family drama, a living re-enactment of history in which even the smallest child plays a part. It starts the night before, when we cleanse the house of leavened bread. In the dark, with flashlights and squeaks of excitement, we find the bits of bread I've hidden. Then, gathered before the orange flames in the fireplace, with shadows jumping around the room, we burn the bread and say the prayers. Now we are all playing the part of our ancestors who fled from slavery in Egypt with their hastily baked unleavened bread.

By the next day, Passover moves from dark to light. The house is sweet with spring flowers and glittering with candles and silver. My mother, may she live to 120, arrives with her feather-light gefilte fish; the house rings with greetings. The more relatives and friends, the better: hospitality is part of the ceremony.

At the table the children join in the drama. One sings, another plays the recorder, and all of them ask the ritual four questions about the meaning of the Seder night. Because the whole celebration is designed to pass on our history to the children, we sometimes stop in the middle to discuss some urgent point. One year we read poetry from Auschwitz. Another year we debate the lines from the Seder service which remind us: "You were a stranger in Egypt...you will not oppress a stranger, for you know the feelings of a stranger." and we connect that to the name-calling in schoolyards and our duty to defend the underdog.

It's like a play filled with light and dark, sadness and rejoicing, climaxes and quiet corners. The children open the door for the prophet Elijah, and the cup of wine set for him in the middle of the table is mysteriously emptied... giggles and wonder and doubting looks at Daddy. Did Elijah really drink?

We talk about freedom, and how we were once slaves to Pharaoh. Black shadows of the Spanish Inquisition, Dachau, the terror and homelessness of our own people and others, dip over our bright table. We talk about spring, and Israel (and this year, about peace), and, as usual, I have to blink away tears of emotion when I say, "Next year in Jerusalem."

The Seder is thousands of years old and yet shaped by the individual quirks and talents and deep thoughts of each family. You don't have to be religious to enter heart and soul into a ceremony so rich. Yes, we started by doing it for the children, and it caught us all up in a bond as strong as history.

Ceremonies—weddings, christenings, bar mitzvahs, graduations, and even, heaven help me, birthdays and parades—always make me cry.

"Now snap out of this sentimental idiocy," I told myself, in what I imagined to be my best Bella Abzug growl, as I sat at the McMaster University convocation last Friday. No use, I felt the old familiar sting under the eyelids as the fanfare rang out, the academics solemnly paraded in their multicoloured gowns, the beaming parents sat tier on tier in the bleachers of what is normally a gym, and the "graduands" began to file endlessly past the chancellor to receive their degrees.

Now, in serene ceremony, three of four undignified years (heady new freedom, intellectual passion, beery hangovers, stomach-churning exams) were signed and sealed in dignity. In their hundreds, the young graduands (so much shining hair, so many scrubbed faces) came in an unwinding ribbon of black gowns to kneel before Chancellor Allan Leal. "I admit you Bachelor of Arts," he said to each one, and not even after the 200th did his voice lose its cheery boom of congratulation. Then the academic hood (like a long loop of silk scarf) was slipped over his or her shoulders, and the young graduate turned to march down from the podium and into the world.

In the moment of turning, student after student beamed at us a tremendous, exultant, partly-embarrassed smile, lips closed so that they wouldn't burst into an involuntary laugh of delight. And each one, striding down the aisle, sought out his or her family in the crowd to exchange a glance of triumph.

Why do moments like that make people cry? The parents of the graduates, of course, have the excitement of pride to justify their moist eyes. But even for bystanders like me, there's an irresistible poignancy about ceremonies. I first started to feel that way in my teens, when it dawned on me that summer did not last forever, and that next year was always turning into this year, and then fading into last year with startling speed.

I began to hoard life the way other people hoard elastic bands or vintage wines, latching onto anything which slowed down the quicksilver passage of time. In my mental bank account, I have a peculiar half-conscious ledger system for keeping track of time won and lost. I hate to sleep in, because that steals away part of the day, and I hate to go to sleep at night. I love summer because the days are long and crammed with the sensual treasures which I stockpile in memory against the turn of the year. A day spent picking raspberries in the hot sun is a day wrestled away from the black hole of eternity. But an afternoon spent in a movie is an afternoon lost forever, an afternoon which trickled away while I wasn't there.

I gloat over anything ancient — words, or Roman coins, or human rituals — because they have been scooped up and saved from the obliterating flood of time. I once seized on and saved a tattered, yellowing handwritten title deed to a Muskoka log cabin whose ruins I was exploring. And I memorized the flowers still growing in the dooryard; someone had planted them, once. In France, I spent some happy hours exulting over the name of a river, a name which, according to the books, had come down from pre-history. Imagine: a onesyllable word had survived since before recorded time.

Ceremonies conquer time, too, and I suppose that's why I love them. Participants in a ceremony seem to me to step out of time for the moment. Caveboys and cavegirls must have smiled just this way (new dignity struggling with exuberance) when they passed their test of adulthood and went forth from the parental cave.

Weddings, funerals, harvest festivals, and religious rites which have come unchanged through the centuries, all snatch us up from the rush of time and hold us still, linked to those who have felt these feelings before and those who will feel them after we have died.

So I forgave myself for my "sentimental idiocy" at the McMaster convocation. And I only smiled tolerantly when I saw my children rolling their eyes at each other in mock exasperation to tease me for my weakness. Just the way, come to think of it, I used to tease my own mother... while wondering a little uneasily what it was that adults knew, what it was that made them blink away tears at ceremonial moments sad and gay.

Labour Day weekend. Time for the annual Canadian rite of closing up the cottage. You're standing in a puddle of melting smelts from the defrosting fridge. He's draining the toilet, cursing already about Monday's traffic jams. The kids are down on the dock arguing about who should clean the dried-up dew worms out of the bait bucket.

Is it worth it, you wonder? Is it worth the drudgery of remembering whether the beach towels are here or there, every weekend? Is it worth the trauma of finding centipedes in the blanket box, and doing without your lovely washer and dryer all summer?

Yes, of course it is. You know it is, or you wouldn't be

standing there with the melting smelts. There's something that brings you back, summer after summer. And it doesn't really matter if the cottage is a rented or borrowed shack on a snag-filled inlet or a palatial summer home that's been handed down through the generations.

Sometimes I think cottage life is the most authentic link in the Canadian identity. Aside from the deliciously acrid smell of spent firecrackers on May 24, what other shared experience is so immediately, palpably Canadian? For thousands of Canadian children, the cottage is the first strange place, a place away from home, where impressions and memories are that much more vivid and provocative: the sharp woodsy smell of unpainted walls; the cold breath of forest that comes in the screened windows at night; the fragrance of fallen pine needles baking brown in the sun, that any Canadian kid would recognize instantly on a mountain top in Tibet.

Cottage life means time, luxurious hours stretching languidly ahead. Hours to spend lying face down on the dock, narrowing the world to the light-sprinkled ribbon of water seen through the cracks. Time to stalk an elusive crayfish through the shallows as patiently as a great hunter. Time to daydream away the afternoon in the cosy cave of the screened porch, where the lumpy cushions seem as inviting as a sultan's divan.

To city kids, the discovery of wild food is even more thrilling than free samples. Who hasn't been lured deeper and deeper into the green underworld of a berry patch, ignoring the scratches and the lulling drone of insects as the pail fills with raspberries?

Wildlife provides a child's first startled realization of other worlds, apart and mysterious, existing parallel to our own. Who ever forgets the baby raccoons tumbling like surprised bandits out of the woodpile? Or the papery snakeskin found in the deep grass, or the fear of a fieldmouse dashing for safety across the cottage floor? Warm in their beds they hear the haunting night sounds...owls and loons...and never forget.

Cottage summers are the time when children can be closer than ever to their parents—sharing evenings by the fire or forest rambles or silly splashings in the lake—and yet freer, too, making their own fun, not needing parent-chauffeurs or subway tickets to have good times.

Imagination gets a new lease on life. Can there be any cottage kid who hasn't walked for three days with eyes fixed downward—hoping every second to find an Indian arrowhead? Or any kid who hasn't fantasized a bark canoe slipping across the glassy water when the mist rises up at dawn? Who hasn't printed her name on a velvet fungus, written messages on dead birchbark, chewed spruce gum, speculated about "deadly toadstools", skipped stones, invented private names for secret discovered places in the woods?

Maybe it's the silence, the space, and the sense of endless time. But one thing is sure: there's more intense learning, daydreaming and sensory richness at a summer cottage than in any classroom a child is likely to come across.

I wonder how many others, when asked to define the word Canadian, would be startled to find the texture of cottage life leaping up in their consciousness. To me, it's still the quintessential Canadian experience. I only wish that all the children in our inner city ghettoes could share it too.

Sure it's worth it. Happy Labour Day weekend.

Saturday was the summer solstice, a day, says my Oxford dictionary, when the sun reaches its furthest point from the equator and "appears to stand still". It was a day that seemed to me to brim over with light, the scent of peonies and the particular lift of the heart that is strangely linked with a lump in the throat. It was the day our son was Bar Mitzvah in the garden.

Many non-Jews have a confused impression, fostered by newspaper stories of gross nouveau-riche extravaganzas, that a Bar Mitzvah is a day when a Jewish boy becomes a man in a gold lamé suit while thousands of guests guzzle caviar. But the Bar Mitzvah, really, is a touching and serious rite of passage when the growing child asserts his or her bond with the Jewish community. First and foremost, the 13-year-old youngster prepares for the duty and honour of reading, during Sabbath services, from the sacred Torah scroll, which is the first five books of the Old Testament written on parchment.

It was last November when our Bar Mitzvah Boy, or BMB, buckled down, like his big sister before him, to long months of study, to arguing Jewish philosophy with other young members of the congregation, and to learning how to sing accurately and in Hebrew from scrolls which have neither vowels nor musical notes. Patiently, he chanted ancient chants at the dining-room table while his basketball idled nearby. Meanwhile, his father and I fretted over a pyramid of details which kept threatening to scatter like spilled marbles.

The day drew near; I stared distractedly out at the sluicing rain. The people from Accurate Tent set up an airy, yellow-and-white striped pavillion in our garden and kept faithfully coming back in the howling winds to check the guy ropes. The BMB, looking a little frayed, had to pause to write Grade 9 exams.

Then it was the day. Sunlight, astonishingly, pooled on the glowing yellow roof of our tent. Inside, it smelled of mown grass. The leafy greens and soft pinks and reds of a June garden glimmered through the clear plastic walls. In the house, unaccustomedly gleaming floors and windows reflected the bowls of floppy pink roses from my mother's garden.

The BMB looked calm in his spiffy new oatmeal-coloured sports jacket and creamy shirt, but I noticed a certain flutter in his throat. In the last two months his descant soprano had suddenly plummeted to an alto-tenor and his trousers had grown three inches too short.

The relatives and congregation poured in. The rabbi, a lovably down-to-earth young woman, smilingly explained that at such a happy reunion of family and friends it was perfectly all right for people to visit and chat during the service.

Outside the tent our foolish dog Rosie snapped at butter-flies in the flower border. Inside, we followed the rabbi in the old minor-key melodies and listened with something like astonishment when our boy stood before the scroll and chanted his portion, and a long reading from the prophets, with lilting ease. He made a little speech, too, in which he described the dawning of his new sense of Jewish community during the past year. His dad stood up and read a poem by Canadian author A. M. Klein, a dear old friend of the BMB's grandpa. Other children, including our two daughters, added their sweet voices to the service, and loved friends, aunts, uncles, grandparents, and teachers joined in.

We felt rich and blessed beyond belief. There are moments when parents stand back in bewildered gratitude and wonder how on earth they deserved so much. This was one of those moments. Then on to joyful clatter. A feast was spread, white wine sparkled, and Serge, a honey-voiced Russian tenor, sang wild, mournful Russian gypsy songs and happy-sad Yiddish ones, out there in the tent where babies clapped in time and grown-ups tapped their toes.

Two hours later, as the golden afternoon dwindled away and guests lingered at ease, the BMB changed into shorts and went bounding off with his friends to try out his new basketball at the schoolyard. "Not BMB any more," the Man grinned at me. "BMM".

Late that night, as I counted out 75 rental spoons and forks and the closest relatives stayed to help with the clean-up, I mused about ceremonials that link families with their community. Sometimes they happen better and more warmly outside the walls of an institution. In the bower-like intimacy of a garden, there were few of us (agnostic or believer) who could escape the tingle of awe and celebration as the Torah was paraded past by our beaming son.

Besides, I would never had gotten my windows shined or my floors polished any other way. And I would not have forever a memory of our young man, standing in our garden, connecting with 5,000 years of history, in the heart of a family of people who love him.

Well, well, our statistics have finally caught up with our private lives. Usually, Statistics Canada limps along behind like a clown who arrives late for the parade, but this week StatsCan panted up to the rest of us to announce that the marriage rate fell by 3.4 per cent in the late '70s.

The wonder is that marriage has survived at all, considering that practically every logical justification for it has long since crumbled away. It's more than a century since a man needed a wife so that she could milk the cows while he ploughed the back forty. In boom times or frontier days, when there's land to be settled or a new flood of consumer goods to be bought, the family is a useful economic unit—which is why governments were so friendly about importing brides for settlers, or shoring up marriages with financial benefits after the last war.

But now? Marriage costs. It's not just the white satin wedding album or the new double bed. It's the prospect of high-rise rents and astronomical mortgage payments. It's the thought that surely as wet follows dry, a $1,500 washer and dryer and an expensive day-care problem will follow the pitter-patter of stork feet on the roof. When the depression hit Canada, long engagements and late marriages became fashionable. Now that economic pessimism has become part of the Canadian psyche, more and more young people will be hesitating to commit themselves.

And, then, why bother? Marriage was invented by men (all those feeble jokes to the contrary) to ensure a clean supply of socks while they were busy in the world—not to mention a nicely certified legal heir to carry on the name and inherit the property. Law reform has whittled away at those cosy conjugal rights: soon a woman will be able to charge her husband with rape; already, she can keep her own name, claim half the couple's assets, and expect him to chip in with the sock-washing since she's likely to be out working too.

Common-law marriage is more popular now, too. In this case, necessity was probably the mother of respectability; the courts just haven't been able to keep up with the number of people who want a divorce so they can marry someone else.

Twice in the past month, women have blushed apologetically while admitting to me that they planned to marry their long-time partner. When marriage loses both its cachet and its cash advantage, the wedding rate is bound to slump. And that's probably all to the good. Many people who never should or would have married without society's pressure will now stay single and stop giving marriage and parenthood a bad name.

Those who do opt for marriage will be able to see more clearly, I hope, why they're choosing it. Once you get past the thrills and chills of the first few years, the emotional roller-coaster of growing up, there's a lot to be said for comfort. And what is more comforting than the utterly dependable "I'm on your side" stance of the loving partner?

Then there's the ease of shared ideas, so that instead of continually labouring over the conversational foothills with strangers ("And do you often come to discos?"), you can start half-way up the mountain and occasionally reach some intellectual peaks together. Strangers—"dates"—can surprise or tickle us with a new stock of witticisms, but there's nothing quite like the shared humour of a couple whose laughter reverberates with a decade or two of mutual experience.

When a couple can enjoy this comradeship of the mind, when a person you've known for 15 or 20 years can still ambush you into laughter or a new idea or a deeper level of feeling, then family life becomes a safe harbour rather than a dead end. A place where children can learn to swim and cope with currents, rather than drowning emotionally.

Every harbour has its snags, its whitecap days, its darker pools, and none of us long-marrieds can afford to be smug. But maybe, now that people are choosing the married state more warily, and despite all its drawbacks, the odds will improve. It will be a glad day for the future's children when men and women together see marriage as a serious commitment to child-rearing.

Marriage as a free choice: no religious and moral whips to keep you there, no economic chains, no chilly breath of worthier-than-thou. I like it. I think it has a future.

Write about the future of the family, said the editor.

Sure, I said. Ulp.

Up there in my head, the statistics go round, chanting the imminent demise of the family: divorce rate going up, kids bouncing from one set of parents to another, sequential marriage, and even, heaven help us, the "post-nuclear" family.

Down in my heart, which somehow hasn't noticed the statistical whirlwind, I'm still a cockeyed optimist. Stubbornly and, it seems, with the tide of change lapping around my knees and the sand shifting under my feet, I persist in seeing the family as the eternal given. Its forms may shift and change (in what era have they not?) but the idea of family is immutable.

Just as I wrote this last paragraph, a book about joint custody landed with a gloomy thump on my desk. It is filled with outraged howls of pain from fathers who have been deprived of their children. And I'm forced to remember, despondently, that for thousands and thousands of men, women, and children, the family has been an embittering trap, a prison of loveless dependencies or stillborn hopes.

So if I write about my rootedness in the family, does that make me ghoulishly insensitive to the one married person in four who will divorce? Maybe not. There are still those three out of every four who *don't* divorce, and, judging by the phenomenal re-marriage rate, even that one in four probably has the same attachment to the family constellation as I do. After all, we all come from families. Willy-nilly, we inherit not only the colour of our eyes but also our complexities, our expectations of the world, and our ways of reacting to it. And for most of us, single or married, a family is still where we expect to find our emotional home.

The family as most of us knew it was that trusted, familiar web of relationships in which we were enfolded — and against which we could later kick without fear of breaking the threads. We, in our turn, remake that web. As parents, we create the world for the new baby, holding at bay the chaos of hunger and panic. And the baby's trust creates us as a family. Out of those two callow young people with their moods, tantrums, and restlessness, emerge two growing adults who will endure diapers and mess and exhaustion to honour that trust and ensure the ongoing of life.

We've learned the hard way, over and over again, that

there aren't any workable substitutes for families. You can't grow happy babies in laboratories. It's the predictability of the thing: the child's knowledge that you can spill the milk, have warts, break the rules, veer from love to hate and back again, and still, indisputably, belong. A family gives us our set of particulars with which we can voyage out into the world. The way the toast smells in the morning, a brother's voice, the patterns in the living-room rug, the inevitability with which a slammed door or a bike in the driveway will bring the expected rebuke...In the certainties of childhood, we trace the world in miniature and steady ourselves for larger uncertainties.

Yes, of course those patterns can become twisted, distorting the lives that should have been nourished. It's all to the good that people are freer now to opt out of poisonous families, or to choose a new pattern for themselves. And yes, some women, with some reason, have wept and raged and railed against the bonds of child-rearing. But I think I'm not unusual in saying that for me the creation of our own family (overlapping with and including the grandparents) was a deeper re-creation of myself.

We have claims on each other, we members of families. Living up to that claim, I've felt all the good in me strengthened. Placing that claim on others, I've helped them grow into humanness, too.

The future of the family? Stormy—until we learn how to adapt to the turmoil of change. Custody arrangements, housing, child care, social supports...all are limping miles behind our new needs and realities. But they'll catch up, at least a little, because the family is so basic to life that we could no more decide to throw it out altogether that we could dispense with our hearts and lungs.

I have so often excoriated the medical profession for its cold arrogance. Now it's my turn to pay tribute to what it does best: rising to an emergency with swift, impersonal skill; fighting with fierce tenderness to save a life; and then, when death must be met, standing back just far enough, but not too far to be kind.

Everyone who has ever kept a hospital vigil knows how eerily the outside world drops away. The hospital becomes your neighbourhood. Within hours, you are intimates, at home with the bench outside the nephrology unit, the ebb and flow of the afternoon and night shifts, the miles of bleak basement corridors to the nearest coffee machine, the fifth-floor elevator button that won't light up, the stupefyingly awful food.

At Ottawa Civic Hospital, my husband's family lived several lifetimes in the three weeks before David Lewis, my father-in-law, died. It was a dizzying see-saw: minuscule good omens sent hope rushing to the brain like an intoxicant; then, suddenly, like blows, grim portents. Downturns. Unexpected setbacks. We would brace our hearts for the worst; a night would pass; the news would be good again; we would gasp for equilibrium.

Through all of this blur of anxiety, we were aware of a quiet army of women who kept the hospital running. Volunteers handed mugs of coffee at lonely midnight. The registered nursing assistants were the caring hands, smoothing a pillow, thinking to move a glass nearer. The nurses, wearing their tact like a uniform, were unassumingly magnificent. You'd see them in the basement coffee shop, giggling over their frightful snacks of Coke and doughnuts, and they'd look like teenagers in a school cafeteria. An hour later, they'd be heroes, transformed, supernaturally alert to a flicker of doom, leaping to pummel a failing heart back to life.

We taught ourselves the rules of life in our new neighbourhood. Tied by an invisible umbilical cord to the hospital, we never went anywhere without leaving phone numbers behind. We smiled and functioned through our daily duties while our minds were elsewhere, and took turns to keep a constant bedside watch.

My father-in-law fought patiently but stubbornly with that serious, almost sad optimism that, to me, was his most endearing quality: that refusal to admit defeat or to countenance despair in the face of the worst that his times had shown him. He was not for a moment defeated. He summoned strength for a smile when we read him a kind letter from

Pierre Trudeau, ending with a teasing postscript that claimed
Liberal credit for medicare.

"That's Truedeau's sense of humour, you know," he whispered haltingly. Long pause. A shadow of that familiar com-
bative grin. "That SOB."

Leukemia had him and it bore him swiftly down. To the
end he fought powerfully, with a mind whose subtlety, depth,
and swiftness had made him a legend of brilliance. It was his
last, only resource. It burned in him, incandescent.

All the strain of those last few weeks was so worth it.
Precious moments were shared, touches and looks. Words
were said that will never be forgotten.

In the medical ward, released from the terrible temporary
hopes of the intensive-care unit, we learned yet another new
country: the calm white geometry of ironed sheets; the soft
light of a lamp throwing its gleam on a polished floor through
the long night watch. The moments measured off by the
harsh rasp of a breathing that laboured, unmistakably now,
toward death.

Some doctors have a special acrobatic grace; to know
when to let go for that last plunge, to let the fall be easy... that
is the humane art. They practised it for my father-in-law.

No gentleness or civility was spared. The ultimate civility
was this: to respect the fine dignity of the man, and not to
torment him with meaningless chemical assaults in his last
weeks and days, when they could no longer have helped.

Afterward, in the stricken clarity of the moment, outside
the hospital room, I saw a young doctor kneel beside the
grieving wife. His white coat swirled out behind him as
though he were a youthful knight. He held her hands urgently
and talked about the beauty of a natural death.

And this was the natural death: all the family around the
bed. No machines. Soft sunlight in the room. The sound of
breath, slower and slower. Another breath. And another.
Pause. And another. And stopped, forever.

Between that last breath and the silence, that good man
slipped away and was simply gone. We were hot with tears,
but awestruck, too, by death's peacefulness. A most complete
life had rounded off. There had been, in the whole of those

last three weeks, not one medical invasion of that life's integrity. Not one indignity imposed through carelessness, haste, or indifference.

Medicine could not, finally, save him. But it could not have held him more sweetly in its arms. The doctor who had so meticulously eased my father-in-law's dying stood with tears in his eyes and spoke of the friendship that had grown between them. I truly think it was medicine's finest hour, wearing a human face, steeped in gentleness, not afraid, as my father-in-law was not, to let life run through the glass as softly as sand, and to end in peace.

BIBLIOGRAPHY

BEAUVOIR, SIMONE DE, *The Second Sex*. New York: Alfred A. Knopf, 1953.

BRADY, KATHERINE, *Father's Days: A True Story About Incest*. New York: Dell, 1981.

BROPHY, BRIGID, *Don't Never Forget*. New York: Holt, Rinehart and Winston, 1966.

BUDOFF, PENNY, W., M.D., *No More Menstrual Cramps and Other Good News*. Don Mills: Academic Press, 1980.

BURFORD, F., CEBRYNSKY, W., PECK, G.W., and PANZICA, N., "The Marijuana Issue: A Headmaster's Perspective", a report published by the Ontario Secondary School Headmasters' Council, 1980, available in reprint from the Insurance Bureau of Canada.

CARMEN, RUSSO, and MILLER, DRS., article in *American Journal of Psychiatry*, October 1981.

CHERNIN, KIM, *The Obsession*. Toronto: Fitzhenry and Whiteside, 1981.

CLARK, LORENNE, and LEWIS, DEBRA, *Rape: The Price of Coercive Sexuality*. Toronto: The Women's Press, 1977.

COFFEY, MARY ANNE, *Inequality at Work*. A report published by the Social Planning Council of Metropolitan Toronto and the Women's Studies and Affirmative Action Departments of the Board of Education of Toronto. Toronto: 1982.

DAVIS, ELIZABETH GOULD, *The First Sex*. New York: Penguin, 1972.

EDELSTEIN, BARBARA, *The Woman Doctor's Diet for Women*. Toronto: Random House, 1977.

EICHLER, MARGRIT, "Canadian Government Policies Affecting Families", a paper presented to the American Sociological Association meeting in Toronto, 1981.

FRIEDAN, BETTY, *The Feminine Mystique*. New York: Dell, 1974.

————, *The Second Stage*. New York: Summit Books, 1981.

GALLOWAY, PRISCILLA, *What's Wrong With High School English? It's Sexist, UnCanadian and Outdated*. Toronto: Ontario Institute for Studies in Education Press, 1981.

MENDELSOHN, ROBERT, M.D., *Male Practice*. Don Mills: Beaverbooks, 1981.

MILLER, CASEY, and SWIFT, KATE, *The Handbook of Nonsexist Writting*. Toronto: Fitzhenry and Whiteside, 1980.

MILLMAN, MARCIA, *Such a Pretty Face: Being Fat in America*. Don Mills: McLeod, 1980.

MORGAN, ELAINE, *The Descent of Woman*. New York: Stein and Day, 1972.

PRITIKIN, NATHAN, *The Pritikin Program for Diet and Exercise*. New York: Grosset and Dunlap, 1979.

TROYER, WARNER, *Divorced Kids*. Toronto: Clarke Irwin, 1979.

ZIZMOR, JONATHAN, and FOREMAN, JOHN, *Dr. Zizmor's Brand-Name Guide to Beauty Aids*…New York: Harper & Row, 1978.

In addition to these specifically mentioned works, I have drawn freely on news and feature stories in both the *Toronto Star* and the *Globe and Mail* for examples, information, and quotations.